Tantric Buddhism

TALKS ON MEDITATION

AND ENLIGHTENMENT

Rama - Dr. Frederick Lenz

LIVING FLOW

Contents

Tantric Buddhism.................... 1
Six Worlds.......................... 13
The Mature Monk.................. 27
The Natural State.................. 37
Freedom............................ 53
Enlightenment..................... 80
Self-Effort..........................88
Possibilities....................... 95
The Nexus of All Pathways........ 103
The Path of Affirmation........... 121
Buddhism.......................... 135
Computer Science................. 146
The Awareness of Meditation...... 153
Focus and Meditation.............. 165
Professional Meditation........... 175
The Best Meditation I Ever Had....185
Metaphysics....................... 193
A Clean Room..................... 208
The Bhagavad-Gita................ 217
Buddhist Enlightenment...........233
The Path of Negation.............. 239

Transience 251
Peak Experiences 258
Solstices and Equinoxes 268
Tenacity 291
Buddhist Yoga 304
Light 317

Also By the Author 321
Copyright 322

Chapter One

TANTRIC BUDDHISM

When you look into a pond or a lake, if there's no wind, then it's a mirror. It's perfectly still. If we throw a rock in, then ripples in concentric circles extend outward. The image changes.

Enlightened mind is often compared to a lake, a pond without ripples. But I don't think that that's completely correct. Because I think enlightened mind also is a lake or a pond with ripples.

We throw a rock into a lake and the pure serenity is disturbed. The ripples cascade; they come and go and then everything becomes still again. I think that's better. It's more like enlightened mind. Enlightened mind is not just serenity. Serenity is an idea. Enlightened mind is beyond ideas. No matter what we think about or how we conceptualize enlightened mind, we're always going to be looking at an image or a picture, not enlightened mind. In all the scriptures it says that enlightened mind is beyond the mind's knowledge. You can't know intellectually what it is. You can't imagine what it is. It's beyond knowing, beyond imagination. It's not sensorial. You can't taste it, smell it, touch it, hear it, feel it. Yet it's there. It's eternal. It's what is.

We look at the world around us filled with cars and jets and people and activities, and it's hard to understand that there could be anything else than this. I mean, the world seems so full of the world. You're on Wall Street, you're on Madison Avenue, and everything seems so active, so busy. The sights, the sounds, the smells, everything is so furiously paced. Even if you go to the forest, the forest is very loud. There are all kinds of birds and noises and winds. The trees creak. There's a lot of activity. Mosquitoes.

A lot is happening in the sensual world. The sensual world, which is the world we're most familiar with, is problematic because we find that it doesn't really make us happy. It always is so appealing. We look at these wonderful fresh images that life brings forth from itself and we're attracted. The promise is so great.

I think sex in a way is perhaps the most exemplary form of that. We look at someone, we're attracted to them, they're beautiful. They take their clothes off, we embrace and there's this cascading sensual experience where everything is so vivid. Everything is so strong. The energies are so intense. This mating ritual is taking place. But then afterwards, it's gone. There's nothing, except memory—which lingers, fades.

The sensual experiences in life are not to be avoided. This is the philosophy of Tantric Buddhism. Nor are they particularly to be sought after. They are inevitable. They come with daily living. A cup of coffee, fasting, the way the sky looks—all of the sensual images of life are there; they can't be disputed. Most people run after them with the sense that if we can experience more, somehow we will feel better.

There are pathways to enlightenment where they encourage us to control the senses, shut the senses off. They feel that the sensual world is a distraction from the world of enlightenment, that it takes us away from reality. They acknowledge that the sensual world is a part of reality, certainly, but it's not ultimate, in the sense that it changes, it never stays the same and it always leaves us empty—alone, really unchanged, perhaps tired, perhaps refreshed—but not essentially different.

They say that Casanova made love to over 10,000 women. Do you think it changed him? Probably aged him a little bit. But I doubt that it changed him. If it had changed him, he probably would have stopped somewhere along the line and done something a little different.

Repetitive sensual experiences don't change anything. They're not necessarily harmful. In other words, Pandora's box is interesting only because we haven't seen what's in it. Once we see what's in it doesn't mean that it's negative, doesn't mean that it's something that's not there, that's not good. The religious hard line, in other words, that the sensual world is in some way negative and not spiritual, is from my point of view not very accurate. I can understand pathways to enlightenment where people shun certain aspects of the sensual world because they feel that these aspects are very powerful; they're not in a position yet to control their appetites, I guess, and so people avoid sexuality, they avoid certain types of food, they avoid, they avoid, they avoid.

Because in the sagacity of the regimen of avoidance there's a sort of a temporary purity that we get from fasting. There's a temporary clarity, an acuity that comes from emptiness, from not doing things, from mortifying the flesh. But it doesn't last. The fast ends. We have a temporary view of something, we feel better. We push the sensual barrage back for a while, although we can never push it back, we're just in a different sensual barrage. The sensual world cannot be avoided. We're in it at every moment. We are part of it.

In Tantric Buddhism, our feeling is that the problem—there is no problem with the sensual world. There just isn't one, unless you have a tremendous attraction or aversion to it. Either one tends to postpone enlightened mind from dawning. If you think that there's some wonderful hidden promise in the sensual world, there isn't. There's just momentary, transient sensual experience. If you think there's some terrible thing that's going to occur because you're involved in the sensual world, well, you're always involved in the sensual world at every moment. Fasting is as sensual as eating. Being celibate is as sensual as having sex. They're just different choices, different videos that you've selected to view tonight.

What matters is not the sensual experience. What matters is your view of it. In other words, what you're doing with your mind. In Tantric Buddhism, we just lead our lives. We don't really worry a whole lot about the sensual world one way or the other. Instead, we enter into the kingdom of enlightened mind. Since sensual experiences cannot be avoided if one has a body, we just let the senses do whatever they happen to do. We don't necessarily try and restrain them, nor do we give them license. We don't feel that there's some wonderful something at the end of the sensual rainbow except more sensual experiences. Without the illusion that there's something bad that we should really find because it'll be good—that's kind of Christianity as it's spoken of today. Sin is good, we all understand that, but we sort of stay away from it because ultimately it's bad. It's this weird kind of dichotomy.

We don't believe in sin. Stupidity, yes, meaning we make ourselves or others suffer. Intelligence, yes, meaning we go beyond suffering personally or we assist others in that process. But we don't feel that there's anything right or wrong about the sensual world. It's all part of infinity. Our interest is not controlling the sensual world; our interest is placing our mind beyond it. Not focusing on it because we find that there are other kingdoms of mind. And to spend all your time worrying about what you should or shouldn't do keeps you right there, highly involved with whatever you should or you shouldn't do. I mean, it's in your mind. You're thinking that you shouldn't have sex because you're celibate. So you just keep thinking about sex—instead of enlightenment.

The tantric path involves taking the mind and directing it beyond the senses. We're not really concerned about what happens here in this world. I mean obviously we're concerned; we try and follow common sense and our intuition and higher intelligence and do things as well as we can to have the most pleasant life we can have, but we're not particularly threatened by the senses. Our method is to enlarge the mind and let the senses do as they will. Again, without the feeling that there's some wonderful hidden ecstasy or that there's anything incorrect. It really doesn't matter. Our attention is placed in other spheres, in other dimensions.

We're all in the sensual world, we've all experienced it; we can do nothing but experience it every moment we have a body. There are no new revelations. It's unavoidable. And it does not bring enlightenment. You can live in the senses forever and there's only more sensual experience, which is either pleasurable or painful, enlivening or boring. There is no major charge one way or the other There's a neutrality that comes with maturation in Tantric Buddhism where it just is irrelevant, it just doesn't matter. The sensual world is unimportant. What matters is enlightenment, taking our mind and placing it in dimensions that we would be completely unaware of if we were totally immersed always in the sensual world.

Some people use avoidance, and for a while they get glimpses of enlightenment. They mortify the flesh, they fast, they avoid, they're celibate. Great. It purifies them in some way, it takes them above their routines. Any discipline has a power to it. But ultimately one will only get glimpses. Celibacy doesn't make you enlightened, otherwise every nun and priest in Buddhism or Christianity would be enlightened. People who don't date and get any action would be enlightened. (Audience laughs.) Fasting doesn't produce enlightenment. A lot of people go on a hunger fast; they don't become enlightened. Nor does being Casanova, nor does eating 5,000 calories a day. It's something else that produces enlightenment that has nothing to do with the senses.

I respect people whose pathway leads them through the discipline of the senses. I've practiced those disciplines personally in this and other lives, only because I enjoyed them. It's fun to fast, just like it's fun to eat. It's fun to be celibate, just like it's fun to have sex. Or sex can be painful as can celibacy. Fasting can be painful and so can eating. It really is irrelevant to the world of enlightenment. What matters in the world of enlightenment is learning to stop your thoughts.

When thought stops, the higher mind opens and we move beyond the sensual world into the worlds and realms of enlightened mind. If mortifying your senses, if fasting, if being celibate helps you to stop your thought, fine. If it makes you dwell on these things more, then obviously you're not stopping your thought, so it's kind of useless.

In other words, Tantric Buddhism is structural. We're structuralists. We don't have a preordained idea of what should create enlightenment or what shouldn't. We look to traditions and if something's in a tradition—any tradition, spiritual tradition, mystical tradition, religious tradition—if we can employ that device that someone else discovered several thousand years ago or last week and use it and it helps us stop thought, we're all for it.

If we try it and it doesn't work, we reject it. Just because there's a precedent, just because it's historical, doesn't mean it's actual. The laboratory of enlightenment is your mind. If we discover something today that no one ever knew about that stops thought, that leads us into samadhi, into enlightened states of mind, then we employ it. We don't care what tradition it comes from or what it's called. If it works, it works; if it doesn't, it doesn't. Sometimes it's chemistry. You know, what works for one person won't work for another, or in a current stage of development you can employ something that will help you stop thought—it might not work a year from now because you'll be different. Or maybe something that you try today won't work today but it will work a year from now.

Tantra is nondogmatic, in the sense that we don't care about the sensual world; we don't care about religious traditions. To not care doesn't mean that we don't learn. Of course, I learn from every tradition, just like we learn from science. If somebody did an experiment 400 years ago and they came up with a good result, maybe it took them 30 years to get that result—we can read about their experiment in two minutes and do it. It took them 30 years to get to that two minutes. It saves us time. So we study Taoism, Confucianism, variant forms of Buddhism—Mahayana, Hinayana, Zen—Hinduism, yoga of all forms, Christianity, Judaism—it doesn't really matter what it's called. People were trying to get high. They were trying to feel and experience eternity in new ways. Anything we can absorb from anywhere is useful, but at the same time there has to be discipline.

In other words, we can just take a little from here and a little from there and end up with a mess. There has to be a template, an overall game plan that we use all of this information in—a system that changes and modifies as is necessary. Otherwise, we're just borrowing, but we're not accomplishing.

The hallmark of enlightenment is in how you treat others. That's a loaded phrase—like every phrase in the world of enlightenment it has countless meanings. It's up to you to decipher them. But by and large as you progress in the world of enlightenment, you should have a sense of decorum. You should treat others well, with respect. And you should treat yourself with respect. So if you become a doormat for others, if you let people abuse you, that doesn't mean that you're necessarily very advanced. Turning the other cheek is not always the answer. In a certain situation on a certain day for a certain person, it's correct. Sometimes a good roundhouse kick on a certain day in a certain situation for a certain person is correct.

In other words, in tantra we don't believe in commandments. We believe in the moment and the truth that is applicable for that moment—as best we can sort it out with our heart, our intuition, our knowledge, our common sense—is the proper truth. This doesn't lead to anarchy, it lends to balance—if we're doing it honestly. But everything must revolve around meditation. It's only meditation that brings us ultimately beyond the sensual world. Not because "beyond" implies that there's anything wrong with the sensual world. But the spirit wants to be free, and the spirit experiences the senses in early incarnations, and it's enough. The sensual world is very fulfilling. There's a lot to learn through sexuality. There's a lot to learn in all expressions of the senses.

But then the spirit wants something more. It evolves. It wants to experience light, true knowledge, perfect oblivion, the dissolution of the self in the finite sense, in the white light of eternity, in variant phrases that just suggest the experience of enlightenment when thought is eclipsed and there's nothing but ecstasy and perfection beyond my or anyone's description. Not because there's anything wrong with life or the senses but because the spirit seeks something else. We've seen the movie enough times. We'd like to see something else. It was a good movie when we saw it. We don't need to put it down for someone who's just starting to view it, do we? Do we have to be so simplistic? Because something no longer interests us, it may be very valuable for someone else. Obviously, we enjoyed it for how many lifetimes?

So we have a mature sense of our development in tantra. We don't need to be bigots. We don't have to put anyone else down for their interests. Because the infinite consciousness of God is evolving through each being at variant levels of gradated mind. And in those variant levels of gradated mind, it is seeking itself in various forms. All we do is seek ourselves. The gopis seek Krishna—another part of themselves, obviously, that creates ecstasy. The man seeks the woman, the woman seeks the man. The Tantric Buddhist seeks annihilation of the ego.

When the sun sets, beautiful though it may be, billions of stars appear. The ego is but one sun. When that sun sets, there are endless suns, endless horizons beyond it. The sun and the earth are interesting for a while but once we've seen them, it's fun to move on and see what other wonders creation affords us.

Tantric Buddhism, then, is a series of methods that we use to expand awareness beyond awareness. Not because we hate life. Not because there is anything wrong with the sensual world. Everything is quite right with the sensual world. We're products of it. We came into this world through the act of sexuality. We would not be here otherwise. So there can't be anything wrong with sexuality.

But sometimes we choose to walk beyond a particular experience because it no longer holds a power for us. If an experience holds a power for you, then we go towards it. That power takes us someplace new in our mind. It shows us something new about God and infinity. It's highly individual, everything. Reality is individual until you reach deeper stratas of attention in which there's no individuality, in which case, reality just is. And one perceives it or not, depending upon one's inclination.

Tantric Buddhism is the study of enlightenment. Enlightenment is part of everything. And so our minds have to be very, very big to encompass all things, to understand all things. To see the tao in a grape, the act of sexuality, meditation, work, play, taking a shower, brushing your teeth, being sick and hurting. Watching someone we love suffer and die and go back into the void. Watching ourselves grow, become strong, become weak, live, love, die, suffer. This is all just sensual. These are just sensual experiences. You're just seeing it. You're tasting it, you're touching it, you're smelling it, you're hearing it. It has nothing to do with reality. It's just a film you're watching, that you're so engaged in that you forgot that you were watching a film and it all seems real. Enlightened mind is beyond the realm of the senses.

We live in a sensual world, and at the same time we live beyond it in billions of dimensions that are non-physical, which we experience when we stop thought. The dimensions go on forever in all directions, some higher, some lower, some neither. No words can apply. They're inhabited by beings, some by nothingness. Universes collide and conjoin inside us. And beyond all of that—not beyond in a spatial sense—is nirvana, the final, absolute resting place of the soul.

It's where all transient experience of the phenomenal world ceases. In nirvana there is no such thing, there is only nirvana, perfection. No pain, no suffering, not even ecstasy. The ecstasy is finite, ultimately. Even spiritual ecstasy is finite. In nirvana, there's just perfection. No words. And at a certain point in its evolution, after certain incarnational experiences have been worked out—where we've had pleasure and pain, loss and gain, fame and fortune, sexuality, the lack of it—we progress to a point where we practice occultism, self-discovery. We go through thousands of lifetimes where we learn to meditate. We study, grow, develop, learn the *katas* of enlightenment, practice them until they're perfect, gain complete control of the mind so that we can let the mind roam, without control, in complete innocence. In innocence there can be only innocence. Purity is innocence, the innocence of lack of self. Desire is innocent unless it's connected with self. It's just an impulse.

The lack of innocence is not sin—sin is a human concept. It's religious. Tantra is spiritual, not religious. It deals with the spirit. Religion is just an applied body of doctrines that's believed or not believed by one or more individuals. Spirituality is the science of metaphysics. It is how we unlock the spirit. It's not random, it's not accidental, it's something that works very definitively. It's the chemistry of the soul. Tantra is the most sophisticated application of the chemistry of the soul.

So I would not be troubled particularly by the sensual world. I wouldn't be troubled particularly by anything. I would only be excited about the quest for enlightenment. And sensual experiences will come and go, always. What I would do is put your mind beyond them.

As you meditate each day, you will gain the mental discipline and control to place your mind in higher states of attention during any sensual experience. Then an experience is no longer sensual, is it? It becomes enlightening. What's going on in the physical level is of little or no importance. We place the mind elsewhere, out of the realm of the senses, out of the realm of loss and gain, pleasure and pain, fame and fortune. Beyond duality.

There is a light that is neither male nor female, black nor white, good nor bad. Beyond duality is infinity. It's a big world; it's where reality really starts.

Duality is the kindergarten of the soul. This world appears dual to you. It doesn't appear dual to me. Which is it? From the eye of enlightenment there's no duality. I don't see duality. I don't know what it is. From your point of view there's nothing but duality. Yet we're both in the same world—or are we?

Perception is reality. In meditation, when you stop thought, perception unfolds. Tantra, Tantric Buddhism is the study of how to stop thought. How to go beyond thought—not into something less than thought, but into higher levels of understanding that are free of concepts, free of the senses, where the mind unfolds itself into infinity and there's nothing but light and pure radiant understanding—the *dharmakaya*, the clear light of reality, where we experience that which is, forever. It's only of interest, that particular subject, to people who have worked their way through the sensual realms, through the realms of game-playing, attaining and losing, fame and fortune, the things we do in basic incarnations forever. Something in us awakens, and that's not enough any more. We're drawn back again by our karmas from prior births to the study of enlightenment. And once again we hoist the banner of the *dharma* up, and we patiently go beyond the senses. Not by giving the senses up; that can't be done. But by placing our attention into the realms of enlightened mind.

To one who's enlightened, there is no sensuality, but innocence. There's no sexuality, but innocence. This culture seems to be so obsessed with sexuality, the good and the bad of it. Every advertisement, every preacher, everybody's concerned one way or the other about sexuality. But from the point of view of the enlightened, from my point of view, as one who is enlightened, it really doesn't matter. There's no such thing as sexuality. It's just an illusion of the senses, like all of life is illusory—illusory in that it is not a complete picture of what reality is.

Sexuality is innocence. Everything is innocence. There is nothing else but innocence, if there's no a priori motivation of an ego. Life itself is perfect innocence. It's only when we're in lower gradated states of mind that we perceive duality and things to be different. How could sexuality be anything but God? It's the creation of life. Whether those beings are very conscious or not, who are in that particular dance, it doesn't matter. Life is experiencing itself in endless forms.

If you go to India sometime, look at a temple. You'll notice all around the Hindu temples—this used to give the British a lot of trouble because they were kind of white and uptight—you'll notice couples, statues and drawings in various erotic forms of love-making. The British had a lot of trouble with this when they took over India for a little while, or thought they did. They didn't, it didn't quite fit—how could a temple of God be covered with pictures of people, in their term, "fornicating." Well obviously, not everybody looks at sexuality the same way. For some people it's part of the cycle of life and it's not a big issue one way or the other, it just is what it is. There's not a great charge on it, other than it's just an experience, like all experiences.

"Be neither attracted nor repulsed" is the message of Tantric Buddhism. Don't be drawn to something, don't run away from it. Just naturally accept whatever comes into life. The issue is not what you're doing with your body, it's what you're doing with your mind—where your mind is. If you want to do something with your mind, meditate several hours a day on the clear light of reality. Practice the mental disciplines, the concentration. Associate with people of like mind, don't be afraid of people of unlike mind. Keep your mind, through all sensual experiences in the *bardo* of duality, on the clear light of reality,[1] on truth, kindness, brightness, inspiration—anything that brings you above the realm of the senses. Use tried and true methods, experiment with new methods but with a sense of purity and integrity. Always. How could you avoid the world of enlightenment then?

The sensual world is available. It's unavoidable. And we play in the jungle gym of sexuality until our spirit suddenly takes us out into a clear field where we see the stars. Or perhaps go to them, perhaps become them, perhaps something that cannot be described, that's more miraculous than words can convey, which is the experience of enlightened mind—the ten thousand radiances of enlightenment. One of those radiances is the dance of sensuality. Sensuality is enlightened mind expressing itself—in a sensual way. Reality is

---

1. "The clear light of reality" is the definition of the Sanskrit term "dharmakaya".

in the eye of the beholder.

Thank you.

CHAPTER TWO

SIX WORLDS

There are six worlds. There are countless subdivisions of the six, but there are six. Now I'm going to disagree a little bit here maybe, with certain levels of Buddhist thought. But none of us can really explain it verbally, so maybe this is just a slightly different translation. Let's look at it that way.

There are six worlds. There's the world of enlightenment, the world of the unmanifest, the world of good intentions, the world of desire—that's this world, the human world. There's a world of astral spirits and beings that are very, very unhappy, and then there's a world of such complete nescience, of such complete darkness, that one doesn't even recognize that it's a world.

The world of enlightenment is not a world per se in that, obviously, we're discussing nirvana. It's nonstructural, nonbonding, noncausal, nonatomic—no chemical makeup. It's the extant portion of that which is. That's where I happen to reside and come from. I've come from there to here, into a physical formation. But where I come from, there are no sunrises and sunsets, there are no todays and tomorrows and yesterdays. There's none of this. There's no duality. There are no other worlds. It's a timeless, perfect, extant, non-bonding reality. Non-bonding means non-karmic. No cause and effect. No structural basis for anything. Buddhist tech talk—you understand.

So in the world of enlightenment, things just are things, except that they're not things. Once again, we're in nirvana; there's no debating team. So if one becomes enlightened as I did in past incarnations, we leave the structural universes behind, and in a way we don't even have past incarnations at that point because the form that had those incarnations has dissolved in the clear light of reality. Sometimes beings come forth from that particular realmless realm. That light incarnates and wanders around through the samsara, kind of looking at itself in various countless forms. We call beings who come from that realm, not that it's exactly a spatial realm, "enlightened."

Then we have the world of the unmanifest—the fifth world, or second, depends on how you're counting. The world of the unmanifest is the undifferentiated reality. That is a world in which there is no form whatsoever. It's the world of *samadhi*. It's a world where there's no dimension, but yet it has a specific existence as something that's not manifest to the senses. When we say manifest, we mean apparent to the senses. Reality exists beyond the senses, obviously. Otherwise there would be no life. But the sense worlds cannot penetrate, or the senses cannot penetrate the unmanifest. The unmanifest is also different than what we would call the higher astral. The higher astral has formations; there is a sense of time there, although it's completely different than the time here.

So we have the world of enlightenment—nirvana. We have the unmanifest, which is again pretty hard to talk about. That's a world of dissolution, but dissolution is a finite state in its own way. Then down from that we have the higher astral—the realms of the happy spirits, the happy haunts, kind of like at Disneyland. Spirits with a sense of humor—the land of good intentions. This is, when one dies, this is heaven. Heaven is the higher astral. There are countless realms and dimensional planes, existences—they go on forever—that are very beautiful, where beings incarnate for a time, where they exist. Sometimes it seems to be timeless, but it does end eventually—which is why we call it structural—and these are the realms of the higher astral.

The unmanifest, which is next up, is not heaven. It's beyond heaven. Beyond heaven is pure spirit. Heaven we think of as kind of a cloud, a kingdom, happy experiences, beings singing, laughing, being in ecstasy and meditation. You see it in the Buddhist *thangkas*, you know, where they're all having a very, very serious party up in the higher astral. Everybody's having a good time. But above that is the unmanifest. You can't put that on a *thangka*. There's no way to paint it. One can symbolically represent it, but the unmanifest is pure spirit. Yet spirit exists and is perceivable by itself, if by nothing else. It knows of its own existence.

The world of enlightenment doesn't know of its own existence. We're beyond both knower and known. There's no conceptual identity whatsoever. Enlightenment is not even conscious of itself—it just is. There's no way to talk about nirvana. It's just riddles.

The world of desire, number four on our hit parade, is this world. That is to say, most of the beings we see on this particular planet or in this particular plane, as I prefer to think of it, are working out basic karmas in the fourth realm. This world is not a middle point in evolution. It's one step down from the middle, in my opinion. There is no middle. The higher astral is one step up, if you will. But you know, Dante and a lot of people like that, and all the Christians, thought of the earth as directly in between the two opposites. Not at all. This is in a slightly lower state, if you will.

This is the world of desire and fulfillment, frustration. This is where one takes a body and one has experiences. And those experiences will determine whether one comes back to incarnate in this realm or one goes up a notch to the realm of the happy haunts, if you will, the happy astral spirits—you have a lot of good karma and you've evolved your causal structure. Or, of course, one can go down to the realm of the unhappy haunts, the realm of entities and what in Tibet they call the hungry ghosts. That's a way of saying dissatisfied. They're hungry; the images are that they go and eat food, but it doesn't quench their hunger. It's a way of saying that they're always in total misery all the time. People in the desire realm are in total misery in a different way but at least once in a while, here you can go to Burger King. If you're hungry you can get a burger, and it can be good. It might be bad. But it could be good! And you will be satisfied for an hour or two before you get hungry again.

One level down on the elevator of consciousness, and no matter how many burgers you eat, you're just as hungry. Plus they never taste good. Here, sometimes it's good, sometimes it's not. On the other hand, of course, if you go up in the elevator of attention a level, then you're in the world of enchanted tacos, you're in the world of wonderful marshmallow ecstasy, hot fudge beyond—you're in a world of happiness. No sense of dissatisfaction at all. None, in the higher astral; nothing but dissatisfaction in the lower. Here, in the middle of those two realms, some days you win, some days you lose. Some days you're miserable, some days you get a little happiness.

Now if you go down, of course, below—if we hit the basement there, we go to the lower realms—again there are countless subdivisions of these basic six relative planes. Nirvana is not a relative plane, so it's not as if this is a simple thing. There are endless realms in each one. Down in the basement, it's very dark. There's no light at all. And the word "pain" is inapplicable. Pain is something that we experience in the second and third realms, this world and in the lower astral.

There's really no pain in the realm of the higher astral. A lot of spirits playing mini-golf having a good time—and of course in the unmanifest there's no body anyway, there's just the realm of pure spirit. And in *parinirvana* there's only perfection, not even spirit. It can't be comprehended by the mind, nirvana, it's so wonderful. It's so wonderful it can't be comprehended by the mind.

To say "pure spirit"—you can kind of get a sense of what that is, if you've meditated for a number of years and you've had meditations where you've stopped your thoughts for a while and the ego has gone away and you've experienced a taste of samadhi or satori; you know a little bit what pure spirit is like. You only know of it afterwards in terms of remembrance, and the ego can't quite remember it, but you've been there and you understand. You have that silent knowing of what pure spirit is. Nirvana has nothing to do with that realm of thought stoppage and samadhi. Nirvana is completely apart—"much better" in Western jargon.

The realm of—the lowest realm—again, it's not exactly hierarchical but it's a way of discussing it, these are just extant realities. But from a dualistic point of view, the bottom of the line, there is no bottom. The bottom line is that there is no bottom line. The lower extant realities go on forever and they're places—I wouldn't even say they're places of suffering. They're places of—in English there really are no words for this. We have special words in Tibetan and in Sanskrit and in some of the Indian languages for these concepts. We don't have anything in English. Hell is not a good concept because hell implies a sense of beingness and going through suffering. Hell is very spatial, and there might be a good day there once in a while. The lower realms are just realms of complete—I don't even want to say darkness. There's a lack of knowing. There's a lack of experience. I guess it's what some people might think of death being like if after death there was nothing. It's something like that. But yet there is a presence.

It's not that the universe is torturing us because we've been good or bad. Life isn't like that. There's just cause and effect. That's all there is. No one knows why. Lots of people have philosophical points of view on the subject, but regardless of their philosophical points of view there's cause and effect. How you handle your karmas, how you orient to the experience of life, will determine the thoughts you think, the actions you engage in, the emotions you allow yourself to feel, what you meditate on, or if you don't meditate—these variant things will determine where you end up.

Just think of it as a big ocean liner. And on the ocean liner there are six different possible ways of going, OK? There are the nicest cabins—just wonderful, great, staterooms, 24-hour room service, everything is great. You feel so good you don't even feel—that would be the realm of pure spirit. Then there are just lots of fun—the tennis set, you know, the young couples on the honeymoon, that's sort of the happy spirits. I mean just everything is wonderful for that period of time. It may not last a long time, but we're on a nice honeymoon, lots of fun, we're getting to know each other. No unhappiness. We're just having such a good time.

Whereas pure spirit, we've got the ultimate cabin and everything is just wonderful. It's not even a sense of happiness. It's a sense of total peace. We're in the right place being perfect. Everything is elegant but without the dry, dead boring elegance of the rich, but with an eminently powerful life force. There isn't anything that isn't perfect in the realm of spirit.

In the realm of the higher astral, it's just fun. It's just, we're on the honeymoon and we love each other so much that we can't keep our hands off each other and everything is wonderful. It doesn't last, it's a honeymoon. It's a certain duration.

Of course, then we have the lower price cabins. And it depends on how you handle it. The view isn't really great; they're kind of small and cramped. If you were a very upbeat person, though, you would enjoy it. You'd say, "Gee, this is really nice. How wonderful, how fortunate I am just to have this nice cabin." You'd fix it up a little bit, put a nice picture of the Buddha up, or Elvis Presley or somebody who inspires you. And in that cabin you'd feel great. Or you could be a miserable prick and just bitch about the cabin, how awful it is—"Nothing works out, I wish I had one of the ones upstairs." It depends how you handle it. It's humble, it's simple. The dining room is not as sumptuous, the entertainment is not as great. But a person could have a good time there, or a person could be miserable, or go back and forth between the two, depending upon how they handled their emotions and their mind.

Then we have steerage. We're down there where it's not a lot of fun to be. It's cramped, it's uncomfortable, it's basically awful. We never get to come above the deck. We never get to see the light and we're just seasick all the time. We're in a big room with countless beings and everybody is frustrated and pissed. It's kind of like a mental institution, an asylum, where everybody is out of their minds and screaming and no two insanities are exactly the same. But what makes them all the same is that they're in complete unhappiness.

All the way down on the bottom, well, you're not even on the boat. You missed the trip. You're in a level of experience that can't be described. Nirvana is not the opposite of that at all. Nirvana has no opposite. Nirvana is just separate perfection without self, without even the knowingness of self. Experiencing self as pure spirit.

How you conduct yourself determines what happens. The state of mind you create and live in inside yourself produces these changes in mental states. In a sense, we always want to think of all of these conversations in terms of a spatial realm. That is to say, the higher astral is a place, the earth is a place, the lower astral is a place, the sub-world which goes on forever is a place, spirit is somehow a place and even nirvana is a place. Not really, they're all coexistent inside your own mind.

We actually are all those realms. Not we as physical bodies or individual egos, but the deeper "we" within us is everything. You have to make the metaphysical leap in understanding to see that. You might be able to intellectually appreciate it or not know what I'm talking about. But if you make the metaphysical leap, you will just intuit how we can be these foolish human beings who have trouble sometimes making it through the day or every day, and yet at the same time we can be all of existence, manifest, unmanifest, *parinirvana,* everything.

How we direct our attention determines what we experience or "who" we even experience, since we are somewhat different in each realm. Yet as we know, there's sort of a spatial world to a certain extent, or at least it appears that way to the senses. There's this planet, another planet; this star, another star; this universe, another universe.

And when I say that the higher astral is endless, that the lower astral is endless, that the plane of desire is endless, those that appear to be spatial planes and that the worlds below the lower astral are endless—nirvana, of course, I can't even say it's endless. That's too simplistic. I'm not kidding when I say that, I mean that's the truth. We just grow so used to looking at the stars in the sky and planets and we think that that's what big means. All the far-flung eternities put together doesn't equal a parsec of nirvana, or even one of the higher astral planes.

Eternity is eternity. It's forever, it's endless, it's perfect, it's shining. Yet there is a system and a flow and an organization to the structure of the universe. Just like there's a system and a flow and an organization to the human body, to atomic structures, to the elements. That system and flow is not apparent to one who cannot see beyond the senses because the senses can't perceive it. But when you look with the eye of intuition, when you use the higher faculties, you can cognize, learn about and experience, in each realm, each aspect of the universe. So in the higher astral we perceive through the astral body, in the lower astral we perceive through another aspect of the astral body, in the desire realm we perceive through the senses, through the thinking mind, emotions, that kind of stuff. Perception alters according to the state of consciousness.

Now the reason I go through all of this is to give you an explanation of your options. In other words, the Christian system just says there's heaven and hell and earth. And earth is in between heaven and hell. Oh, there's this subvariant purgatorial situation you can go through—it's like transient hell. You can kind of get the "Get Out of Jail Free" card and maybe get out, or go around, miss a few turns, roll doubles. But the Buddhist mind is more complicated than the Christian mind, obviously, so it comes up with more complicated—we have endless heavens, endless hells, endless earths, and then we have something lower than hell. We have endless subrealms that make hell look like Club Med and we have endless nirvana, which it can't even be endless since it's nirvana; it's beyond such things as beginningless and endless.

It's just more complicated. And we say that all those realms exist inside your own mind. Now it doesn't mean they exist in the cells in your brain. That's not what we mean by mind. That's a very physical definition of mind. We see mind as that which we are, which is never definable. We can never define what mind is. There's no way. We can never see it. We can only be it. Yet it's forever and it encompasses all things. Except of course nirvana, which can't be encompassed since it's not a thing.

So now you know where you are. You're somewhere in infinite mind forever. If you don't know how the universe works and how to get around it, it can be very painful. When you understand the system and you realize that there is actually a system to life, to incarnation, to states of mind, then you can very intelligently make selections, and that will determine not only where you end up, how you end up, but who you end up as, or what, or as nothing.

The role of the Buddhist teacher, vis-a-vis the Buddhist monk in training, is to explain your options and to show you what creates karma. All our discussions are basically karmic until you're fully engaged in samadhi, when you can go into the breathless state for an hour or two a day, where you basically don't breathe and there's no thought in the mind. Then at that point the teaching process changes, and we don't really discuss karma, we start to discuss the nonbinding states of reality, which are above the higher astral.

Naturally we go to the higher astral sometimes in dreaming, if we have a discussion in dreaming. We might meet in the higher astral realm, which isn't a dream, we're just both in the astral body and we run into each other in a lovely realm and we have a discussion about the *dharma* or something going on in your life or just look at neat things that are pretty to look at just because it's fun to do. It's ecstatic. Or we might run into each other in a lower realm. If you happen to be there and I happen to be passing through, I might ask you what you're doing there.

Enlightened teachers get all kinds of assignments. Sometimes we end up in the higher astral, sometimes we end up in the realm of pure spirit, sometimes we end up in the desire realms. Sometimes we go down to the lower astral to teach, you don't really teach there, you just sort of are—because everybody is very confused there. They don't understand anything. They just hate—themselves mostly. Sometimes you can even teach all the way down. There you just meditate because there's nothing to say. Just by being there you try and send energy and understanding.

Why is the universe so complicated? Why does infinity embody itself forth in all this complexity? I have no idea. It's not really a concern of mine. Philosophy is not a big subject for me. I'm more of a structuralist. I'm just interested in how things are, what are my options, how do I get there, that sort of thing. Some people just have more of a philosophical bent. I'm not particularly philosophical. I'm a structuralist. I just like to know how things work and what are my options. Who am I, what is there, is there any way out of here? Is there a better place, how do I avoid fucking up, that sort of thing. I'm very structural—no, people are all different! I'm very structural in my viewpoints, very non-emotional. Emotions are interesting, but I find them a little bit tedious, personally. They require a lot of energy to experience.

If I had my choice I'd hang out anywhere. I mean, it doesn't matter. It's all God, it's all the same. There's only nirvana for the enlightened. And everything else, even the gradated realities, are viewed as such. That's when you read in the Tibetan books, they say "samsara is nirvana." That's what they're talking about. The only person who can say that is somebody who is enlightened. And it can't mean anything to anybody else, so they obviously just say it because they enjoy hearing how it sounds, since no one can possibly understand what it means. They don't even understand it, they just are it. Enlightenment R Us, that sort of thing.

So it doesn't really help to think about nirvana because you can't. Even the realm of pure spirit is something that's very ineffable, and when we experience it we don't have a sense of experience of it because we have to transcend the ego to experience it. And we do that as meditation improves and you enter the breathless state in which there is no breathing, no conscious thought, and the ego dissolves in the clear light of reality. The clear light is the light above the spirit, the spiritual light of the fifth realm—or second, depends if you're counting or not, and how.

So then, what one does with an explanation like this is, consider how big the universe is. It's endless. Its realms are endless. Consider that behind all of this is a nonmoving force that we call *spirit,* which somehow makes all of this happen. It's a big screen on which all of these images appear and it is the perceiver of these images, and beyond all of that, beyond the unmanifest creative force and all the manifest creative forces, there's *nirvana.* Again, it's not spatially beyond. But this is all perfect light. *Clear light.* It has no definite color. This is all perfect light. That's all there is. But it is perceived by variant beings in variant states of minds and variant worlds. That's how it all looks anyway.

With this information, the intelligent person begins to understand that there's *karma,* and the state of mind that they're currently dwelling in can instantly be modified at any time. And the realms to which one is born can be easily modified at any time. The study of Buddhism is essentially the study of modification—how we modify the state of mind we're in, how we modify the realm we're in. That's really all it is. How to better one's state of mind and better one's place of existence, since it's easier to study the *dharma* in higher realms. If we're not in one, we find out how to get there, so we run into a Buddha that exists in whatever realm we're in and the Buddha will explain—Buddha meaning one who is enlightened—how to get to the next realm where it's easier to study all this, which would be the higher astral. Once you're in the higher astral it's a lot easier than it is here. But wherever we are, we meditate and we go beyond the realm we're in and we experience beyond the senses the realms of perfection.

Buddhism always points you. There's always a picture on a thangka of the

Buddha with his hand pointed in a particular direction. There's usually a big wheel in front of him if we're doing the six worlds, which again I interpret a little differently. And he's pointing beyond the wheel of all the realms. Now, I've included nirvana as a realm, so my wheel's a little different than some of the others.

But—translation. He's always pointing, he's saying, "Look, don't get involved here. You really don't want to get involved here. Go to enlightenment, go to nirvana. Go directly to nirvana, don't pass go.[2] Don't worry about the 200 bucks, it's just a wrap—they're just trying to hang you up while you're collecting the 200 bucks, who knows what you'll get involved with. You'll meet a girl or a guy, you'll get married, you'll have kids, you'll grow old together, you'll be born into another realm where you'll forget that there was even nirvana. You know, it gets complicated. Fifty billion incarnations from now, maybe you'll remember the guy who told you to go get the $200, and what realm could he be in by now, and who could he be or what could he be? You'll probably never catch up with him and even if you did, that would take another 50 billion incarnations to be involved with revenge when you could have been in nirvana, forever. You know, it's complicated.

What you do with an explanation like this, I have no idea. But I think it's nice once in a while to admire the universe in its complexity and its diversity, along with its simplicity and purity. There's an understanding that one gains from all Buddhist thought and icons that cannot be explained in words. The purpose of all our explanations is not to have you understand anything, but for you to snap from the understanding of the intellect to the understanding of pure spirit, where you just know things. All our explanations work backwards.

You usually want an explanation in the West—you want to hear something explained so that you can understand it. We know that all understanding is illusory and fallacious, meaning it's incomplete. So we don't want understanding. We've had all the explanations. We've had life explained

---

2. Rama is referring to the game of Monopoly.

to us so many ways that it doesn't mean anything any more and we know that all the explanations in the world aren't going to give us the pure experience of ecstasy, of enlightenment.

So we use explanations backwards. We use an explanation to take you to a point where there are no explanations. If we explained absolutely everything in the cosmos, you will realize at the end of all of our explanations that nothing has changed for you and you're still not a bit happier nor more aware. That then forces you, if you're a go-for-it type, to jump beyond explanations to the realm of pure intuition and understanding, in which case we click up to realm five, the realm of pure spirit. That's what a Zen koan is supposed to do—or really anything in Buddhism is pointed at taking you into not a conceptual leap, but the leap beyond conception.

All our explanations are not intended to explain anything but only to get you so frustrated with explanations, which all seem so wonderful in the beginning and prove to be so pointless as time goes on. All our explanations are designed just to kind of confuse you and get you so involved in explanations that finally you say, "I can't take another explanation!" And you just sit down and meditate. And you stop your thought because you're sick of hearing your thoughts trying to explain everything to you and rationalize and work it out, and everything—thought stops, the universe stops, and you're in the realm of pure spirit and you just know.

Now you can stop there. Most beings do. Or you can go beyond spirit because even the explanation, even the sort of the nonexplanation of spirit—now I sound like Marshall McLuhan, right? Spirit is definitely a hot medium, right? Even the nonexplanation of spirit is a wrap. You see, now that you didn't skip—you didn't get hung up on the $200 and now that you own Park Place and everything else, and still, now you're just stuck, you're stuck with this board, and maybe you know how it works, maybe you've even—but you know, you're still playing the game. Even if you're winning, you're losing in the game of life.

I mean you can't lose for winning and you can't win for losing. See what I mean? These explanations will drive you crazy! Make the ganglia twitch, right? So then, we don't want to win, we don't want to lose, because we realize after a while that we're the same being and that they're actually the same experience. There's no difference between winning and losing. I mean, OK, you go to the track, you lose a lot of money, you win a lot of money, you say to the guy, "Hey, you trying to tell me there's no difference between winning and losing? I went in with money, I came out with none. I went in with a little, I came out with more. Of course there's a difference. What are you, stupid?"

What we mean is that they're the same type of experience. Ultimately winning and losing are sensorial, affixed to an ego, blocked in time and space, and none of them ultimately make you happy for very long. If you're going to win or lose you might as well win, I mean, let's have some common sense. But winning eventually will turn into its opposite. It can't sustain itself forever because everything changes. Beyond winning and losing we have a better experience and that's the realm of pure spirit, and of course you can get stuck in that realm. If you've got to be stuck someplace, it's not bad. Even the higher astral is pretty nice. But the realm of the dissolute, unmanifest, perfect reality—samadhi and satori are our terms—in which there's only light and not even a sense of oneself perceiving light—that's the higher astral—but just light extant of itself, in itself and through itself, that's not such a bad place to get stuck.

Remember, it's not a spatial place, it's a place inside your mind. You see, it gets frustrating so that you'll make a tremendous leap beyond all this discussion and this conversation to stop your thought, fold down the ego and be the pure beingness of the fifth realm. But no one can explain how to get to nirvana since no one remembers. Since no one is who they were when they went there. You give up being someone.

You see, that's the fun of Buddhism. We do have a wild card in the deck that can't be explained, that changes value continuously, and that's enlightenment. That wild card is inside each one of us, if we could but find it. We've just sort of misplaced it. Or did it misplace us? You could go crazy thinking like this. Or you could become enlightened. Is there really a difference? Some say no, some say yes.

Life is an endless experience of God's. And God doesn't even exist in nirvana, yet God exists in other realms. What does all this mean? You'll have to sort it out. But it does mean something. It suggests that there's more to life than HBO or 99 channels. Life is infinite ecstasy in the planes of infinite ecstasy. It's infinite suffering in the planes of infinite suffering. It's infinite boredom in the planes of infinite boredom.

What all of this suggests is that you have a choice. Most people aren't aware of that, they don't even know that there are other things to choose, let alone that they can actually choose. Buddhism suggests that you have that choice—you are in the driver's seat. Hertz or somebody has put you there. You have an absolute choice about what you experience in your mind.

The sense world is unchecked. Anything happens there. But within your mind you can experience nirvana, you can be, etcetera—there are no words. Spirit realm of pure unmanifest spirit, the higher astral, the lower astral, the desire realms or realms beyond cognition of nescience and darkness. Pain isn't even a word. The other side of light. The absence of light. Light can be absent from itself. It's a very interesting trick that creation can do.

I've journeyed through all these realms—because I like to travel. I just love getting around. And so do you, evidently. All of us are doing this forever, but it's nice to wake up in an incarnation and realize that we have choices and conscious control and that we can better our state of mind and better our life both in the physical, astral, causal, and beyond. There is nirvana—inviting, shining, perfect, refulgent, unknowable, yet attainable. How interesting. What an oxymoron, from the point of view of reason. Yet as real as reality is.

Thank you.

CHAPTER THREE

THE MATURE MONK

The universe is in your hands. It's in your hands, it's in your eyes, it's in your feet, it's in your breasts, it's in your back, it's in your body. There's a wonderful scene in *The Last Temptation of Christ* where Christ is on the ground and he's writhing and God is inside him. And it's not pleasant; it hurts. This is a very different point of view than we get in the usual stories about Jesus in the Bible. It has upset some people, but there's some truth to it.

Spiritual growth and development is at times very painful. At times it's difficult, like any growth and development. But there needs to be a recognition of who we are and what we are and what the truth is. The truth is that the universe is in our hands and it's in our body. Self-discovery and enlightenment is not something that is outside of us physically. It's here. We are it, and it's in everything. Everything is the eye of God. God is in everything, and God is everything. To not see that is to be blind.

There's a resonance inside us, a sense of who we are. We're a multi-bodied traveler. We're an essence. We're a feeling, an awareness that has an ancient existence. The world of meditation puts us in touch with that being. Happiness is not something that you'll ever find in life, in the world. It doesn't exist there. There's no place that you can go to on the earth that will completely fulfill you. The Himalayas are beautiful. Ladakh is a very nice place. But if you go there, it's still just a place.

You've been to lots of places and it's fun to visit them. Each place has its own powers, its own beauties. People are interesting. There are all types, shapes, colors, sizes. They have different types of minds; you can experience them. But they won't make you happy.

It's interesting to have a successful career. It's worth working towards because it gives you a sense of self-discipline; it trains your mind. But having a successful career, having a great car, having a great lover, having everything doesn't make you happy. It just passes the time. That's all it does. There's only one thing that makes you really happy and it's not found in this world. Otherwise everyone in this world of things and places and experiences would be happy. The only thing that makes you very, very happy is to go beyond this world to a world where there is what they call heaven—an absence of pain, ecstasy, a sense of completion, not just a sense of completion, but actual completion.

God comes in different forms. There's the form we see with our senses, and there's the form we know in meditation that we feel during the day and during the night if we extend our awareness. God is found in silence and in noise, but we get a deeper side in silence. Noise can take us to silence. Flesh can take us to spirit. Pain can take us to ecstasy. We use all the routes there are in our quest for enlightenment, perfection. But you should know that you'll never be happy if you just try and get things and avoid things because then you're in a world of pain and fear, loss and gain, of ego, time and space. Happiness is gained by getting outside the circle of all of this, the circle of self.

Enlightenment. Enlightenment is knowledge of who you are in a very real sense. Not just who you are in terms of what your personality is like, your likes, dislikes—that's a simplistic overview of the personality structure. Who are you? You're not a person, certainly. We take that form. We're an essence. We're an awareness of God's. We're made up of countless, countless realities. To come to know that is to know the truth, and the truth always frees us.

As Buddhists, and particularly as initiates, as Buddhist monks, we seek to find the truth wherever we are. But it's with an understanding that the temporal truths that we find in the sensorial, sensual world, that those temporal truths, while an expression of the infinite, will not give us what we're really looking for. We enjoy them but we don't expect something from them that's not realizable. Therefore we don't get frustrated when the place we live doesn't feel perfect, the job isn't perfect, the people we know aren't perfect or we ourselves are not perfect. We don't place our expectations upon the physical. We place our expectations upon nirvana, upon the world of enlightenment.

We can elevate our minds and our spirits and direct our bodies to know, live in and flow with the world of enlightenment and spirituality. Or we can be destitute. We may be making $150 an hour, but we're destitute because we have no light. We only have the small transient fulfillments of God in the temporal world.

Living in a spiritual world is very easy, once you grow accustomed to it. But initially, it puts you through some changes. To not go where the crowd goes and seek what the crowd seeks, nor to just avoid the crowd and the noise and be afraid, to be somewhere in the middle. To be looking for truth in all the wrong and all the right places is the only excuse for living.

A Buddhist monk has a responsibility first and foremost to themselves, and that's to find the truth each day in every part of their life. In the morning we get up, take a shower and we meditate. Now we can fall asleep in meditation, but we were just asleep. We just woke up. Or we can meditate; we can make our mind stop thinking. Through the practice of concentration and various techniques, we silence the mind and we enter into a flow of perfect light. We go outside of the parameters of mind and thought and experience nirvana. We hold ourself in that state as long as we can, as high as we can. Then when it's done, we bow. We touch our head to the ground as our way of saying, "Thank you for elevating me to a place that I can't even consciously feel. And I trust that you will flow through my life—forever."

We seek to unify ourselves with the endless light of truth, of God, of nirvana. And while the concerns of the world may not be such, that's of no concern to us. We recognize the infinite playing through all beings and all forms, but we only have to concern ourselves with ourselves. We develop our bodies because it's important to be strong, to be able to conduct the higher light and energy and to be able to deal as highly sensitized beings with the material world and the beings who permeate it.

We go through the day without a sense of superiority, without a sense of inferiority, but with a sense of being special. We're connected to the Buddhist order, to the mind of enlightenment. All day long, we draw the power and force from that world, from all the teachers and all the adherents of the practices and the principles, who for countless lives have enjoyed the beauty of the viewpoints of the enlightened mind. We're in the world, but not particularly of it, which doesn't connote a spaced-out sense but a very grounded, integrated sense of dealing with the physical properly. But also more absolutely, a sense of assurance that our lives are not in vain, that there is a definite purpose, that every effort does create an effect and that happiness can never be known here, not in the physical—only transient pleasure and pain.

Happiness is something we know inside our mind when our mind is stretched towards God. When our mind is stretched towards God, we feel free. Needless to say, we are the God that we stretch towards in another form. Here we are, there we are. We're trying to connect. Yet when we're in the world, we must be extremely practical, pragmatic, down-to-earth, funny, loquacious. We must be able to deal with ridicule and scorn, which it always seems that Buddhists receive. But we feel that that doesn't matter. God's laughing at us; God's laughing at God. I mean, we must seem pretty funny to create so much upheaval—such small groups of people, the Buddhists, seem to upset a lot of people. So we feel that God is laughing at God, and we can take a joke too. We're pretty funny.

But we just keep walking. We have somewhere to go, and it's not in this world. It doesn't matter what anybody says, we know in our own conscience where we're at, what we want. We know that we don't mean harm to any living being and that we just wish to merge our minds completely with the eternal light of consciousness, and that's all that matters. And we forget that sometimes. We forget who we are and what we are. We get very complicated with our lives. We think, "Well, I need this and I need that to be happy. I have to have one of these and when I get to this point, it will all be different." No, it won't be. It'll just be another place, another state.

What makes the difference is when we take our mind and put it into the scriptures, when we read the Buddhist Canon, the Pali Canon, when we read the Tibetan books, when we read anything inspiring, somebody else's journey into the world of enlightenment, anything that takes us there to that place of silence or stillness. Sometimes surprising things take us there, something that we might not expect. Something that seems, perhaps, antithetical to stillness. It doesn't really matter what it is because the ten thousand eyes of God are everywhere, always seeing and always looking at perfection in different forms.

Enlightenment is real. It's something that you grow into every day. The experience of satori, which is the lightning flash—the moment we step into it, the transmutation, the epiphany of perfection—is something that we have many times a day, briefly, a moment, an intuition, an insight into something beautiful.

But don't be frustrated when you're not happy. If you're not happy, it simply means that you're frustrated because you're trying to be happy someplace that happiness can't be. You have a longing for perfection but it will never be realized in anything physical. Yet we're physical and other things are realized—enjoyment, pleasure, pain, suffering, the dance of the senses.

All kinds of things happen in the physical. But happiness is only gained when your mind is in extended states of attention, when your mind is merging with the infinite. Where else could it possibly be? We go to work, we practice martial arts, we live our lives, we keep our houses nice and clean, our paperwork nice and neat, simply so there's no clutter in our lives. Not because we feel there's a residual value to anything in particular, but because it is necessary to do commerce and to transact in the Western world. We're not living in a monastery. And there, it's necessary to do commerce and transact for the existence of the monastery. Monasteries are very complicated. They take a lot to run them.

Our monastery is the world. We're networked electronically and psychically. We're involved with the world of computer programming, meditation and martial arts. And fun. But in all of it, don't lose your purpose—to be enlightened, for you, just for you. No one else knows or cares. They crucified Christ, you know. They don't take real well, necessarily, on this planet, to the people who see things differently. Times haven't changed all that much. There's no alarm, there's no death. The only losers were the ones who did it because they didn't get to hear what he said and see the doorways he would open for them to other worlds that he lived in. The only loser who walks away from a wise man is the one who walks away. It's not the wise man. So never be concerned with insults or lack of understanding. Be brave and be who you are, but turn to the silent mind.

In the quiescent mind, within your own mind, is enlightenment. It's not just in my mind. It's in every mind that exists. You have to find it. It's a harmony, a ray of light. There's a little path of Reese's Pieces or something that leads to it. You have to follow the trail. You'll get off the trail and you'll know it because you won't feel good. You'll be frustrated, you'll be trying to gain satisfaction from the physical. You'll know when you're on again because you'll be smiling and not thinking about how things aren't fulfilling you. But rather, you'll just be experiencing the aliveness of the upward stratas of consciousness.

Meditate each day with your whole being and you will be free. Work, work, work to make the great vehicle, the diamond mind, the Vajra Sutra, perfection, a machine—so you can get back home again, real soon. Sitting around idly contemplating doesn't produce much. But in work you can discipline your attention, forget about your misery, and it doesn't matter how anything comes out; what matters is it was just fun to do. This is all just for fun. The meditation, the computer science, the martial arts, making money, spreading enlightenment—it's all just for fun. The day it's not fun is the day to think about what happened and to get back on track. It's just for fun, for enlightenment, that is.

The eye of God is inside us. It's looking through us and it sees whatever we look at. Sometimes I think we could give God better things to look at than the things we focus on, don't you? As Buddhist monks it is our job to inspire others simply by our own presence. They look at someone who's calm and serene even though they're freaked out. They look at someone who is looking past this world of continual change to something that's permanent and unending, someone who can laugh in the midst of adversity. We're the best hope that humanity has, so humanity is clearly in trouble. (Audience laughs.) Buddhists have always known this. But we have to do our best. Our best is to just be as happy as we can, remembering constantly that nothing here will ever make us happy. Yet we have to do quite well here to have an uncluttered life.

An uncluttered life will awaken within us a very pure, simple view of infinite mind. A cluttered life will just keep us cluttered. We will just somehow never get to what mattered—the world of enlightenment. Going off in the desert and meditating is fun. But one can be as cluttered in the desert as here. Simply going out there doesn't change anything. You have to simplify your life and your mind. You must think more of infinity and less of yourself. You need to spend time quietly working and letting your mind go beyond your work into infinity.

All there is is infinity, but so few are very aware of it except in the most simple, sensorial ways, and of course, a life of continual ups and downs, pleasure followed by pain, youth followed by maturation and by old age and death—it's an endless cycle. But the world of enlightenment bodes a continual renewal. When we step into light, we're free. We simply have to close our eyes, stop our thought and we're free. That's all it takes.

During the day with our eyes open, we witness things. We silently witness the passing of eternity in all of its forms and shapes, and we recognize those forms and shapes as part of our own essence—distant cousins, sometimes very distant cousins, your relatives, not mine. Somewhere out there in the great infinity, everything is connected.

Our interest is not the form but the formless, not matter but spirit because matter just changes; form just changes and it does not fulfill. What creates ecstasy is the formless void, the realms that are beyond description but are very experienceable, the realms of light that we touch when we meditate, when we have any type of experience that brings us into a sense of quiet, perfect exultation. That's what we look for, the peak moments that take us above the horizon that we're so familiar with, which is our boring old life and mind.

Enlightenment is very available. It's in every single moment. It's in every single being. But our task is not every single being. As Buddhist monks, our task is to bring ourselves resolutely more and more into light, to forgive, to forget those who create problems for us because to remember them is only to keep problems in mind.

You all know the story about the two sexist monks who were crossing the river and there was this gal on one side and one of the monks picked her up and helped her across, and they got to the other side and he let her down and she went her way. They walked on for a while, and the other monk said, "How could you let that woman touch you? How could you carry her?" The one sexist monk turned to the other sexist monk and said, "What do you mean? I put her down at the edge of the river. You're still carrying her."

I say they're sexist because they carried her. If they weren't sexist, they would have had her carry them, you understand?

So what are you still carrying? No, real question. What are you still carrying? Are you still carrying everyone who's insulted you, injured you or in some way defamed you or bothered you or hurt you, attacked you or interfered with you? That's a lot of weight. I'd let it go, personally, and just move on and forget. Whether you forgive or not doesn't matter. Forgiveness is a silly word. Forget is the correct word. Be in the moment. Don't even notice. Personal power means that you cannot notice things. You see them in your peripheral vision but they're not worth focusing on them because you only get caught up in them and to get caught up in them distracts you from someplace you want to be—eternal awareness of light.

The only issue is, how long will it take you to wake up? As long as you choose, it's completely within your control. The more deeply you meditate, the more quietly you work, the less excuses you make, the more you simplify your life, the less you expect to be happy here, and the more you move your mind into the upward radiances of the ten thousand lights of enlightenment, the ten thousand radiances of enlightenment, that's when you'll be happy. All this work is simply to gain the mental control to put the mind in alignment with the ten thousand radiances of enlightenment and experience them in various gradations forever. That's our only purpose. All of this is only to do that. That's the total purpose of a monk.

There are teaching monks who remind others of the things that they forget. There are enlightened beings like myself who project the radiances to any who show signs of wakefulness. But what happens in the world is immaterial because it will change again and again and again. You keep up with it, just like you keep up with cleaning in the house. You keep it clean. But you know it will get dirty again. If you're going to cry every time your clean house gets dirty, you're in for misery. If you're going to be in ecstasy every time it's clean, you're going to be in for ecstasy and you'll bounce back and forth. That's life for most people.

But if you just do it because it's what we do, it's what a mature monk does—we just keep up with our lives, pay our bills, go our own way quietly. Then you can take your energy instead of losing it in all the little hassles and all the little battles you could have fought with opponents who didn't matter, who were so confused that they didn't know what they were doing or even who they were or what they were. Instead, if you put that energy into pushing your mind into the ten thousand radiances of enlightenment, you'll find that you'll be enigmatic, practical, purposeful, funny and quite happy. But if you try and become happy leading your life, it's impossible.

Look at the world—happy one day, sad the next; laughing one day, crying the next. But if you put your mind into the Diamond Vajra Sutra, into the ultimate spiritual vehicle, the ten thousand radiances of enlightenment, if you think about it, dwell on it, meditate on it, program about it,[3] let your mind dwell on the kingdoms of enlightenment that are endless—they're there, they're real, they're more real because they stay the same. They are permanent, whereas the transient world of form is impermanent.

Meditate on enlightenment. Read the exploits of the great teachers, the great saints. They'll inspire you. Their power is there. Accept that you've become a monk—unless you choose some day to give it up—to discover something, to lead a different kind of life. Be proud without being vain. Feel special without debasing others in your own view. And seek a stillness, whether it's in the city or in the woods, seek a stillness. Avoid the noise and the commotion unless it's very good rock and roll. Avoid the noise and the commotion; it doesn't empower, it drains. It just looks like it'll feel great but then afterwards, you feel lousy.

---

3. Rama indicates that programming can be a spiritual vehicle.

As a monk you have a responsibility to meditate many hours a day. Not just to sit there but to think of the ten thousand radiances. When you get sleepy, to wake yourself up. If you're meditating for 90 minutes and you're losing it, keep the Tibetan book in front of you and open it up and read a page every 25 minutes to remind yourself to keep your mind there. Don't just sit there thinking for 90 minutes or two hours. It's a waste of time.

Think about enlightenment, live in enlightenment, experience enlightenment and don't care what anybody says about enlightenment, except the enlightened and those who seek it.

Chapter Four
THE NATURAL STATE

They say that faith can move mountains. So can bulldozers, so can nuclear weapons—I'm not sure if that's really what faith is intended for. I guess if there's a mountain that has to be moved, and you've got nothing else to do it with, you could probably do it with faith.

I think faith is intended to enable us to discover who and what we are, what our purpose is in life and what life is. It's interesting—when you talk to someone in the West and very often in the East too, but particularly in the West, about the meaning and purpose of life—it is assumed that the a priori structure of life will remain in place, and we're talking about a substratum modification of how we live. That is to say, we're being philosophical.

Philosophy implies nothing active. Philosophy implies a passive expression that really has nothing to do with day-to-day existence. On the other hand, an ontological review of existence as such, with serious revisions of life, is the nature of self-discovery. In other words, self-discovery suggests that you will reach cosmological points of view, not philosophical but actual dialectical changes in the way the flow of consciousness passes in, above, around and through your mind, that will so change the reality that you perceive, even on a sensorial basis, that there will be nothing that is the same.

Self-discovery is not a submodification of how we live. It's not a methodology per se. We're dealing with changing the structural operation not of the mind—that's a submodification—but actually delineating new aspects of mind and experiencing them and literally removing that which was ourself and our perception, to move from the human level of perception—we'll take it that we all know what that means—to another method of perceiving life. To walk down a hallway and instead of seeing what you see today when you walk down a hallway, to experience life—those moments of walking down a corridor in hundreds of states of mind, seeing the atoms move, perhaps, perhaps seeing everything in streams of light; perhaps being aware of hundreds of realities simultaneously as part of that hallway, perhaps seeing the corridors of eternity intertwined with the simple hallway that runs through a structural building. To see your life again and again as not just your life but as eternity; to be so completely integrated in the experience of perception that there's no sense of a perceiver but just the fluid moment of ecstasy that is reality unfolding itself to itself.

The politics of consciousness, the dialectical change of mind that occurs in Buddhism, is not simply the assimilation of a new philosophical basis or religious basis for viewing and interpreting experience. Rather it is the complete structural revision of that which is, from our point of view, that which is us—the mind, the perceiver. Life.

In the 1960s, the psychedelic revolution occurred and Timothy Leary, Richard Alpert and other people experimented with LSD, psilocybin, mescaline. They didn't do anything new. Similar psychotropic substances have been used in the Far East, in the American Indian culture, all over the world, for a long time. These drugs seemed to open up the doorways of perception and allow one to experience reality, what we've grown used to in the nine-to-five sense, as something totally different—to take a bubble bath and suddenly find oneself in a hundred universes and the bubbles have a meaning.

Everything, every atom, every part of life has a meaning, implies a meaning that cannot be thought about because we're in a pure dialectical state of attention in which there's no thought. The idea is that every atom of existence is reality and is perfect and is enlightenment. But in the dead world of the Western mind, all that is seen are shades of gray. There's a cloud over every experience. There's no possibility of divine incarnation, divine intervention, let alone that one's self in every moment is divine, endless, continually shifting through infinite radiances of the perfect diamond mind of the universal godhead. There's no possibility in the cosmology of the West for such things.

THE NATURAL STATE 39

So in the 60s people started experimenting with these drugs, and they found that reality was not what they had perceived before. It was, certainly, but they found that there were alternate ways of perceiving reality, and so on and so forth.

Now whether these experiences are valid, invalid, hallucinatory or not, these are issues for philosophers and lawmakers to deal with. Whether they're dangerous to society, I have no idea. That's not my province. I deal with the world of Buddhism. In Buddhism we use not drugs but energy, which is developed through the practice of meditation and through mental exercises and by leading a certain style of life that enables us to create effects that LSD, psilocybin, mescaline and these things—they're toys. They're minor shifts in awareness that obviously don't last. A person has to take the drug again, I guess. These experiences are minor compared to the experience we produce with meditation, which, of course, is permanent and unending.

The realization of satori, the day-to-day enlightenment, the nine-to-five enlightenment, changes one forever—to experience satori for what in linear time we would call a few minutes. You will never see life the same way, let alone self. A permanent change is made in one's structural awareness. More circuits of the mind come on. Forever. Each time you experience satori again, when you're able through your extremely hard work, perseverance, willpower, to stop your thoughts for protracted periods of time—it's very hard work.

You have to want to do it very badly. You have to want to be high. You have to hate being where you are, in these gray, endless, dead states of Western mind, in which the possibility of incarnation, let alone of one's own divinity or the divinity of every moment, doesn't exist. Religion is confined to a book. The possibility of the spiritual experience is nonexistent in the West. It happened a couple thousand years ago, and you either met the guy and you had it or you didn't. Once in a while there's a saint who has a minor revelation.

In the Western philosophy you can't perceive infinities at every moment. It's not there to do. What you must do is shuffle through the variant choices that you're given, which are boring and dead in that the grayness holds us into these lower sentient states of mind. The lack of belief, the lack of possibility prevents us from seeing what is there. Endless states of mind do not exist per se in another dimension that you have to physically go to, or another world or a place you have to die to get to. They exist wherever you happen to be sitting right now. Rather, it's a question of moving your perception from the state of what you would call the normal—I would call the very abnormal—waking consciousness into infinite states of perception.

That is done with the will; with the power of one's will we stop thought and move into alternate forms of perception. We gain that power through practicing very, very, very hard each day when we meditate to stop our thoughts. We gain the ability. We also store energy by leading a conservative life, and we continually discipline and direct the development of the mind so we can sustain our journey into enlightened states of mind. Anyone can do this who wants to. It is a great deal of work. It is more than satisfying. The work is nothing compared to the ecstasy. But you have to admit the possibility of a world, of a universe, of such brightness, of such ecstasy in its own presence.

Ecstasy does not require a physical experience. It is perception in its simplistically pure form. That is to say, what we see in this world is a gross abnormality. The human consciousness, the development of human beings, fails to perceive the very simple, divine nature of every atom in every moment. The cloud of negativism and doubt is so complete that it eliminates the possibility of enlightenment. We can't even imagine what it is or that it could happen to anyone, let alone to us.

In the Far East, it's understood that beings are born enlightened, that there are cosmological cycles other than the one that we're engaged in. A larger universal view of time and eternity is held by the most common peasant in rural India. The peasant has no problem that someone can be born from another universe into a human body, walk up to their hut one day and ask for something to eat, sit down with them, transport them by their mere presence into infinite galaxies of awareness, walk out, and that that person's life will never be the same. They will have shown them infinity without having to say a word, just by the pure power of their presence because that individual is perceiving life directly, and just to be around them in their aura, one sees it at least somewhat that way, which suggests the possibility of experiencing our own divinity from moment to moment in any circumstance or situation.

The issue in Buddhism is perception, gaining control of the mind and directing one's attention, to raise the kundalini energy so that it flows with such volatility and force that we simply perceive life correctly. The gray aura of humanity caused by the billions and billions of individuals who live on this planet makes it very difficult just to see what is. Nothing shines because of the deadness of the human mind.

The aura of billions of people coats all experiences like a thick cloud of smog. Just to live on the earth is to live in that smog. If billions of people meditated, then everything would shine here. If no one were here at all but yourself, the world would shine in a way that would amaze you. But the human mind generates an auric field that covers up the naturalness, the innate divinity of life. That auric field is a field of doubt. It's a field that runs contrary to existence. Obviously it's a side of existence, for it is existence.

So the province of Buddhism is the stretching of perception. It's pushing the mind to its—we call it the "natural state," to indicate how unnatural the normal human consciousness is. You know it's kind of funny when you're first reading some of the Zen texts or the Tantric Buddhist texts, and you hear Tilopa, or one of these guys, who are saying, "Abide in the natural state." And you think, "My God, what I have to do to get to the natural state. How can he call it 'natural'? I have to meditate for hours every day, straighten my life out, I have to do all this incredible stuff to get to what this guy calls the natural state."

What he's saying is that everyone has sunk on this planet to such a low state of consciousness, and that [state of consciousness] has become so defined and striated in the individual mind of every single perceiver, and it's taught to every child by every mother and every father, by every political regime, by every philosophy—the total denial of what is. It's kind of an Emperor's New Clothes situation in reverse. It is the natural state we have deviated so far from, the path of it, in this age of darkness, meaning the darkness of the human minds that are on this planet.

In this age of endless violence and repression of the human spirit, we are so far below the natural state. I mean, human beings are a kick. With their technology, humanity actually has the gall to feel that they are more advanced than they were; technology somehow defines intelligence. Technology has nothing to do with intelligence. If technology enables you to kill more people, that doesn't define intelligence. An intelligent species survives, perhaps increases its numbers, but it survives in a high level of style.

The planet Earth is a subworld. Not the planet—the planet is just time and space colliding—but the basic level of awareness on this planet we consider to be subnatural, way below what's average, because if an enlightened being walked through New York City today, no one would see him or her. They would just see a person. They wouldn't see the glow.

There is a wonderful moment in the *Last Temptation of Christ*, where Mary comes up to Christ and she doesn't want anything to do with any of this and she says, "Hey, come on home, son, I'll make you something to eat. We'll sit around and talk like we used to." He looks at her and he says, "I have no mother, I have no father here. I have a father elsewhere." Meaning, this human parent thing, come on, give it a rest. I've existed forever and I happened to pass this way; I went through that particular toll, and I've paid the toll and that's enough. But I can't perceive life the way you do. You perceive life vis-a-vis one lifetime in this very simplistic way. My perception shows me that you were just another minute experience on my agenda.

So then, whoever is with Mary turns to her—after this conversation Mary is heartbroken—and Agnes, or whoever it is, says, "Well, didn't you see what was going on?" And Mary says, "What do you mean?" Her companion says, "Well, didn't you see the thousands of wings, the thousands of angelic lights that existed and went on probably forever? Didn't you see into all those dimensions when he was standing there?" And Mary says, "No, not only did I not see, I don't want to see. I just want my son back."

If someone enlightened walked down the street today, no one would see the glowing light, the thousands of emanations, because the description of the world, the deadness of the aura of the human mind is so complete that it literally blocks out reality. Ever have a conversation with someone where you're trying to explain something to them and they don't want to hear it? No matter what you say, they keep changing the subject, or even if you say it, they will not absorb it.

The entire structure of the human mind works that way. It blocks out most of infinity. To a certain extent it's necessary because otherwise one would be insane, unless you have a very developed mind to deal with the endless permutations of infinity simultaneously. We don't need all information to make good, logical choices or to have a pleasant time. Sometimes too much information just creates a clog. But the human mind works in such a way that it actually blocks out most perceptions. We don't realize that because we don't realize there's an option, because we're brought up in a world where we are taught not to perceive but to avoid direct perceptions of reality and to substitute instead this kind of one-dimensional view of life. We don't know that there's anything else to do.

With everyone doing it on the same planet, the overall auric vibration, which stretches out and touches every mind here, is so complete that it's impossible to see anything divine—unless we really push ourselves. We have to learn to redo the circuitry in the mind. We have to think in new ways. We have to perceive in new ways. This is what Buddhism is about. It's how you actually restructure the mind. Not to come to some abnormal, unique perception, but to get to what Tilopa calls the natural state—what is just ordinary perception in the universe for anyone who's not totally blind.

The Buddhist study is that. We don't feel that enlightenment is particularly unusual. We feel that it's the natural state. Enlightenment means simply perceiving life directly as it is in all of its infinite, ever changing wonder, in all of its varied, myriad states of mind or as *parinirvana,* or whatever. You know, pick your favorite words. The words mean nothing. The perception is.

Black belt doesn't mean much—the point is, can you knock somebody down? If you've got a black belt and you can't do that, then the belt means nothing. To say one is enlightened means nothing. Anybody can say it. To say it as [if it were] exceptional, like, "I'm enlightened, I'm this great thing." Well, no, it doesn't mean that at all. That's just, well, obviously we're not dealing with someone who's enlightened. We're dealing with an asshole, a major asshole because this person, in their confusion, might actually believe they're enlightened, but how could it be extraordinary or special when it's simply the natural state?

There are beings that descend from other cosmic cycles that drop by for a while. They have extraordinary powers and abilities, certainly, and I think that we should respect all life and all forms and cycles, particularly from a common sense point of view, if it can be beneficial to us. If we have a cousin who's a multi-millionaire and we're having problems just making it financially and they drop by for the weekend, I mean it really doesn't pay to be nasty to them. (Audience laughs.) In the quest for infinite truth, I don't see any point in buttering them up if that would cause you to fall from a higher state of mind. But if you could maintain the higher state of mind and at the same time make friends with the extremely rich relative, this is—in Buddhism we're very big on common sense. We have to be. There aren't many of us and there's a lot of everyone else in the world, even though Buddhism is the world's largest religion. Still, there are very few of the true practitioners of the way, and there are a lot of human beings out there who are very hostile towards anything that rocks their perceptual boat. They'll kill you in a minute rather than deal with truth. It's more convenient because then they can forget about it and rationalize your death.

So Buddhists, serious practitioners, have basically over the years walled themselves off from humanity. Remember, monasteries were built not to keep people in but to keep people out. We lived up in the Himalayas because it was the last place anybody wanted to go, except the people who happened to get stuck being born there. It's a very unfriendly environment. It's cold! And since it was the least favorite piece of real estate on the planet and at an altitude high enough to avoid a lot of human aura, we would go up there to meditate after India became too crowded and China, and so on and so forth.

We live in a world that's crowded now wherever you go. The human aura permeates everything. But it hasn't really changed anything. Perception is still the same. The natural state is still the same. It's what we seek. We seek enlightenment. Enlightenment is not something unusual; it's just how life is—seeing it directly. Powers are a little different, knowledge of other cycles.

Enlightenment, in other words, doesn't mean that you know a lot of things. It just means that you are perceiving endless life, and everything glows that you see, including yourself; and that there's no sense of a stable self. There's no fixed personality, nor is there schizophrenia. There are endless refractions of infinity, which we are, just as we are endless refractions of nothingness. All of life is moving in and out of itself in constant, fluid, perfect change at every eternity.

Meditation is the pathway to enlightenment—always has been, always will be. Meditation just means holding the mind in a state of quiescence with no thought. That's not unusual. I think, to think a lot is unusual, personally. It's thought that creates the grayness. So as a Buddhist monk, one concerns oneself primarily with leading a life that doesn't make one think too much. Obviously one thinks when necessary—one perceives right and wrong, what is correct and incorrect, what is always happy and that which should be avoided. But to endlessly have the mind just jabbering on, covers over the diamond, the jewel in the lotus.

We believe that there's a jewel in the lotus with a diamond inside us. We don't mean that in a symbolic, mythologic, allegoric form. We mean directly, that there's a diamond, something that shines with infinite facets right at the very core of your mind. It is the core of your mind. But you don't perceive it as such; you don't see the glow. You don't see the infinite facets, all the realities. You don't see God in yourself, let alone God in anyone else unless they're very, very advanced in meditation, in which case they glow so brightly that if you're with such a person and you direct your attention towards them, their glow is so strong because they have become the diamond, the wisdom.

A very advanced master can glow so strongly that you see the divine in them. You see that glow. You look into them and you see infinity constantly changing, evolving and radiating in new forms. We call such beings avatars, something like that, meaning advanced enlightenment. Not just the ability to perceive the endless flow of reality oneself but one whose mind is so powerful that it just simply radiates. Such beings are very unusual. Very few students, Buddhist monks, ever encounter such a being. It's really not necessary, to be honest. What's necessary is to learn to stop your thoughts and become enlightened yourself. If one has the opportunity to meet such a being, it creates substantial change in one's awareness in life.

Most people never meet such a being, most monks. They wouldn't know what to do. They read about "the" Buddha who was one such being who lived in 600 B.C., whatever. Maybe they read about Milarepa, who was one such being, and a few other names. But in the whole Buddhist tradition, there have been very, very few beings at the level of enlightenment that you could simply look at them and see the diamond mind of the universe without a lot of effort—very few, very rare. There have been a number of enlightened beings, meaning people who live in satori; people who have stopped thought completely; who perceive life in unending, shifting, perfect form without a sense of self, meaning personified fixed ego that has definitive past history, identities, and so on. But very, very few ever have, at least in this world, passed through, whose radiance is that bright. It's unusual.

It's not really necessary for the student of enlightenment to encounter such a being. All that's necessary is a good place to meditate, a knowledge of what meditation is and someone to study with who has learned to make their own mind completely tranquil, who can show you how to deal with the variant difficulties and opportunities of mastering the mind and your society and your environment, [dealing] with your history, and so on and so forth—someone who can show you the steps, who's taken the steps, understands the difficulties, the hardship, the humor, the variant sides of the experience of gradually making the mind natural. That's all that's really necessary.

To deal with someone from other infinities is problematic at times, to deal with a true master of all the realms of the yogas. We call them someone with the seven seals of enlightenment, meaning that their gradated perception has passed through all the realms—these are human words. I mean there's no way to explain it, particularly in English, let alone even in the Eastern languages, it's difficult. There are words for such things, but the words themselves are still words.

There are beings who, from time to time, come into this world. Not simply with miraculous powers, which we call the *siddhas,* but with a miraculous awareness that is so strong yet so subtle that anyone or anything that touches that awareness is transformed forever. All their *karmas* are shifted. That transformation, of course, it's hard to say how it will work. It's always a teaching, let us say. Some people might encounter such a being. If that was your fortune, it might cause a lot of what you would perceive as problems and difficulties in your life. But those problems and difficulties are not really problems and difficulties. Those are the doorways to freedom. In other words, when you encounter a being that's beyond what we would consider the natural state, beyond personal enlightenment, and they use words like avatar, and so on—any word is just going to be confusing. But when you encounter someone like that, all they do is exist in complete purity in all universes simultaneously—you know, the words break down again.

But let us say that they just teach by their presence. They don't really have a message for humanity. It's irrelevant at that point. They're just a fluid, perfect embodiment of what we call the *dharmakaya* or the enlightenment of nirvana—nirvana in human form, if it's in this world, nirvana in other forms in other worlds. To encounter such a being is considered the ultimate karmic blessing in the sense that your life will be so configured that every single variant problematic karma will surface, which means that you have the opportunity of passing through them all correctly, going over the ocean of the samsara and reaching nirvana yourself.

It's kind of like meeting God in a human body. It's tricky. What do you say? "How's it been?" But suppose it hasn't been, from that point of view, from the infinite mind of—maybe there's no past. Maybe this is all that's ever been, this one moment particularized forever in infinite and variant forms. Maybe there are no variant forms. Maybe this moment doesn't even exist as you perceive it to—it's complicated.

That's why it's best to just keep your life simple and not worry about these cosmological matters. But it's interesting to know that there are beings that do walk through this world occasionally like that. Sometimes it's one's karma to encounter such a being and it creates tremendous changes in the multi-life configuration, not simply the life configuration, because when you're dealing with a volatile energy field that's that strong, it enumerates not just the kind of pro temp mind in the current body, but the field of energy is so strong that obviously it would have a protracted multi-life effect. That is to say, it's kind of like radiation; it's the rads.

You see, if you're exposed to a person who has achieved what we call satori, they go into samadhi many hours a day, they've eliminated personal selfishness, you know, all that sort of stuff—a saint who lives in an enlightened state. They put out, what, 30 rads? When you encounter their aura, when you spend time with them, you could pass by them and not see much, but if you're open to them, if there's a symbiosis between the mind states, yours and theirs, then you'll be lifted into very pleasant states of mind. You will find them very inspiring. When you leave them you'll be more in touch; there will be a stillness, a peace inside your mind.

Such a person can, if you just meet them once, affect your life forever. You'll walk away with a very quiet, very beautiful feeling, perhaps a deeper understanding of life that actually comes from touching their aura, and again, there's no aura that's "our aura." It's the radiant mind of the universe manifesting itself in a particular way through a particular being, but it's a one-life affair. We refer to it in Buddhism as a multi-cycled being from the realms of the *dharmakaya,* what we could call a complete Buddha. Maybe that's a better word. The Hindus use the word, *avatar*. It's complicated because they have a cycle and there are only so many [avatars]. We believe that there are innumerable Buddhas.

A Buddha is a being who is complete, integrated enlightenment, through every cycle, through every awareness, forever. When you run into such a being, if you run into not just an enlightened person but a Buddha, then that energy field, the rad level is so high it's incalculable, and their effect on an individual is for many, many, many, many, many, many lifetimes. Simply by the sheer vortex of the energy emanating from them, from their soul, from that part of the universe, which they have—they've so integrated themselves with deeper levels of enlightenment that it just flows through them.

Enlightenment is not a finite state. It's not something that you just do and it's done. It goes on forever. I wouldn't say that there are levels of enlightenment because that makes it too simplistic, too uniform, too diurnal, too yin and yang. Let us say that enlightenment is not something that just happens one day and that's it, and you get the totality of it and there's no more. There's no way to explain it. I can simply say what isn't, certainly, and it certainly isn't that. There are beings whose enlightenment is further. They have suffused more of the diamond mind of the universe.

There's no end to enlightenment. That's the good news, of course. We call "the Buddha" someone whose mind has become so integrated with the deeper levels and structures of infinite mind and infinite being that there is only reality for them. There is no delusion of any type. Yet they come into a body, take on an incarnate form, experience the joys, the sufferings, the thrill of victory and the agony of defeat, all that sort of thing.

In Buddhism we like to talk about our Buddhas. We've named our "ism" after one. But the theory is that we are all incarnate Buddhas. We just have not realized deeply, not simply philosophically or in thought, we have not moved the mind, what our friend Don Juan calls the *assemblage point,* to that deep a level. The idea is that you can move the assemblage point, where the mind joins together and creates life, to deeper and ever deeper points of understanding and perception.

Your journey is to see how deeply you can interface your mind with infinity. That's the journey of a monk, to see. "Monk" simply means that you've decided that the most important thing, the only relevant thing in life is that. You've been properly initiated by a teacher who has put you on the path, empowered you, given you directions for meditation, and then off you go to meditate and to live your life as purely, simply and excitingly as possible. Excitingly in the sense that your perception is that life is glowing more every day because your meditation is clarifying and the way you lead your life and the thoughts you think are continually clarifying your perceptual body. If, on the other hand, life is glowing less, obviously you're not doing yoga properly and you have to start over, hit the reset button and learn what yoga is. You've fallen from the path and it's time to get back on it.

This happens to most monks a number of times. Where you just—you're not practicing yoga at all. You're not practicing real meditation. You're practicing ego or practicing laziness or practicing confusion. It happens to everybody and we don't feel bad about it. Since we don't have a self, we don't have to worry about it, we don't have to account for what we've done or not done, we simply have to get back on the path. Being on the path means we again meditate with joy, we again deal with the suffering of life and the pain of existence without perfect enlightenment with a smile. It means that we clarify our lives and we have a quiet place where we live, we keep it clean and simple, and we have a quiet life with lots of fun in it and brightness of course, but quiet in the sense that we don't fill it with unnecessary clutter, with cluttering emotions, cluttering perceptions, cluttering hates, cluttering jealousies, cluttering vanities because these things simply cloud the mind and they don't afford a very perfect view of existence, rather an imperfect view.

The perfect view of existence comes from an unclouded, uncluttered life and mind whereby the radiance of perfect attention of the mind of the universe floods us at every moment. This is Buddhism. This is being on the path. Meditating with clarity so that at the end of one's meditation the world shines brightly. That means you've meditated. If the world does not shine brightly, even just the physical, sensual perception after meditation, you have not meditated. You have sat and thought of things that were not real. So we have to be dynamic, we have to push ourselves to stillness, to the natural state.

Eventually the natural state becomes so natural that it really doesn't require effort. We abide in it perpetually. But it's only by modifying the mind and one's perception of life continually for a number of years that that occurs, with a grand sense of brightness, enthusiasm and humor. But life should be continually brighter. We are seeking an innocence that escapes humanity. We are continually seeking our own innocence. We want to recapture it for eternity. It's in there, but we lose touch with it.

We come to the path because we know it's there, we feel it there, we remember it being there, whether as children or in another life. We seek our own innocence. We have to continue to seek our own innocence in a world which doesn't care for innocence, which doesn't even acknowledge the divinity of existence. In a world of beings basically gone mad in a sense with their societies and their structures and their technologies, but who are completely oblivious to the religious experience of every given moment.

How absurd to have all the worlds and all the technology and all the power and not to perceive life in its infinite ecstasy, to have all the stuff, but none of the fun. Doesn't make much sense, does it? Well, it doesn't have to. It's an individual matter that each of us considers.

Your life is either getting brighter from moment to moment or it's not. If it's not getting brighter, it's because there's no risk. There's no risk in sitting, thinking instead of stopping your thought. There's a lot of risk in stopping your thought. You might experience ecstasy. You might enter new dimensions. You might see yourself or reality differently. There's no risk in doing a lousy meditation or not meditating at all. There's no risk in being convenient and comfortable. There's a lot of risk in the world of enlightenment. There's the risk of perpetual freedom. But this is a world that defines everything backwards, a world in which good is called bad, brightness is called darkness, up is called down, enlightenment is called abnormal behavior and abnormal behavior is applauded as reason. In the prison camp, the Gestapo state brain-police planet Earth, what is normal is insane and what is insane is normal. But it doesn't pay to tell that to the local politicians or other structural organizations that run the place. They didn't crucify Christ because they liked what he said, clearly. That is the reaction.

Normally, Buddhists build walls to keep others out so they can simply see life as it is—happily, brightly. And we do not seek to interfere in the politics of the world or in other people's methods of perception since we acknowledge that all are God-perceiving, as they will. But we still know what we know. We know that God is in everything, and that to not perceive that at every given moment is illusion—delusion—and to perceive God in the radiance of perfect reality in every given moment in everything that we do, see and are, is normal. It's not saintly, it's normal. We call someone a saint in a world in which everyone is abnormal. The normal person becomes extraordinary. But there's nothing extraordinary about being a saint—that's just someone who's somewhat online with life.

In the world of enlightenment, a Buddha is normal. In the world of

Buddhas, in the world of enlightenment, to be a Buddha is just another aspect of perfection, in infinite perfection. Everything depends upon your state of mind, in other words.

Thank you.

CHAPTER FIVE

FREEDOM

Our subject is freedom. It's always the same. How do we become free, free from the limitations of dimensionality? The way we become free is simple, and it's complicated. It's simple in theory, that is to say, all we have to do is stop our thoughts. When thought stops, a doorway opens into dimensions that are pure and unassociated. They're nonbinding realities. They're non-samskaric, which simply means that they're beautiful, they're ecstatic. The consciousness of the worlds that we can get to through thought—those dimensions are very limited. They're limited by time and space, a sense of past, present and future.

We seek a freedom we haven't experienced yet, and we seek an ecstasy we haven't known. Mostly, I think, we seek our own innocence, a state of joy in which we don't feel age, a body, desires or aversions. There's a very pure feeling of beingness, of aliveness that's always there.

We become used to thinking that attainment in self-discovery is external. We get used to the idea that we have to go someplace or that something can pass us by. In other words, we think of inner attainment as having a dimensionality, a physical structure, because that's how our mind looks at things.

Our mind is very visual. We look at the world and we see up, down, back, forward; we're caught up in calendars and watches; we like to look at things very physically. We like to think that consciousness and the mind are dimensional, and they certainly are not. Dimensionality only exists because the mind can perceive life that way, but that's only one simple method that the mind has for perceiving itself, for perceiving life.

Freedom is a difficult thing because we think it's difficult. If you were sitting in a pastoral environment—perhaps you lived in Hawaii, your needs were simple, the rent was paid, the food was provided and there was an instructor you could go and see on a fairly regular basis—perhaps in an environment like that, a stress-free environment in paradise with nothing else on your mind, you could sit and learn to meditate. Perhaps. But as you know, life for most people isn't like that. We have to make a living. We have to deal with automobiles, insurance, income tax. We have to deal with health, hygiene, shopping.

We have to deal with a lot of things, which is why a long time ago they invented the ashram, the spiritual household, where a certain amount of time was spent by each individual in maintaining a physical location, in cleaning the house, in maintaining the gardens, maybe growing some food, but a lot of time was set aside for meditation and prayer. That was the ideal. The idea was you could go lead a fairly simple life, get out of the social system, which is so demanding, and have some time to meditate, hopefully to be with an instructor of self-discovery who was much further along in their understanding of freedom and their attainment of personal freedom than you were.

The problem, of course, with monasteries, ashrams, convents, is very often the director of such an institution is no further along than the people who study there or that the structure becomes so political. Ideally, everyone would be selfless and kind and working for each other's enlightenment, the enlightenment of the whole universe. That's usually not the case. Usually there are people who mean well, who obviously have an aspiration of some type for truth or just want to get away from the world, but usually these institutions become extremely political. In other words, they're really small societies, and much of what you hope to avoid in societies you just find there.

I personally have lived in a number of spiritual communities over the lifetimes and directed a number of them. I feel that in today's world, one is better not to live in such a place because one can, with a minimal amount of effort, earn a very large amount of money these days since there isn't as much of a class system as we had in other lifetimes. A person can really set up their own little ashram, their own little community, in their own little apartment or condominium or house, do commerce with the world and not be undone by it. I've devised a way, through computer science largely, of making a great deal of money in relatively short periods of time and in a way that will actually develop the mind, further the mind's awareness, and that will assist one in being able to meditate, in other words, and be free.

If your ashram is your own, no one's going to tell you what to do. You don't have to deal with a power infrastructure. You don't have to deal with whether someone likes you or not. You can cut your own way through the universe. I think it's better. I think that we just give up one dictator for another when we leave society and move into an ashram. I think it's better to make our own way and have our own spot and then we can call the shots. If we make mistakes we make them, and if we succeed, then we succeed.

But before launching on your career of self-discovery, I would make a few suggestions as to what matters and what doesn't. To begin with, what you're trying to do is to be free. I think it's good to keep it simple. There's a lot of religious jargon and mystical jargon and a lot of people seem to get caught up in jargon like they get caught up in ashrams and power structures and they never become free, but they become masters of jargon and power structures. I think freedom is a good word, and it's an English word and it will do—freedom from the limitations of the world, freedom from the limitations of the mind as we know the mind in day-to-day life—the thinking mind, the doubt-ridden mind, the fearful mind, the aggressive mind, the desiring mind.

In other words, what we're seeking to be free from are the constraints of civilization, if they're going to try and interfere with the process of trying to live a free life. But if we live in a somewhat free society, the issue then is strictly being free from our personality, our sense of self. It's a very low-tech operating system, the self, the personality. It limits us and binds us to being one very conventional person with likes, dislikes, history, hopes, desires and fears. That's a very unhappy state compared to what else is available in the world of mind.

Self-discovery means that we're going to push back the envelope of personality. There's something outside of personality. There's a deeper, more complete self outside of personality. It's not a personal self, which is a little bit frightening to some people initially, because we have become so used to who we are, even though we hate it, we're afraid to lose that. We're like the person who's made a little bit of money and they put it in a bank. They're afraid of investing it because they might lose it, but at the same time the inflation rate is greater than the interest rate, so little by little what they've saved is being lost. But they're afraid to take a chance and lose it.

Self-discovery requires a bit of courage and a belief in a feeling. I can't define it more than that for you—except to say that there's a feeling of ecstasy, of freedom, which is available to a person depending upon how gutsy they are, how patient they are, how hopeful they are and how tough they are. You have to be very, very gutsy to look the world in the face, society in the face, families, power structures and to walk away from all that. To decide that you're not going to fit in, nor are you going to try not to, but you're just going to follow the beat of a different drummer—your own. That's pretty gutsy because everyone is applying pressure for everyone else to conform. If you think about it, the constraints that humankind has set upon itself, what they've agreed upon as acceptable, is so narrow, so rigid. If you just don't wear your clothes one day, they'll lock you up. No, that's pretty rigid! That's a pretty simple action. In other words, everything's been so defined that it doesn't really leave one a lot of room to move.

If you seek to practice self-discovery, you've got to be pretty gutsy. You have to be willing to buck the system, to buck everyone you've known, who for some reason seems to have a vested interest in how you turn out and how you are or who you are. Essentially what a person does is you either leave everybody you know and go start off on your own, or you have to be willing to tough it out and manage to be who you are or what you were becoming in spite of pressure from those around you, if you choose to stay around them. One way is not better than the other; it's strictly a personal matter.

I don't recommend that people leave everyone they know and leave their relatives. I don't recommend that they stay. It's a personal matter. But what must occur is you must be able to change who you are and maintain that new identity. And then change it again and again and again. If you find that you can't do that around people you know well, then it's better to not know people closely. Or if you find that you can do that and you enjoy the people around you and you're strong enough not to allow what they say and don't say to influence you, then that's fine too. It doesn't really matter; it's a personal thing.

You've got to be pretty gutsy because the party line is pretty heavy on the planet Earth. Always has been. It gets heavier—every 50 years or so it gets heavier. As education has advanced us, it's also defined us more. There's very little room to move, as I said, in the structures of the human system. My advice is to blend. To do what's necessary, unless you're in a political system that's very bad, in which case you have to get involved in overthrowing it. Obviously, if you're in a situation with a dictator, you can't live with that and their taking away all your freedoms. But if you live as most of us do in a fairly free society, political involvement is really not necessary.

If the boat is going in the right direction, then we leave it to the captain and the crew to run it. If it's going in a direction that isn't right or headed for the rocks, then we have to have a mutiny. If we can't talk the captain and the crew into turning it around, if we can't convince them, then the mutiny is necessary to save all of us.

There are always those who will press their advantages, press their desires, press their egos—their own personal needs or views of what life should be for themselves—forward, and they really don't care what happens to anybody else. Everyone else is expendable, in their view. Such leaders have to be overthrown. Hopefully the world will eventually have a democratic system everywhere. It is the best system, obviously, because it gives us the most latitude.

But the democratic system is still ruled by the people in it, and the people in a democratic system are not necessarily very aware. From the point of view of a person who seeks personal freedom, they're still bound very much by the myths of their culture, by their religious structures, which they don't even necessarily understand but have just been handed down to them. They're bound by sociologies, psychologies, by the limitations of culture, by ethnic limitations, all kinds of things.

A person who seeks to be free wants to blow past all of that because they sense, feel, perhaps remember or project that there is another condition that can be attained—a condition of ecstasy, a condition so far different from what the people of planet Earth experience that it's not even discussible. We're not discussing a minor change in how a person perceives life but such a radical departure that it's as if one were not human. Yet, of course, we're just redefining human. We're saying human can be something more than most people experience it. But it's so different from the normal human psyche that there is no point of comparison. It's as if you were going to leave, as in the movie *Cocoon* where some of the old folks decided to leave the planet Earth and go with these beings from another world, the Altereans, and learn a whole different way to be, a different way to live, a different system in which you don't grow old, you don't die and there's no aggression, there's no hate.

One pushes the forefront of awareness back not just a little bit but through eternity. What is the mind of God like? That's what we want to find out. What is the mind of infinity like? What is it like to not have a human mind but to have a mind that's like the sky that goes on forever, that can embrace feelings and awarenesses that the structural human mind, as most people know it, can't even begin to contemplate, let alone experience.

So the occultist sets their sails in a different direction. It's not a physical direction. Whatever you can do physically here is just in a physical dimension. It's an inner direction because we know that within the universe there are different possibilities, there are different dimensions. We call them states of consciousness. If we can place our mind in those dimensions, then we're free.

There are larger views of the world. There's reincarnation, where we wake up a little further and we see that there's a cycle to life, we see what happens before birth and after death, which most people don't know about. There are cosmic cycles where we can, with deeper understanding, view how the whole universe works—well, I don't know about the whole universe, but parts of it. We can gain those understandings. There are understandings of dimensions and how they work, just like there's physical science, understanding matter and energy.

But the real undertaking, as I said before, is pretty simple—it's to be free, because those understandings can trap you too. You can get so caught up in learning all about reincarnation, you can get so caught up in learning about structures, fascinating though they may be, that you're not free; you're just studying something else. It's a different textbook, that's all.

Freedom then is an inner issue. To find freedom, what you really need is a very quiet life. It's a life in which you really don't interface too much with almost anything. You don't want to define yourself. This may sound nebulous, but it's not, it's exact. But it's exact outside of the world of words.

If you define yourself too much, then you know who you are. It's a trick that the mind plays on itself. What you want to do is be like one of the characters in the Bugs Bunny cartoon, or Daffy Duck, rather, where the guy with the eraser, the guy who is writing the cartoon, suddenly comes down and erases Daffy, and Daffy goes, "Wait a minute you guys!" He gets very put out, and they erase part of him and they put part back and there's a surreal moment where the illustrator suddenly appears in the cartoon itself and he's erasing this duck in front of us.

What we're trying to do is erase ourselves. We're trying to take a big gummy eraser, one of those big art gum erasers, and erase ourselves. We want to erase our past, everything we've known, everyone we've known, everything, no matter how beautiful or how horrible. We want to erase it. Simply because we've done it. It's a wrap. We've seen it, we've experienced it. We know that what we want lies elsewhere. If we keep reviewing where we've been and who we've been, then that's where we are and who we are. Whereas if we can erase all that and just forget about it and through the principles of self-discovery and occultism hurl our mind, our spirit, our energy and our life force in an outward bound mode, if we can push ourselves further and further into the stillness of eternity, then we've formed lighter identities, new identities, and those identities will fade and we'll erase them again, and so on and so forth.

It's an ever-outreaching process whereby the personality structure and the mind become more lucid and what we experience is a lighter, gradated reality. We experience a much more ineffable sense of being. This is the process of occultism; we're erasing ourself because we've been there. We reformat ourself into a much lighter, brighter, happier, deeper more conscious being.

Then, after we've explored the limitations of that particular new form, we blow it away and we do it again.

We're continually reaching towards infinity. Infinity is not out there. We always like to think of it as external. It's not in there. It just is. We want to get to know infinity because we don't feel it's intrinsically frightening, it's what is on the other side of life. Since we are life, since we exist, we don't feel that this process is bad or evil or fearful. We've come out of nowhere and here we are. Is there something wrong with that? Is there something to fear? Is there something to be afraid of? We're going to die. Why should one be afraid of death?

In other words, life has made you who you are. You must trust that life will make you, unmake you, change you, shift you around. What's to fear? Why don't you trust the very thing that you are, that has created you and all of what you experience? Why are you so afraid? Of what? Of dying? Of living? Of pain? Of pleasure? There's nothing to be afraid of. There's only life and it goes on forever. Fear is personal. It's inside your mind. It's an emotion. You can push it aside and never be afraid of anything.

Life is just a series of experiences that the mind touches. The mind is unmodified by them unless it consciously adheres to them. If your mind consciously adheres to experiences then you will remember them. Then they become a part of your inventory. Then you identify with them. But by itself, life is just itself. It's forever. It will always be and it always has been and it will never stop. You're part of that, and you can't divorce yourself from it because that's how it is.

You and I are both life. Our bodies will pass away; between now and then, there's just the experience of every moment. We like to call them moments—there isn't really such a thing, there's just is-ness, there's just eternity. Those moments can be in more limited states or less limited states or beyond states. It just depends what you want, and if you like limitation, then you'll stay in limited states. If you'd like less limited states, then you'll find out how to get to those. If you don't want any limitations at all, then you'll learn how to go beyond all states of mind. It's there to do.

You can do whatever you want, don't you understand? There's no real mystery to self-discovery. It's just that most people are so basically unconscious all the time, even those who practice it, that they never sit down and think, "Well, God, I could do anything. I could become enlightened if that's what I want to do. I could get married and have a lot of kids if that's what I want to do. I could become rich if that's what I want to do."

The only thing you can't do is become younger. Can't do that, not till your next life, and that's inevitable. But you can push back from the body consciousness and see your spirit, which is eternal, which never grows old or grows young or does anything. It just watches everything from somewhere inside us. It's a patient watcher. It just observes everything you're going through. All your desires, all the little dramas, all the fears, the anxieties, the hopes, the pain, the difficulty, the depression, that's just your own mind. It's all inside your own head, this magic theater that you call life. It's just inside your mind. Nobody else has exactly the same scene going on, the same drama.

And you get so caught up in it. You get so caught up in the little dramas. It's fun to go to a supermarket or a park or a shopping mall or someplace where human beings convene, where they do commerce. It's fun to watch these beings and if you can stand back for a minute and you get a little distance, if you're not so caught up in your own drama, if you can stand back, you realize that each of these people that's walking around, they have a motion picture theater inside their mind. Each one is completely into the film they're watching; they're the main character. For some people it's a tragedy, for some people it's a comedy, for some people it's a melodrama, and other people—everything just comes in and out of their little drama. But they're so caught up in their own personal reality, literally, as to not see each other or see life, except in terms that add to or detract from their movie that they're making inside their mind. It's the funniest thing to watch.

Everybody's just off in their own little webs of fear and desire and melodrama. You see the old lady sitting on the bench poisoning pigeons, feeding them the little strychnine gumdrops, right? (Audience laughs.) You see the young couple trying to get into each other's pants, as if there was any question of whether it was going to happen. (Audience laughs.) That's why they're together, that's not the issue. It's funny, the gal's worried about the little pimple she has on her face today and will Joey care? And Joey is not looking at the pimple, I assure you. That's the least of his interests, it's a little further down in the anatomical structure. But to her that's the whole world, that pimple—you know, the human drama is so basically boring. It lacks much depth at all.

Philosophers are no different; they're all caught up in their philosophies. That's their house of cards. Religious leaders are caught up in their religious movements to the point where they forget about freedom. They get so busy making sure that everybody else gets free, and they get so frustrated in their religious movement and what happened to it. Everybody's got their drama going, except the advanced occultist who just looks at it all and laughs and keeps becoming more and more free, very quietly gliding through different dimensional planes, doing the little bits of homework each day that allow one to work through the *samskaras* and through the *karmas* and gradually just becoming more and more free because they like that. It's not a better condition. It's just more real.

As an occultist, as you view the people of the world, they're just like watching five-year-olds playing, and some of them are dangerous, they're violent, they're in that phase, Some are nonessential. None of them are helpful, particularly. If what you seek is freedom, the only person who can teach you anything, the only person who can help you is someone who's already done it, who knows the way. No one else can do a damn thing for you but slow you down.

Let's face it. If you knew how to do it, you'd be there now. You're not. So the only person who can help you at all in the whole wide world, or persons, are individuals who have climbed Mt. Everest inside their own mind and gotten to the top and gotten back down and are different from it. If they just go up and come down and they're the same—you can go into samadhi but after you come out of samadhi, if you're still the same old creep, then what good was it? Then it's just a rush. It's just a brief journey into infinity, but then you come back and if you haven't changed, if your view of life is not better, if there's not less self, if you're not more free, what good was samadhi?

You can go to India, and you can see gurus go into samadhi. Yeah, they really do. They can stop thought for half an hour, forty minutes. But then when they come out of samadhi, they're nasty. They're egocentric. Yes, they're really going into samadhi; when you're with them you can feel a lot of energy. But then they're not very nice to the people around them, only when others are watching. They don't really have a deep regard or understanding of what life is. It's just a little trick they can do, a one-trick pony. They go up into samadhi and down. They go up the elevator and down. But if it doesn't integrate with life, if you haven't learned more about what life actually is, as opposed to your little dream of it, your little fantasy.

If you just want a larger fantasy, you don't have to do self-discovery. You can just sit down and think anything you want. But that has nothing to do with the reality of the dissolution of the self and climbing outside of the structures that cause you so much pain or even the structures that bring temporary pleasure, which when gone causes pain. Or even the pain of relative happiness, which fools you into thinking how happy you are, placates you so that you don't see that the happiness you're experiencing is so limited because it's an ego structure. You're in the world of time and life and space and death.

Occultism is a step-by-step method whereby we extract ourselves from the human condition because we feel it crowds us. Yes, obviously if somebody doesn't feel that, then it's not a concern of theirs. But some of us just feel crowded wherever we go. We feel crowded by other people, we feel crowded by societal rules, we feel crowded by ourselves, mainly. We want to be in unhorizoned skies. And so those people practice self-discovery. They find out what it's like, and they do it very well because it's to their advantage. Whereas most people we observe who practice self-discovery just get caught up in a new description, a new "ism," a new religion, a new god, a new political system, new language, new terminologies. But nothing changes. A few of them make it to the point where they go in and out of samadhi, but they don't change. They just, as I said, they do a trick. They're free for twenty minutes or a half an hour and then they're back into the mire of "them," their "them-ness;" they're stuck in themselves.

I don't have anything to do with any of that. I don't teach that. I teach how to be free. I've learned myself. I keep changing always. I became enlightened because I couldn't see any other alternative. I got so frustrated with myself, with any self. To be in oneself at any given moment for more than an infinitesimal time just doesn't make any sense. Enlightenment just means you don't have a structural self. It means you've flipped through the gradated realities. Nothing binds, nothing clings to you. You're unaffected by everything. Ramakrishna compared it to air. When smoke gets in the air, the smoke will pass through the air and it won't stay there. The air is unaffected. It clouds up and then it goes away. Whereas if the smoke passes through a building it gets all over it and it gets sooty, it stays there.

An enlightened person simply doesn't have a structure. They'll experience the desires, they may experience whatever is in the universe. But it doesn't stick to them; it doesn't form a new personality structure. They're nonkarmic. Since there's no structural self, there's no sense of history, there's no karma, there's no cause and effect chain. A metaphysical principle, but it's true. Whereas a person who has a structure, they have a seed, a core structure within themselves. Things affix to you—pasts, futures.

Enlightenment means you're always free to roam through all states of mind, all states of infinity. You have just reached a more pure awareness, which is the mind of God. The mind of God is very pure, sometimes. There are other parts of it that are very bound up. It's infinity, the mind of God. All states, all possible conditions are there, are apprehensible. There are things, of course, that there are no words for. We sit here on the oasis of human consciousness and the verbal plane trying to talk about something that we have to just go and see and do and feel and show and tell, touch—infinity in its different parts and forms.

People come to self-discovery for all kinds of reasons, and whatever you come to will be fulfilled. But hardly anybody seems to come to be free. So whatever dream you have, I'm sure it will come true. If you practice meditation, if you get involved with the occult principles, it makes you very powerful, gives you the power to fulfill your desires sooner. You'll do that, I'm sure. But real self-discovery is about being free. It's something very quiet.

It's something that you experience personally. It's your own view, your own experience of reality. It happens when you meditate.

Naturally, you have to have enough money to be able to live in the right kind of place that's conducive to meditation. You can't be at the mercy of society, otherwise you can't meditate well, there are too many demands and pressures. Naturally you have to be able to afford a teacher. Naturally you have to be able to clothe yourself, eat, do all those things. If you're sophisticated, you're going to need a sophisticated environment; if you're simple, you'll need a simple environment. But the world is expensive. If getting involved in the making and sustaining of one's life is so complicated and takes so much energy and attention and gets you so bound up in the world, then you're not going to do much self-discovery.

You have to convince a teacher to take you on. That's not easy. It's a complicated matter teaching someone about truth because the individual has to show certain signs. They have to show that they have tenacity, that they have a sense of humor, that they can be patient and at the same time, that they have an essential energy to try things that most people would run away from, not because there's anything problematic about them but just because people run away from freedom. Who knows why? I mean, I don't try and understand the insane. As Spock would say, it's not logical.

Freedom is a very simple matter, yet—boy, what we have to go through to do it, huh? We have to unwrap the self, we have to unwrap the illusions, we have to stop making the movie we're making, get off the set and go someplace else to another condition inside our mind. Where is it? How do you get there, how do you do all that? What makes it happen? Words like meditation, karma, samskaras—they're just words. As I said, you can get into the jargon, you can speak it, but that doesn't mean you'll be any more free. You can get stuck in that. You know, it's the riddle, the riddle of self.

What is self? Self is the mind viewing itself. That's all. The mind stops viewing itself and turns towards infinity. There is no self, there's only infinity. Whatever we view is what is. The mind enjoys viewing itself. You like looking in the mirror. "Mirror, mirror on the wall, which is the fairest self of all?" Then you'll see whatever you'd like to see. As I said, bodies come and go, ages come and go, *yugas* come and go, eternities come and go. Selves come and go. As long as we remain self-reflective and keep looking at who and what we are, as long as we keep our analysis that way, then there's no freedom. We're just trying clothes on in front of a mirror and admiring them. We get tired of one, we put on another, but we remain the same.

It's when the mind is no longer self-reflective and instead turns towards infinity—infinity is not frightening, unless you want to be frightened by it. You can't die. Bodies come and go but your spirit is eternal. You're the stuff that life is. Can't be created or destroyed. It just changes form.

To have the detached eye of the occultist, to look outward, to not be so self-reflective and to learn to step through the various viewpoints of consciousness that we call occultism does lead to freedom. It's a step-by-step process. It works. It creates enlightenment, nonbinding states of reality. That's there to do and be if that's what one seeks. Or you can get caught up in the drama of religious study, the politics, the language, the frustrations. You can get mad at yourself when you didn't turn out how you thought you were, when you failed to complete the list of tasks you set up for yourself.

The tasks don't matter. All that really matters is, are you more free than you were? Is that what you want to do? Why frustrate yourself with trying to be free if it really doesn't matter to you? Then you should just dream whatever dream comes along and enjoy it. Know that it will have its limitations, that it will end as all dreams do. That's not necessarily sad, unless you'd like to be sad for a while. Then a new dream will come along.

You don't have to seek freedom. You can become involved with the world of occultism or just be able to fulfill your desires more quickly. Why pretend to yourself that you really want to be free if you don't? In other words, why put yourself on the crucifix of enlightenment? Why do that? Why hate yourself for not becoming something that you really don't give a damn about anyway? Why not just admit that it doesn't interest you particularly. What you'd like to do is fulfill your desires. You want to go on different rides in the amusement park. It's all God. It's all life. Why feel the guilt when you don't do what you really didn't give a damn about?

In other words, unless you're confused, I really think you do whatever you want to do. If you don't do it, you really didn't want to do it. Why hate yourself for that, see what I mean? In other words, people go into self-discovery and they practice. You become a monk and you practice and the teacher tells you what to do. All the teacher is telling you to do is what is necessary to be free—showing you the steps. They're not laying a trip on you, if they're real, and if they're free themselves. Now if you find that you have a resistance to that, and the resistance is strong, it just means you're not that interested. So why go through it, then put yourself through some sort of torture when you find that, "Oh God, I didn't do it. I didn't try that hard." It means you weren't that interested.

In other words, we get caught up in an idea of how we think we should be. That's just another mind fuck. That's just another way of torturing—"Well, I'm supposed to be advanced. I should really meditate hours a day." But you don't because obviously you don't really think that. You just are enamored of a view of how you think you should be. You read a spiritual book and it describes some character who probably never existed. And you fancied yourself as that. So you went to a great master, or a not-so-great master, an insignificant master, and you said, "Teach me, oh master" because you were kind of romantically infatuated with the idea of yourself as a religious person, a person who sought freedom—you, in your imagination, thought of yourself as having a high and noble mind when probably you're just a base slob. (Audience laughs.)

You get so caught up in the drama of it you will go to any extreme to fulfill something that you don't really even care about. So you'll do hours of discipline and not enjoy it, or you won't do the discipline and feel guilty and feel that you haven't come up to your higher nature, which you don't even have!

In other words, if one is truly inspired to seek enlightenment, there is no sense of hardship in the practice. (Someone in the audience sneezes.) Now, let me do that again; you sneezed so you couldn't hear it. If one is truly inspired to become enlightened, there is no sense of hardship in the practice. If you feel a sense that it's very hard and very difficult, then you're not really inspired to be enlightened. Then you're just kidding yourself about enlightenment. You're setting a goal that's not necessary at this time and then you get very frustrated when you don't attain it, if you work hard, because you didn't work quite hard enough. Or you don't like the work or you don't do it at all, in which case you feel guilty, you see? I think that's a waste of time.

I've never found self-discovery difficult because I love it. I get up in the morning and I meditate because there's nothing I'd rather do. Not because I feel I have to, but the idea of going into the world without meditating I find abhorrent. I've tried it and it's very unpleasant. So no one has to convince me. I meditate as long as I can because I like it. I like the difficulty of the practice. I find it challenging. I always have. I enjoy stopping thought for sustained periods of time because it's really hard but I just like that feeling. I like the hardness of it. That's a normal, natural feeling when you're practicing a discipline that you enjoy.

If you enjoy martial arts, you don't have to drag yourself down there. You just are drawn. When you get down there and it's a hard workout, even though it's hard you like it because your spirit obviously wants to do that. I think we spend a lot of time hating ourselves over things that we really don't give a damn about because we have some stupid view of ourselves in which we see ourselves as someone who we are not at this time, who we do not need to be at this time.

You can enter into the world of meditation and touch it lightly and just enter into a few different states of mind, gain a few powers and have some fun. Why set yourself up as a serious religious aspirant if you're not? If you are, it will come naturally. In the meantime, enjoy it at any level that you can. Unpressurize it for yourself. If you seek enlightenment, it will be very obvious to you. Nothing will stand in your way and you'll accomplish it because it's the most fun thing there is. You'll be drawn to the best teacher that's around, and you'll do absolutely everything they say times ten because that's what you want to do. You're so drawn to it, you're so excited by it, there's no other possibility.

Otherwise you really don't seek enlightenment, you seek a more pleasant state of mind, you seek power to fulfill your desires more quickly or to avoid things you find unpleasant, and there's nothing wrong with that. The person who seeks enlightenment so avidly, obviously, in other lives has done that. They've gained more power through different occult practices and found that when they could fulfill their desires completely and avoid the things they wanted to avoid completely, it still didn't get them where they wanted to go. But you have to have that experience, you see?

So why hate yourself when you haven't done something? I have a training course for people who are interested in enlightenment. I have another training course for people who want to make a lot of money in computer science and who enjoy the philosophy of enlightenment. But they're not the same thing. That's why they're separated. Computer science is great and if you combine it with the Buddhist philosophy it gives you a very nice lifestyle. You're a high-minded person, it's fun to hear about the *dharma*; it's wonderful to make a lot of money and just have a nicer life because maybe you have a refined sensibility. But that doesn't mean that you have to hate yourself because you don't push yourself to enlightenment, because you don't. It's not what you want to do now. When it is, it will come very naturally.

I think it's good to unwind yourself a little bit and not push yourself so hard and just enjoy your life because it's all you've got. I think it's a better way to be. It's a more pleasant way to be. Self-hate doesn't create enlightenment. It just causes you to not enjoy the current moment. In the philosophy of consciousness we feel that all life is perfect, all life is ecstasy, all life is infinite and that there isn't anything that's problematic, ultimately, in the ultimate picture of things. I think there's more peace in that.

This is the study of peace. If you hate yourself because you're not becoming something you really don't want to be but you're just sort of enamored of the idea, then you don't have much to do with self-discovery, if you see what I mean. That doesn't mean you shouldn't meditate at all. That doesn't mean you shouldn't practice. That doesn't mean you shouldn't see a teacher if it adds something to your life—why not?

But I'm saying, don't feel that you have to be a black belt if you just like to work out once a week. Why? Why go through that? Why compare yourself to people who are very inspired? Very few people on the planet Earth seek enlightenment. Otherwise we'd have a lot of enlightened people. It's not that hard to do, if that's what you want. It's impossible to do, if that's what you think you want but you really don't. Then it's just frustrating. So I would suggest that if you're a person who just is interested in consciousness, if you find some of those different states of mind more fun than the ones you were in before, then dabble. If you like seeing a teacher, see a teacher. Do what you want to do. But don't hate yourself for not being someone who it's not time to be yet.

It's like someone in fifth grade hating themselves because they're not getting a Ph.D. yet. It's sort of pointless. They'll get there in time. It will happen. It's inevitable. But you may have thousands of lives to go through between now and then before you're a real hard-core seeker of enlightenment, hard-core meaning that you just love it, there's nothing else that matters, there's nothing else that you'd rather do. If you find yourself resisting anything, it just means you don't want to do it.

Now teachers are different. I'm an easy-going teacher, as you know. I have very few requirements. No, I do. I have very few requirements. Some teachers have endless requirements. But I don't have that many, just a few. If you're an intermediate level student, if you've become a monk, naturally you have to meditate for required periods of time each day. Naturally you have to give a certain amount of money, which I use to sustain myself and spread the *dharma* and get involved with projects I get a kick out of, essentially. Because I've worked hard, hard, hard to get to where I am, and if someone wants to avail themselves of the empowerments, I don't see in this particular society anything wrong with them paying for that. They pay for everything else, and it doesn't give them much satisfaction. Why not pay for empowerments? They can do more with one empowerment than all the things they can buy in all the years of their life. Let's face it, it's simpler that way.

In other words, I've set up a system whereby you do not have to be a strict ascetic in order to study enlightenment. Normally the qualifications to study enlightenment with someone who is actually enlightened are very, very stringent. It's rigorous, very rigorous. But I don't see why that should be. I've taught in monasteries where it's been very rigorous and very few of the monks were ever admitted into an actual program where they got very close to an enlightened teacher. But I don't see that that's necessary. In other words, I don't see why this has to be the experience, why some of the things that you study in intermediate enlightenment have to be limited to people who are just totally gung-ho.

If I thought that, none of you would be in the room tonight. Not one. Because no one here, at this time, has shown the signs of a person who's seriously interested in enlightenment, meaning to the exclusion of all other things. To my eye. If you think that that's the case with you, then I suggest that you go compare yourself someday to someone who really is eagerly seeking enlightenment, and I think you'll find that you're not in that position at this time. I have not in this lifetime yet met one person who earnestly seeks enlightenment, in the West. Not one person.

I've met some people who in their own mental melodrama are very convinced that that's the case. But that's because they have the illusions of wanting to be that person. They think if they were that kind of person they would be happy, or they fancy themselves that way. But I've not yet ever met someone who came to me in the twenty years I've been teaching meditation—the hundreds of thousands of people whom I have seen in meditations in California and all over America and Europe—I've not met one person who has ever said, "Please, show me how to become enlightened," and who really meant that in a happy way and then would go through whatever is there without any resistance, and they want to do it really badly.

I've had a lot of people say that to me, but then you say, "Oh great! Well OK, you want to build a house, this is how." You tell them what to do and then suddenly they hate you. They're angry that you told them they had to do these things. Well, that means that the person really didn't feel that way. They were just enamored with the idea. They didn't think you were going to take them seriously, maybe. Maybe they didn't think you really knew how. It's kind of like California bullshit talk, right? You know, where you just say to somebody, "Oh yeah, like, let's do enlightenment. Like, let's go visit the teacher," and what you're supposed to say is, "Oh, like really, like, Hi teacher, how are you? Please, like, show me how to be enlightened." And the teacher doesn't take you seriously, they just say, "Ah, you have a good day today and say the mantra and call me in five incarnations."

But I always believe people. If somebody says to me, "I want to be enlightened," I believe them immediately. It wasn't until after living in California for many years that I realized that you don't believe what anybody says, ever. Whatever they say, they're just making a movie. It's just a part they're playing, and they don't really believe the lines, they just like the way they sound. They like the image they portray. So now, when someone says to me, "I want to be enlightened," I immediately take a vacation because I know that the person isn't serious. I've never met anybody who's serious about enlightenment. I've met many people who like to be in empowered states, and when they meditate with me, if I place them in an empowered state by projecting the kundalini and different lines of energy, they enjoy that. Well, sure, who wouldn't?

I know people who just like hearing the *dharma*. They enjoy an elevated state of mind where they hear higher teachings taught. And that's a nice way to be. I know people who like making a lot of money, who like leading a different kind of life, who like getting away from a lot of the clutter of day-to-day life and who enjoy variant states of mind. But I've never met anybody who seriously wants to be enlightened. Not yet.

I think it's important to recognize, to feel good about the fact that you don't have that driving necessity. You might have it for half an hour once in a while. No, really. For that half an hour, that's all that exists and you want to blow away everything else in your life. That's a touch of it. Someday maybe you'll feel like that all of the time. What I'm suggesting is, when you do feel that way, it's very natural, it's very normal, it's entirely healthy, and there's no sense of having to become someone you don't want to be. There's no sense of having to go through disciplines—you don't think of them as disciplines, it's just the next fun step to get you where you want to go. That's truly what it's like.

If you don't feel that way, then maybe what you should do is see yourself more realistically in a happy way and feel good about the fact that you like hearing people talk about things that are less mundane, you like meditating, you like empowerments. Great. But there's no sense in casting yourself in a role that is not applicable at this time, when it will only cause you personal misery. You'll either try to do things that you really don't care about and you won't enjoy them, or you will not fulfill the expectations and hate yourself. You see what I mean? You're just setting yourself up for misery. Why not just take it at whatever level you choose?

So when a person studies with me on a basic level, there are no requirements at all, basically, other than they pay a general admission to come in the door so we can pay for the hall. On an intermediate level, there are very few conditions. The payment is larger as is due, in my opinion, and a person is required to meditate, and that's it, really. There are assignments from time to time. They're usually pretty enjoyable—viewing a movie, reading a book. That's about it. I also teach computer classes that have a different set of demands and create rapid advancement in computer science, which some people like. There are desert seminars, and there's a physical requirement for attending them simply because the desert is a very rigorous place to go. There are a number of ways just to demonstrate that you're very healthy, that you do yoga x times a week, or martial arts or aerobics. But that's really about it.

Now you can wind all that up very tightly or you can go see Sai Baba and wind that up tightly, or any teacher, or you can just see it as it is, and unwind it a little bit. Maybe lower your expectations of yourself and find that you're a lot happier. Perhaps you're not the next Buddha. Perhaps you're not the Maitreya.[4] Perhaps that's not your job in this incarnation. Perhaps you don't need to be that. Perhaps you don't have to fast and meditate for thousands of hours. Perhaps you have to enjoy life and learn about it through relationships, through careers, through whatever way that you find yourself going. Maybe what I'm trying to teach you is to enjoy yourself more and hate yourself less. Maybe that would be a good thing to learn in this particular life.

Because as we hate ourselves less, we tend to hate other people less, too. If we don't have to get violent with ourselves and castigate ourselves and ostracize ourselves and excommunicate ourselves because we didn't live up to

---

4. A future Buddha, the last incarnation of Vishnu at the end of the Kali Yuga.

the standard we set down for ourselves, then maybe we don't have to do that with other people. Maybe that's your lesson in this life.

There are teachers other than myself who teach different things. I have a particularly defined program for people who are involved with computer science and meditation. I put the two together because I enjoy that, unless it's a very basic class, in which case I just teach meditation and recommend that a person investigate the world of computer science. But at an intermediate level you can't separate the two because I enjoy that. Since I only do things that I enjoy, unless I can't help it (Rama laughs), and I'm in a position to do that, that's why I do it. We know the result is exciting; I find it exciting. I'm doing it obviously for myself because I get a kick out of it. That's why I do everything.

Why, when you get to the point of an advanced level of attention, when you've done all the work and gone through all the challenges to get to states of mind that are absolutely euphoric, would you ever want to do anything that you wouldn't get a kick out of? It wouldn't make any sense. In other words, you don't become enlightened to become an indentured servant to humanity. I realize that there's a thing called the *bodhisattva* ideal, and it's a very nice pinnacle of attention to get to the state of mind whereby you say that you will lead every life forever to liberate all others. I've felt that way at times. It's a nice state of attention. But it's just another transient state of attention. When you're in that state of attention, the right thing to do is say that. You say it, and then you get sensible. (Audience laughs.)

No! It's a wonderful mood. But it's a very indulgent thought to feel that in some way you are an instrument of immortality, which has to be around to liberate everybody. It's a very egotistical thought, ultimately. It's very binding to *samsara*, like everything else. But it's a neat feeling to feel that way. To really feel that way is wonderful; it's very genuine. But it's just another illusion. It's just another drama. That's the bodhisattva's drama that they're playing out in meditation hall after meditation hall with all those people who come to see them. They're in their own illusion. They're as equally wrapped as anyone else.

Enlightenment is freedom. To have to liberate everybody doesn't sound very free to me, it sounds like a lot of work. You know, you're going to go liberate people who maybe don't want to be liberated. See what I'm saying? You could set up the whole universe just to fulfill your fantasy. It hasn't anything to do with enlightenment. Enlightenment is a personal matter in which you erase the self, until there's no self. You do it for ecstasy. Why else would you do it? That's its nature, it can't be anything else. When all illusions vanish, there's only ecstasy. Someone who's reached that pointless point, so to speak, of infinite ecstasy is certainly not going to go do things that they don't enjoy, which includes teaching.

I teach because I get a kick out of it. It's fun. It's a very fun, exciting, silly process. If I didn't enjoy it, I wouldn't do it. I don't do it because I feel that it's particularly noble. I can feel that way if I look at it from a certain point of view. But ultimately I do it because I enjoy it. I set certain criteria because they're sensible in a teaching process because what I do really works. I actually teach people how to become free and how to become enlightened. I know how, and I teach it.

But I also teach people a lot of other things. Mostly I teach other things—about how to enter into different states of mind, how to astral travel, how to become more successful, how to fulfill your desires. That's not unspiritual, that's quite spiritual. Spirituality means assisting a person in gaining a full view of reality. It doesn't mean taking people to some state we call enlightenment. You drag people to some state that they're not prepared for—that's not assisting them. That's causing misery.

So, are you trying to drag yourself to some state that you don't even know about, you just have a hypothetical idea that you call enlightenment? Are you making yourself miserable in the process? Most people who practice meditation are. Most of the people I observe who meditate are much more, after they've meditated for a while, unhappy than anybody else. I've had people come into the meditation hall, new people, and they say, "Gee, I wouldn't want to study with you, Rama, because everybody here is so unhappy." And I would say, "Well, you know, that's just part of the experience."

That's because they're all trying to be enlightened and drag themselves to enlightenment or hate themselves when they're not becoming what they think [they should]. That isn't what I teach, that's just their own trip they're going through, and I just happen to be in the room. Each one is off in fantasyland, and I'm up here enjoying myself teaching. But no one hears what I say. They just put it into their fantasy, in any way that seems appropriate.

Enlightenment is about freedom. But to be free sometimes we have to first be ourselves and learn about ourselves and experience different sides of ourselves. You can't push away who you are. It has to dissolve. It's like Speedy Alka-Seltzer. You take the little tablet and flip it in water. There are a lot of bubbles and there's no tablet. No ugly residue. (Audience laughs.) That's what enlightenment is. It's effervescent. You go away. It's kind of fun, there are a lot of bubbles and you're gone. But you can't do that until you've experienced all the different sides of yourself. In the tantric process we accelerate that. We enable you to experience all the different sides of yourself much sooner than you had thought possible.

If you want to be evil, we'll show you how to be real evil for a while, because we'll amp you up. If you think there are other powers and forces and you want to go to other dimensions and live out fantasies there, go ahead, we'll enable you to. Whatever you want to do, we can teach you how to get the power to go do it. Because I guess you have to work through that drama for a while. Don't hate yourself for that. But we do have general guidelines that we suggest you employ as you progress through infinity so as not to create too much pain for yourself or others, simply because if you create too much pain for other people, sooner or later they're going to blow you away. People don't like that.

We also teach you things that will enable you to avoid the snares of others who are wrapped up in their own little dreams, who would make you part of their dreams. That's abrogating your freedom. We'll teach you how to avoid weird people and weird beings and weird forces and powers that seek to dominate you. But then what you do with all the power is pretty much up to you.

As I said, all I require is that a person pay an admission; and if it's at the intermediate level that they meditate; and if it's a computer science course, of

FREEDOM 77

course, that they do good computer science; and if they go on our desert journeys that they, through any method they choose of three methods, indicate that they are in fact in good shape to be able to go out into the desert when it's 20 degrees in the middle of the night—go on our desert journeys in the study of occultism. But other than that, that's about it.

So I would unwind yourself a little bit as we approach 1990 or whatever we're approaching—infinity. Why don't you take the time to enjoy yourself for a change? Why don't you like being you for a change? Just be different, and don't hate yourself, and feel very good about all your different desires and all the things you didn't want and want; and why don't you go get them all, and see what it's like?

If you like studying meditation, great. If you like empowerments, great. I provide a tantric schoolhouse in infinity, where you can come in and take from this whatever you choose and employ it in any way you want, and the worst thing that could happen is you might learn something about yourself and life.

Naturally, if you use this power to annoy anybody else in the class, I have a problem and you'll have to be asked to leave if you don't stop because that's against our rules. But other than that, it's really up to you what you do. That's the process that I use. It's called "living in the teaching and learning of the enlightenment." It's called "living." And I think a lot of you have wound this into a process in your own mind that has nothing to do with what I'm doing. You're all people at a mall walking around in your own dreams of self-discovery, and it has nothing to do with what I'm teaching at all.

I'm providing empowerments and teaching you how to release the *kundalini* through a process we call meditation—teaching you how to lose things that take your energy and bind you to a particular self-form or reality structure, and how to affix yourself to things that create a sense of freedom and mobility through different planes of consciousness. I'm also teaching, through our computer seminars, how to do very good computer science and to make a tremendous amount of money, which creates mobility or just enables you to fulfill your desires.

The computer seminars are expensive. The enlightenment seminars are very inexpensive. They're nominal, in our 1990 system. In our computer seminars I actually teach some of the philosophy of enlightenment because I feel it's very complementary to computer science. A good, clear mind enables you to do very good computer science. Doing good computer science, of course, does foster a mind that is better prepared to meditate, if that's your interest.

So I would ponder this a little bit. I would think, as we're moving towards 1990 or whatever infinity we're moving towards, I would think about self-discovery in perhaps more realistic terms for yourself. Think about yourself more realistically and think that you don't really have to hate yourself; you can be whatever you like and learn from that. If you put your hand in the fire and get burned, you'll be the first to know and I'm sure you'll withdraw your hand. But that's part of learning.

You can't live without pain. You can't live without pleasure. They come and go. You can live without self though, interestingly enough, even though it sounds incongruous. It's quite true. I do it, meaning no particular self. That's the study of enlightenment. It's all the study of enlightenment, isn't it? I mean, isn't that all there is? The only difference is that you're receiving empowerments and particular training in the subject of occultism, which just enables you to do things more rapidly because you seem to enjoy doing things more rapidly.

But don't set so many goals for yourself. I don't set them for you. There's no need for you to hate me because I set a lot of goals for you because I don't have any, just nonviolence and a certain amount of meditation every day, and if you're in the computer science courses, you pay for them. If you attend our meditation seminars, there's a nominal charge just to cover the room. But it's strictly segmented that way. There's a charge for the desert seminars. But they're three entirely different things. On an intermediate level, there are four-night computer seminars, for whomever I decide to allow to attend them, and there's two-night Buddhist seminars, and then there are, for those whom I decide to allow to attend, desert seminars. They're three completely distinct products.

I've done that because it's realistic. The philosophy of enlightenment permeates all three because I enjoy that, but they're distinct. One is career-oriented, one is enlightenment-oriented and one is strictly power-oriented. They provide different accesses for different places inside one's mind, different experiences. They're like different rides at Disneyland.

So I would think a little more about enjoying yourself and not feeling that there's anything wrong with you or your desires, and allow yourself to naturally experience life. If you're supposed to be the Maitreya, if you're going to be the next Buddha, then I'm sure you will be. But sometimes it's best just to be who we are for a while and then allow ourselves naturally to change.

If you meditate and you experience these empowerments, it speeds everything up. If what you seek is enlightenment, that will be sped up. If what you have to go through are other dramas, that will be sped up. There's no right or wrong in the study of enlightenment. There's only experience.

CHAPTER SIX

ENLIGHTENMENT

I've read a lot about enlightenment and thought about it quite a bit, and I find that it doesn't have much to do with enlightenment. Now fortunately, I can see both sides of the coin since I happen to be enlightened and I've gone through that training process that culminates in the dissolution of the finite self in the white light of eternity. But at the same time, I'm an avid reader and I like to ponder things, so it's kind of fun to step in and out. And I notice that the two are not really the same. The description and the reality are very different.

Enlightenment is a timeless void. It's an emptiness that's filled with the most excellent light. That light is suffused through every part of your being. It is your being. There's no sense of separation between yourself and the light. There's no self but the light. That's enlightenment—timeless, stillness, perfection. It's not in the words, it's in my voice. It's in the voice of anyone who has crossed that frontier of self, taken a big machete and gone after the illusions and the desires, even the spiritual hopes and aspirations that can bind one to a spiritual, more refined self—hacked through the Amazon jungle of hope and fear and desperation, always in search of perpetual brightness. What I seek, what we all seek, is something we can't define—because if it's definable, it's limited. And if it's limited, we grow tired and bored with it, with ourselves.

Beyond the parameters of the self is an ocean—it goes on forever. It's not circular, it's not square, it doesn't have a definite color. All we can say is that it's large, from the point of view of one who looks at it as being separate. And it's most excellent.

The world that you see is a phantasm. It's like a motion picture. For a while we go into the movie theater, put our feet up when the attendant's not looking. We'll get a Diet Coke and some popcorn. Soon we're engrossed in a film and we've forgotten that we're sitting in a movie theater, if the film's any good, until the attendant comes along and tells us to move our feet. We grudgingly do so, hopefully not sending any bad energy to the attendant because he's just doing his job. And we put our feet back up as soon as he's gone, and go back into the film.

Enlightenment is an ocean of awareness that slides through the human part of us and dissolves it, and leaves us forever in eternity. But eternity is not cold. It's not lonely. It's warm with its own life. It's filled with the very pleasure of itself. In a lot of self-discovery, there are a lot of people against pleasure. The anti-pleasure movement in self-discovery is very strong. I have big news for them—if they ever get to enlightenment, which is unlikely the way they're approaching it, they're going to find enlightenment is very pleasurable. And if you have a problem with pleasure, you're going to be surprised.

Enlightenment is the pure pleasure of the universe enjoying its own being-ness. The universe doesn't hate itself. That's human beings who do that. The universe doesn't think it's bad because it creates myriad worlds and destroys them. It doesn't have guilt. The universe doesn't have a problem with sexuality since it created it and creates itself through it. The universe doesn't have a problem with money. The universe doesn't have a problem with creating and sustaining loathsome beings who harm others. It doesn't have a problem with creating and sustaining boring beings or with most excellent enlightened beings. It creates all of it. It is all of it. It doesn't moralize, it doesn't equivocate, except through a few of its instruments, the human beings. It just is.

You can think whatever you want, you can create all the labels you choose, but the universe just is. So you can come to terms with it or not. If you don't come to terms with it, we say you live in illusion. When you come to terms with it, then you're in the reality. As long as you think of it as other than it really is, that's what we mean by illusion. It just is. It's real. Enlightenment is the seeing of reality. And reality is most fine and most wonderful, most warm and nubile. It's definitely beautiful, reality.

It's the seeing of things that makes them so. I think Shakespeare talked about that a little bit. Enlightened people talk about that. It's the seeing of things. You can see everything as glowing light or you can see everything as dark and foreboding, shadowy shapes. You can see everything as dull. You can see everything as hopeful. What makes that is a state of mind. Reality is not any particular way. If you're in a hopeful level of attention, then you could be in the pit of hell and see possibilities in it. If you're in a dead state of mind, then heaven would not entrance you, if you were there.

We concern ourselves, in Buddhism, with not so much the movement of outer structures, but inner structures within our own mind. We feel changing the world around is not going to make any difference. Changing ourselves around, on the other hand, makes a world of difference. To change ourselves around we have to learn something about the structure of the mind. The mind has a definitive structure. It works in a certain way. There's no way to explain that. A person has to experience it. In other words, I could say, "There are thousands of states of mind," but all your life you've been in about the same state of mind, so that doesn't really mean much to you, does it? Whereas if I meditate and generate a lot of energy and cause you to step from one state of mind to another, then you say, "Oh, I see what you mean." Suddenly all of life is different.

The funny thing about states of mind is, of course, they're all inclusive in the sense that when we're in one, unless you're quite advanced in your Buddhism, you forget about all the others. You can be in a state of mind for a few seconds and forget that you were ever in any other state of mind. That's what we mean by illusion. We see a little kid and they're crying. They're so obsessed with the broken toy that they're crying and crying. They can't step back from that for a moment and realize that they'll be smiling later. They've forgotten they were ever smiling.

So part of what we seek in Buddhism is the sense of quiet observation. We like to draw back to a place inside ourselves whereby we can remember. We don't get so involved in a state of mind that we forget that it's just another transient state of mind, no matter how much ecstasy or agony or mixture of both is involved.

Perspective comes from the ability to stop thought. When you meditate each day, if you practice meditation, what you're doing is consciously creating a sense of perspective. It's a measurement. We like to measure things. How do we know an inch is an inch? How do we know a centimeter is a centimeter, or a meter is a meter? Well, they have somewhere, frozen at a controlled temperature, a bar of metal that is an exact inch, that is an exact foot, that is an exact meter. And the Bureau of Standards and Measurements measures everything by that.

Well, how can you measure life? How can you measure states of mind? You need a standard, a way of always gaining perspective, and that's the stoppage of thought. When you stop thought, when you can do that, which is meditation, and when you can do that at any time, you can bring a sense of perspective into any moment. No matter how involved you get in something, you can step outside of it simply by stopping your thought. Because as soon as you stop your thought, you step outside of all states of mind into something other than states of mind.

Remember, the entry into the stoppage of thought is not another state. In other words, when there's no thought whatsoever in the mind, no impressions, no images, no self-supportive reflexive views, we enter into another condition, which I would *not* call enlightenment. It's an *enlightened* condition. And if we can sustain the view of no thought, if we can keep the mind in the state of no thought, then we've entered into another country and that country has many conditions, many sides to it. It's not a simple thing. To describe it—"Oh, no thought"—we assume it'll be the same every time, but that's not the case. It's always the same country, but there are many parts to it.

We don't discuss that too much in Buddhism because there are no words for it. But don't shortchange it in your mind. Don't assume stopping thought is always the same, that it's a condition, that it's another state of mind. It's not. It's outside of all conditions and it goes on forever. It goes on forever. It's the nameless—I couldn't name that. Some people have tried, but they're just trying to define it and make it into another condition when it's not.

Enlightenment itself is not simply the stoppage of thoughts. Otherwise, a mental acrobat who's simply learned to stop thought for long periods of time would be enlightened. Enlightenment is a suffusion of perfect awareness. It's the light in the darkness that supports itself without a source. It's the province of wisdom, of perfect intelligence, the pure beingness of the universe without any structures superimposed over itself. It's part of all of us.

You know, people say, "I'm not enlightened." It's true. You're not. But yet, strangely enough, you're an emanation of enlightenment. The very fact that you exist, that you live, that you breathe, that you function, that you have consciousness, that you have unconsciousness at times, that you dream, is because enlightenment, which is the universe, has created the hallucination that is you, in a form that shifts.

We are all part of the substructure of enlightenment. And so, it really doesn't matter whether you become enlightenment or not. You are enlightenment. You are that. It's purely a matter of personal enjoyment, but you can't divorce yourself from enlightenment. The whole universe is enlightenment in varying stages, on varying stages. There is nothing else but enlightenment.

Naturally, to be aware of that, to have the whole consciousness of immortality flowing through you—as opposed to being in a self-reflective, sentient state of mind—is a little bit different. And those who quest for that view, those who seek that will undoubtedly find that. They're seeking themselves. All you can do is experience yourself. With no self, there's no experience to be had. This is not jargon, it's true. What you experience is yourself. Everywhere you look, you see yourself. There isn't anything else. Unless you go beyond self, in which case you enter into the province of enlightened mind, enlightenment.

I've read a lot about enlightenment and pondered it—the images, the cultural images that planet Earth people create of enlightenment and the enlightened—and they make it so religious, which I guess is perhaps the case. I don't know—if the brightest star were to appear in someone's mind and they walked down the street and everybody saw them and they saw that star, I guess they'd react like people react to most things they don't understand—with apprehension, with fear, with worship. Emotionally, they'd react emotionally. Some would react rationally and try and figure it out. Some would moralize, some would turn it into a major motion picture, some would sell the screen rights immediately and the book rights and the comic book rights. But none of it would have much to do with what it is. You're dealing with that which can't be understood.

Human beings, when they encounter that which can't be understood, they either run away from it, run towards it blindly or just rationalize it out of existence. But you can't do that forever—because it is forever. When you die it swallows you up, eternity does. When you live, it swallows you up—it's just—you're more asleep maybe than when you're dead. Sometimes I think death is a greater awareness than life—because life gives us the illusion of immortality, whereas death gives us the certainty of immortality.

The universe is a matrix. It's a doorway into itself. But that doorway remains invisible if you don't have enough energy flowing through you. You don't see it. All you see is the senses; you see physically the structures around you. If you have a little more energy then you see the occult, you see the different dimensions and what goes on in them. If you have a lot more energy you can get above dimensionality and see what we call the *unmanifest*. Those are the planes of pure and perfect being, which do not have dimensional form or a time/space continuum related to them. But what you're really seeing is your own mind, aren't you? I mean, those are all parts of your own mind. Your mind has a side that's very dimensional. It has a side that's very sensorial. It has a side that's beyond dimensionality, it's pure radiant light, and then there's enlightenment, which is beyond the mind itself—which is an obscure way of just trying to say it's beyond the stars.

We see the stars. At night we go outside on a clear, cold night. We see millions of stars all over the place, bright and beautiful, each one shining, forever. And each moment is forever, it's shining in each moment forever. And each moment is forever. We connect the dots in the drawing with our mind and we give them a meaning, a figurative sense, which is self-reflexive in that it creates us because we are the experiencer of the moment. All the eyes of God are looking through all the stars. We're looking at the stars through our eyes. There's only the eye of God everywhere, seeing and being in perfection, always.

We fall into states of illusion and we forget all this. We get caught up in desires, frustrations, political movements, creeds, philosophies, religions, the getting of a living, the pain of a body, the pleasure of a body—we forget everything. We forget about the space between the stars, the pure and perfect space that's also the eye of God. To penetrate the mystery is to become the mystery. To penetrate infinity is to become infinity. To penetrate light is to become light. Who is so brave and so noble that they could hurl themselves at infinity without any question, with complete trust and complete certainty that infinity will destroy them forever—in such an absolute and perfect way that they would sacrifice themselves and all that they are, all their fears, all their dreams, all their dramas—who has that absolute trust, that perfect and pure trust? Consciously, not as an emotional whim, not as another egotistical embrace of the self, but with a quiet dispassion and yet with a quiet passion to fling yourself into immortality, to let it do with you as it will, with all the permutations and possibilities of "as it will," be it horror or ecstasy or boredom. Who has that perfect faith and trust? Only such a person with that faith and trust can be enlightened.

Only when you recognize the universe as your own body; when you recognize all deaths, all births, all horrors as illusory, as interpretations; when you see the universe in its perfection as your perfection; when there is no difference—there is no difference. Until such time, we read about it, we ponder it. But only with that pure and perfect trust, which is an intelligent realization that the universe can create horror for you forever and that that's quite fine if that's what happens, only then can we go beyond self, beyond boredom—even beyond freedom.

Freedom just implies a change, a conditional swap, a movement into something else from something. Beyond freedom is limitless reality. Only when we can look all the faces of God in the eye and claim them as our very own, that they are us, that we are them, that we are all projections of the one perfect light, the perfect being-ness of existence—only when our mind is so saturated with that that there is nothing else, is there reality. Everything else is illusory, meaning it's transient, it changes. You're looking through the kaleidoscope of God and seeing God's face in so many ways—as friends, as strangers, passersby, country roads, jammed freeways, the cancer ward, the maternity ward—all the faces of God surround you at all times.

But what does God really look like stripped naked? That's the province of enlightenment. The formless, perfect face of existence. To contemplate that, to be aware of that, to live in that, is the world of enlightenment. The rest is for humans and other beings—the states, the conditions, the perpetual ways of viewing and seeing things, endless permutations of the kaleidoscope. But to see the flawless face of perfection forever is nirvana, is enlightenment.

The contemplation of enlightenment elevates the spirit for a while. Like a kite that flies up in the sky when the wind comes and then eventually it comes down—better for the flight in that we enjoyed the flight. We were that flight. You don't have to equate your moments, you don't have to add up the black and white stones. You don't have to do the judgment of yourself. It's pointless. Beyond the judgment is the clear light of reality. Beyond the illusory heavens and hells and other *samsaras* of your own mind there is the clear light of reality beckoning. It's inevitable, freedom. Life is not what it seems.

Thank you.

Chapter Seven

SELF-EFFORT

Spirituality is breaking the link between the mortal and the immortal consciousness. The mortal consciousness is the awareness of time and space through a body and a perceptual sensorial field. The immortal consciousness is nothing that can be described in words.

Divinity does not require humanity's understanding. It exists because it exists, because it exists. Humanity is terribly limited in its understanding of anything and everything. As long as humanity chooses to avoid divinity, it suffers. But divinity does not. Since it is immortal, pure and perfect, it is beyond suffering. Its self-luminescent light propels itself through infinity without any abrasion.

It is not the part of divinity to go to humanity and to modify itself in any shape, manner or form; rather it is up to humanity to make itself available, accessible, if you will, to divinity. Anything else is a misconception. If you feel it is the responsibility of God to come to you and to work it out, you're mistaken. Rather, it is your responsibility to go to God and work it out.

You can use extra-logical arguments to say, "Well, we're all God," or "There is no God," or anything you want to, but it doesn't change how things are. Those are just ideas. So as long as you wish to separate yourself from the immortal consciousness, you will suffer. You will experience the pain of the separation, the lack of luminosity, the abridgement of infinite mind in finite form. Divinity, enlightenment, if you will, sits on top of its mountain and is somewhat bemused by what it sees. It sees itself in another form trying to approach itself or being afraid of itself and running away, or completely unaware. But it is not moved by that at all. What makes enlightenment enlightenment is its dispassion.

In the West they use a term—compassion—to try and bring across a feeling I think that they would like to think enlightenment has. In other words, I think there's a great amount of plagiarism, if you will, in the scriptures, in the discussions of enlightenment. Because it's suggested that enlightenment has some tremendous compassion, some driving necessity to help humanity. I don't think that's the case at all. I think humanity wishes it was the case, and since it's humanity that writes the various scriptures, I think it's a self-reflection, but it has nothing to do with enlightenment. From the point of view of enlightenment, none of this has ever even been. All time and space, all the conditions—that are apparent in the absence of enlightenment—are unreal. It doesn't matter.

You can sit in your room and think someone should bring you food. And you can sit in your room in your house alone day after day and no one will arrive. No matter how strongly you think that should be the case, unless you go out and find food it's not going to come to you. That's up to you. To think that in some way—as people think both in the East and West but more so in the West—that the knowledge that brings freedom from all limitations is in some way supposed to come to you and be at your service is ridiculous.

It is up to you to avail yourself of that knowledge. That knowledge doesn't need you. It doesn't care. Since it's not in this world, it is completely oblivious to your suffering. The idea of a compassionate God was formulated, obviously, by someone who didn't want to do any work. If you look around you, you'll see that that's not how life is. Creatures are born and die. They go through terrible suffering and no one intervenes. Some people get angry—I guess those who don't want to do anything—and they say, "Well, there is no God because if there was a God, God would stop all the suffering." Nonsense. God is oblivious to suffering. God is beyond suffering. That's what makes God God, by definition.

That is to say, we refer to God as the part of being that is beyond suffering. Obviously everything is God, but in our definition we view the part of being that experiences the dualistic consciousness, which brings about suffering, we call that humanity, squirrels, plants, astral beings, whatever it may be. But some people have a very strange idea. They think that in some way that that immortal essence, which we call God—for lack of a better word, or maybe it's the right word—should in some way come to you and assist you, should answer your prayers. Why, when it exists in perfect ecstasy beyond the dualistic consciousness? It's totally oblivious to you. It has no interest in your life or your death, it doesn't matter.

It exists. It is perfect. But it is up to an individual to go on a journey of self-discovery through their own self-effort and discover that, to meld their mind with that perfection and make that perfection their life. Then an individual is beyond suffering because all caring brings about suffering. So how could you ask God to care, because then God would suffer, you see?

This is where Buddhism differs from Christianity, Christianity as it's presented to us. Buddhism suggests that simply because you were born in a certain religion, because you were baptized, that has nothing to do with salvation. There are no elect. Everything rests upon your own self-effort, which is the good news because that means you don't have to wait around for some nebulous God to help you. You can pick yourself up and go do what you want to do, and if you want to remove yourself from the world of suffering, you can. The universe is not seen in Buddhism as some giant machine, some cold mechanism—not at all. Nor is it seen as a big human being that thinks like a big human being.

Most people's Gods are self-reflective. God just has to be like you. You get concerned so you assume God must get concerned. You get pissed off, so you assume that God must get pissed off. You're attached to things that you create so you assume that God would be.

God doesn't care. God is a pure and perfect awareness that has no knowledge of any of this. It's beyond all of this. You have to elevate yourself to that point and bring your mind into the Godhead, into nirvana, into that perfect and pure radiant knowledge. It will not come to you. It never does. Why should it? It's oblivious because it's ecstasy and in its complete self-ecstasy of perfect being-ness, why should it be aware or aroused by your suffering or your joy?

One can stay in the *samsara*, in mortality, forever. One does—unless through one's self-effort, one moves one's ass and does something about it.

You can read all the books, think all the thoughts, but unless you start to discipline your consciousness and accept the very simple reality that the infinite mind is oblivious to your suffering, nothing will change. That acceptance is reality. The reality of just what is as opposed to the idealizations.

Idealizations are problematic because they prevent us from acting. If you're sitting in your room alone and you're getting more and more hungry and it's beginning to hurt, but you really think someone's going to come through for you, you may just sit there and no one will. But if you know no one's going to come, and if you're going to eat you're going to have to move it and get your body up and down the hall and down the stairs and out to where there's some food, then you'll move.

False hope implies a Messiah. The very concept of the Messiah is ludicrous. It's a great misunderstanding, in other words, of what is. Yes, there are beings who reside in the human form and in other forms who have reached complete enlightenment. But to assume that they just come and make an appearance and take care of everything is ridiculous. They simply point the way. They suggest to you that something is doable by their advent on earth. Obviously, if these were human beings and they've climbed beyond all the limited states of consciousness, that tells you it can be done. Some might even explain how. But they don't care. How could they? It's just part of their operating system to explain how. You would like them to care. You would like to think that, because then you would think, through that caring, they might do something for you and therefore you don't have to do it yourself. That's a mistake.

You, as they did, must go through every step of the self-discovery process. You must win the ecstasy. You must win freedom through your self-effort. Otherwise nothing will occur. You can pray incessantly and some being out there might hear you and they might help you a little bit today, but tomorrow you'll be back on your own. You can beg on the street and somebody might give you some food. But it probably won't be what you want, it might just get you through. But you have to go out and get a job and make money and make it happen. Otherwise you're completely dependent upon the charity of others, which is not necessarily what you might like or what you might need.

Therefore, yes, there is help. This is the difference between Mahayana and Hinayana Buddhism. In Hinayana Buddhism, they don't feel that there's any help at all. In Mahayana Buddhism, which is tantra, we concede, yes, there's help. Yes, somebody might give you a handout, but they'll give it to you today but don't expect it tomorrow or necessarily ever again, or it could come every day. But you can't count on it. It never hurts to ask, but you don't sit around waiting for it to show up. You go do it.

In tantra we believe you can appeal to the Goddess and help may come, but you don't wait because it might not. You have to do it yourself. And if you'd like to ask, and if that's an extra, well, great. We don't feel there's a prohibition. But certainly it won't just come. The idea is that the Savior came and simply by the coming of the Savior you're saved. Nonsense. Human beings wish! If that were the case, we'd live in a perfect world and obviously we don't. There's as much tragedy and pain today as there has ever been, no more, no less, in any human life. And if you seek to be unusual and go beyond that, then it will only be accomplished through your self-effort and by following the examples and the methods of those who have successfully done it. Otherwise you'll just sit in limitation forever. Literally forever, since there's no end to infinity. Why should it change?

To think that God is compassionate is a terrible mistake. To think that God is wrathful is equally stupid. God isn't emotional. You are. To superimpose your emotions on infinity is typically human. But the infinite is made up of light. Light is dispassionate because it perceives life in such a different way than you do that it doesn't even see what you see. What appears to you as necessity is not necessarily a necessity. Five years of pain from your point of view is nothing to an infinite consciousness that is aware of infinity. Five years is nothing. So why should it be concerned about some being who doesn't even perceive reality properly—[their] five years of pain, which is nothing in infinity. Why interrupt the ecstasy of perfect awareness by entering into limited awareness?

It's a mistake to think that anything's going to change. That's the message of Buddhism. It's a mistake to think that things can't. Buddhism suggests that there is enlightenment. Definitely, it's there. Even though it's not perceivable to the mind or senses, it's there. That there are those who have attained enlightenment, and enlightenment is absolute freedom, and that there are a number of methodical ways, meaning ways with methods to attain enlightenment, and that until one does, one will eat it heavily. It will be extremely unpleasant; the absence of enlightenment itself is pain. There's only growth, maturation, old age and death forever, in variant forms, in variant universes. And that until one sees this truth and begins to follow the path out, paying no attention to one's neighbors—it doesn't matter what anybody else does, you're only concerned with you, one body, one stomach.

It's nice if you wish well to others and you hope that they will become enlightened, but it really doesn't matter. It's a strictly individual situation. And how can you possibly assist anyone in their enlightenment unless you happen to be enlightened yourself? It's a joke to think you can help anybody become enlightened until you become fully enlightened. Don't even waste your time thinking about it. Get real. The only issue is your own enlightenment. Anything else is only an interruption of that process. If you do have a genuine need for some reason to assist others in their enlightenment, the greatest thing you can do is become enlightened as quickly as possible and then you will have something at your disposal—right knowledge to assist those individuals. But otherwise, you're just being self-indulgent and ridiculous.

A little truth goes a long way. It goes forever. The truth is that you are alone. That you've always been alone, and that you'll always be alone in an infinite series of infinities. And the truth is that at this point in infinity, at this moment, you have become aware of your aloneness, and you have become aware that it is only through your self-effort that that aloneness, that separation, can end. You can wax philosophical, religious, logical, extra-logical, it doesn't matter. As Joe Friday used to say, "Those are the facts, ma'am, just the facts".[5] If you choose to ignore them, it's to your disadvantage. Your self-encased fantasies will end in pain. And if you accept that, then the mere acceptance of the reality causes a transmutation. You're

---

5. Joe Friday was a police detective in the 1960s television show, "Dragnet."

motivated. And then you begin your search.

As long as the pain is not sufficient, there isn't really motivation. If your life is pleasant enough and you feel no need, then there's no need. No one can force a person to become enlightened. It's something that a person seeks because they have come to certain realizations about themselves and how life works. And they see no certainty in living whatsoever. They see that today they're alive and everything is wonderful, and tomorrow they'll be dead and alone. Today they're healthy and happy, tomorrow they'll be sick and miserable. Today they have ecstasy, tomorrow they'll have depression. Today everyone loves them and pats them on the back, tomorrow everybody despises them, says terrible things about them, tries to destroy them. There's no certainty in this world, or in any world. Even the higher astral worlds don't have certainty because eventually they change, even while they may exist for a number of eternities, eventually they change. They become something other.

The only certainty is dissolution, to step beyond change into the world of perfection, into the eye of God. The practice of Buddhism, the practice of yoga, of unifying one's consciousness with nirvana, brings an end to all limitations. Not only does it bring an end to pain, but it brings complete ecstasy forever—the ecstasy of the experience of infinity, of infinite light, which has no limitation since it's infinite.

CHAPTER EIGHT

POSSIBILITIES

The 1990s. It's strange for an enlightened teacher to talk about a time period since we don't believe in time or space, as most people know it. We live in a continuum of perfect attention. Yet there is time and space in a relative plane. And there's astrology.

Astrology is the science of time and space. It is the science of karma. It has to do with places in which you locate your body, and energy fields that affect you. What we seek to do is push all energy fields away from our bodies so that we can perceive life perfectly and clearly. Astrology is an indicator of karma. You're born in a certain geographic place, in a certain dimension. At the moment of your birth, a variety of energies are present and they lock at the moment of birth for you. From that moment on, there are only the various choices one can make from that location, from those energies, with whatever you enter an incarnation with, which is karma—with the knowledge you have, with the knowledge you don't have, with the tendencies you have and the tendencies you don't have.

Astrology offers us the possibilities. It simply shows us where we came in, what we came in with, what we don't have, and the likely possibilities, the karmic permutations according to the time/space continuum of our entry or at any given moment in our life vis-a-vis location. The earth is also revealed through astrology. It has its own little horoscope, you might say. And the planet Earth is going through a series of major transits in the 1990s, meaning not the earth as a place per se but the people on the earth.

The 1990s will be a determining period of time for another cycle. If humanity during this time chooses to throw away a lot of the mirages and illusions it's fooled itself with, then we will enter a very bright and golden age after 2000. It won't all happen in one day, but a trend will be started and it will be an upward trend in terms of the evolution of consciousness. If, on the other hand, during this period of time there's a descent in consciousness, that movement will be locked and we will enter into a much darker age than the age we are currently in. It is not decided.

Of course, as most prophets and mystics have said, there is a very large chance of a major cataclysm of some type, particularly in the area of 1997, 1998 or 1999. It really runs from 1997 to 2003. There's a karmic flaw or variation there. There could be a giant cataclysm in which all life as we know it on the planet Earth is changed in some way. It's not guaranteed, but it's there; it's a possibility, and many people perceive it and they're correct. Some say there's going to be nuclear war; there's no certainty of anything. Life isn't that certain. What we're dealing with are karmic variations, possibilities of cause and effect that are working themselves out on a global scale. It's not that certain. That's what makes life exciting—that it's not that certain.

Self-discovery teaches us to push past karmic possibilities in cause and effect and create entirely new realities that are not based upon anything that's ever happened before. That's its purpose. The purpose of astrology is to show us our patterns, to show us our life, and then give us a way to push through everything that's supposed to happen, to skip it and move on to something more interesting. But in order to do that, we have to know who we are and where we are and what the possibilities are from which we can pick. Most people don't know that.

The 1990s are, of course, a time of continued population growth on the planet Earth. The consequences are devastating, needless to say. The earth is too crowded already in terms of aura, and it's growing at a rate of 20 percent a decade. Every 20-percentile growth every decade, of course, is a much larger jump than the previous decade. So the earth, by the year 2000, will be a very crowded place, if you think it's crowded already.

But the most important thing about the 1990s is that it's a time of tremendous freedom. People will look back upon this time as a very free time. We've become used to forgetting about hope. We think that hope doesn't exist; everything is worked out against us. That's the view of the average adult.

Not true. Please cast your eyes, as we're starting the 1990s, to Europe. Look at Czechoslovakia, which ushered in a new government today, the first democratic-based government in many years. No one could anticipate that this would happen. The people have had a bloodless revolution. They have chosen freedom as opposed to communist oppression. The 1990s have begun with some very, very positive signs in Eastern Europe. It's a time when decisions will be made which will last for thousands and thousands of years.

I suppose that's true at any time, but not like this. The 1990s for the planet Earth people are like a Saturn return. We're born when Saturn is in a certain position; Saturn signifies karma. We follow a karmic progression for 29 years, till Saturn returns to its original place. The same progression can continue, but at 29 there's an optimum moment, there's a window that opens whereby we can totally change our life. That can be done if you have enough personal power and vision and perseverance and luck, at any time. But at 29 it's very easy. It's very hard for people who do not meditate, who do not practice intermediate self-discovery or advanced self-discovery to change. But at 29 something happens to everybody.

So let's say the earth is about to be 29 during the 1990s. We have returned to a certain position. It's a position of freedom. South Africa is poised on the verge of the potential end of apartheid, probably this year. Countries in Eastern Europe that no one would ever have considered would become free, are about to become free. The Berlin Wall has crumbled as we approach 1990. And this is just the beginning of the 90s.

Now, there's exterior oppression. There's a degradation of the environment. But the real issue is inner oppression and the degradation of one's inner environment. The 1990s is a time when it's very easy to shift your life and your consciousness around. Everything is extremely mutable, changeable. It's not always so easy. It's a wonderful time to practice yoga. It's a wonderful time to take patterns that have existed for countless lifetimes and change them finally. It's not always so easy. It's a Saturn return. It's a very, very hopeful time. It is perhaps the most hopeful time that the earth has had in millennia. Things that would be impossible to do become relatively easy. But if we don't try them, assuming that they will still be impossible, nothing will change.

The spirit seeks the spirit. Matter seeks matter. This is a time of tremendous potential for spiritual development and growth for individuals on the planet Earth. The radiances of energy are very positive for the 1990s. Those radiances are always there, but they're hard to access, they're hard to get to.

Personally, this is a very important time for me because as an enlightened teacher, it's time for me to assert my aura fully, as it is for everyone who's involved with enlightenment. Because this is the time when we can do the most good, because things are mutable. If we assert our auras as fully as we can, we maximize the possibility for individuals to choose personal growth as opposed to stagnation.

This will be, for all people who teach enlightenment or engage in any part of the practice, their most active period. It's a time of work; it's a time of adventure. After 2000, it matters, but not as much. The karmas will be locked. They can still be changed on a case-by-case basis, but on a world basis, it's very hard to do. This is perhaps the most wonderful time that will ever be. And you're living in it. It's a time of hope, it's a time of adventure and it's a time of testing, of challenge. It's a time to change.

All this can be said of any given moment and is always talked of by teachers of the occult arts. Yet at this particular time, in this particular interdimensional configuration, things are possible that are very difficult, if not impossible, for a planet at this time in its evolution. It's a wonderful time. It's a time of awakening, potentially. Potentially.

So will the great wall that divides you fall? Have you hung onto your beliefs that you had so long ago, and can you bring your optimism up again? Can you end apartheid inside yourself? Can you throw off the totalitarian suppression of forces and powers that have held you down for so long? It's time. If you're going to do it, this is the time. It's always there to do. But after the year 2000, it will be much more complicated. On a case-by-case basis it can be done, but it's much more complicated. I don't envy the task of people who begin their self-discovery after 2000. But if they practice the methods that have proven true throughout the ages, it will work for them. It will just be hard, but worth it, always.

There's an ease and a grace to the next ten years that's beyond comprehension. But if you don't press the door marked "exit," it doesn't open. If you've pressed it many times and it hasn't opened, you might assume that to press it again would be a waste of your time and energy. This time if you press it, it will probably open. If it doesn't, get dynamite. (Audience laughs.)

The 1990s is the most important time period to come along in human history in millennia. What will happen, no one knows. That's what makes it exciting. On a global basis, tremendous changes are already taking place, just as we move into the aura of the 90s. The 90s are an eclipse. Let's assume there's a kind of heaviness, a darkness that seems to have been pervading this planet for a long time. But an eclipse of a reverse nature is happening. We're eclipsing the darkness, and the eclipse is just beginning. It reaches totality around '97. Then it really ends around 2000, 2003. It moves faster as it goes on; it's not an even-paced eclipse. But totality is around 1997, then it disappears fast. It's done by 2000. It fades a little bit to 2003, there's a little residual activity, but we're in it already.

Today is the 10th of December and it's begun. Already the world is changing in ways that no one could have anticipated—changing towards freedom. Oppressive leaders are being thrown off. The Soviet Union may not be communist for very long. If it falls, all that's really left is China, and already there have been powerful demonstrations that people there want to be free.

All this is just the mirror of the human spirit. To choose the light or to choose other things is always the question. So it's a time of great self-examination, a time of great adventure and a time of hope. Yes, it's a dark age, but there's a ten-year intermission. Certain things are still difficult—the earth is crowded, there's a lot of dark aura, there are a lot of heavy karmic patterns—but there's an era of hope and it's already begun.

The most important thing one can do during this time—if someone were to say, "Well, Rama, what can I do during this period of time to maximize the possibilities of feeling good, of finally clearing it all away," I would say, just to be truthful with yourself. To be honest with yourself.

There's no point in getting angry with anyone else. It changes nothing. There's no point in getting frustrated at yourself. Just be truthful. Determine where you are and where you wish to be. Then use all of your self-effort to make that happen, following the guiding principles of all the Buddhas and Bodhisattvas and seekers of the dharma, of enlightenment. Believe in yourself, step one. Believe in the order, step two. Believe in the teachings, step three.

Self-discovery works. Countless individuals and countless universes have practiced it and achieved enlightenment, or just gone into higher states of knowledge. If you follow the principles, they're true.

The order of self-discovery—those who practice—deserve your respect. If you respect them, you respect yourself. It's easy to be critical, but it does no good, that kind of critical. What's important is to be supportive of all who practice. Anyone on any level, even if they don't call it self-discovery, who is seeking to awaken to their own potentials and possibilities, to the inner freedom, deserves your respect and support. It doesn't matter what it's called or even if it's called nothing. The recognition of the waking of the spirit deserves your respect. If you respect it in others, you'll respect it in yourself.

Believe in yourself, always. You have no idea what you're capable of. You haven't tried. Try. You'll be surprised, very pleasantly.

We're entering an age of hope and of brightness. Certainly, in every bright sky there are a few dark clouds, otherwise there'd be no definition, no perspective. But inwardly there's a high gradient aura in which all the karmas are loosening. It's a time of right belief and if you follow that belief, you won't be disappointed.

It's a time then to forget everything that we've been distracted by and get back to business. It's a time to remember who we really are, what really empowers us and what gets in our way, and go about the business of enlightenment, individually and collectively. It's a time to return to old sources that are still good, that perhaps we've forgotten about. Or the wells that seemed to dry up—they're still there, they're still good.

Return to the sources of your renewal and define new sources. Realize things that we've engaged in—practices, states of mind, activities, methods that do nothing for us that we cling to out of desperation, out of apparent necessity, out of boredom, out of routine—and just blow them away. It's time to be truthful with yourself and say, "Wait a minute, who am I kidding?"

The strongest source is meditation. To meditate with full effort produces infinity, freedom. Next are the tasks and next is just to enjoy beauty. But it's a time of martial combat, of martial arts; it's a time of battle. Oppressors don't just go away, you make them go away—externally or internally.

Passive resistance is good in some circumstances; in other circumstances active resistance is the only way. You don't have to choose one or the other—you can choose both. To achieve a revolution you have to apply whatever method is applicable in any given situation, otherwise there's no revolution. The path of least resistance is the best. Passive resistance is fine if it works. If it doesn't, active resistance must be considered.

It's interesting, the Dalai Lama, in accepting the Nobel Peace Prize, said that he's been trying passive resistance for Tibet, but he's beginning to consider the possibility that something else may be required to remove the Chinese. I salute him for being able to step outside of his own convictions in the eye of reality. Step outside of your own convictions and deal with reality instead. Just see what is necessary to clear your mind, purify your being and return to a state of perpetual innocence—a childlike state of hope and belief and the stillness of the sage, the vastness of nirvana.

This is the best time. There will not be a better time. There's always a better place to get to inside. But in terms of the ease in this particular universe, it will never be easier than now. Unless of course, humanity chooses wisely and the entire age begins to shift and break the downward pattern that it's in and starts up. Then of course, well, this is just the beginning of something that will get better and better. Otherwise it just becomes more difficult.

Personal growth always gets better and better, but it's more difficult in an environment, in an aura such as the world has had of hate, fear, negativity and the complete denial of the spirit. Or the rationalizing of it and the packaging of it to the point where it has no power—the local church, the local synagogue, the local guru who says nothing, means nothing and accomplishes nothing.

So it's an exciting time. It's a time of battle. Not celebration yet. Battle. Battle and journeys and teaching and learning. But it's an open time. Who could ask for more?

CHAPTER NINE

THE NEXUS OF ALL PATHWAYS

There are two ways to become enlightened—the easy way and the hard way. I suppose that could be true of anything. The easy way is through a complete focus on that which is most positive. The hard way is through a focus on that which is negative. Both positive and negative come from the same source. So if you follow either path, the path of affirmation or negation, eventually you'll come to the source, if you follow them to the source.

But positive and negative, what we call yin and yang, light and dark, are circles. In the Far East, we look at life in terms of circles. In the West, they look at life more in terms of squares and rectangles. We look at life more as circles. In the West when you talk about yin and yang, people normally think of yin and yang as something that's linear. There's a single line, which is yin, and juxtaposed to it is a single line, which is yang. But in the East we tend to think of yin and yang as circles. They're two circles that actually can lie on top of each other, yet they remain separate. But if it's easier for you to think of it that way, you can think of them as being next to each other.

Now, yang, which is positive, affirmative, and so on, is a circle, and you can come into it at any point of the circle and go around the circle. When you've gone around the circle, at the end you'll come back to the beginning of the circle. And then you'll go around the circle again and again, forever. The same is true of yin. Being on the circle of yin or yang does not necessarily mean that you will ever go beyond the circle because the source of the circle is not necessarily connected to it.

To reach the source of the circle, you have to get off the circle. But going around the circle, one can build up a kind of a momentum, a speed. And as you go around the circle more and more rapidly, you can gain enough momentum so that you can lift above the circle, and vortex, or do a pirouette, into the source of the circle. When you enter the source of the circles of yin and yang, it's what they call *tai chi*, the undifferentiated reality, which is a way of saying it's beyond description. But it is not something that can be separated—because what we're seeking is the nexus of all possible worlds and states of mind, which is within us. The source of yin and yang is within you.

But within us there are a number of different points or configurations where we come together and join as intelligence, as wakefulness, as something that has an aliveness to it. The points are progressions, the locus points, where the nexus that we are conjoins, creates what we call *bonding reality structures,* states of mind in a more vernacular usage. And these locus points cause perception.

Yin and yang are outgrowths, positive and negative. Affirmation and negation are negatives and positives; they're outgrowths, syntactical outgrowths of a nexus within the mind. But there is not one nexus within the mind. There are many. And self-discovery, the pathway to enlightenment—particularly the tantric method of attaining enlightenment and liberation and emerging into the clear light of reality, the *dharmakaya*, the rootless source of all being, the ultimate groundless ground, so to speak, what they would call God, nirvana—[is] that assimilation, that jump, that trajectory, to move from the states of apparent reality, which we call the *samsara,* in which occur birth, growth, maturation, old age, death and rebirth—those circles are absorbed or are extensions of the mind. The mind is all that exists. There is nothing else. Everything that we perceive, including the action of pure perception, is an extension of the mind. Without the mind there is nothing.

The nexus of the mind, the central nexus, the first one you encounter, is that part of the mind which creates the pageant that you call life. The pageant of life is divided into yin and yang. They're two circles. You can follow either circle and manage to develop enough speed to move beyond this world or other worlds, dimensional realities. But the thing that the novice normally misses in all of this is that all states of mind are internal. That is to say, what creates reality is the mind's self-reflection.

Let's imagine that there's someone far, far away in another dimension—very far away. They're sitting by a lake in a world that's made of light. It's not a world like this, but it's a world of light. And they're looking into the lake, and out above the lake there's a horizon that goes on forever, which is made up of lights that continually change coloration. And the being is made of light and the lake is made of light, yet the lights are variegated and seem to have a slightly different density in that they resonate at different frequencies. So as the being is sitting by the lake looking into it, they see a reflection. They see their eyes and their face, which is also light. And the light is moving. The light of the lake is moving, the light of the being is moving. The light circulates and shifts and changes hue and vibration. And as they look into that lake and they look into their eyes, they see a world very far away, maybe this world, and they see a person in that world, maybe you. And maybe they're inside that person living a life, experiencing a world for a while. But where are they really? They're looking at a lake of light, which is an extension of their mind, which shifts and changes, and has different hues.

Reality is perception. And within the mind there's a lake that contains everything—all possible realities, all possible universes, all possible perceptions. Not just of external things, but of oneself, as oneself as a god or a goddess, as oneself as an ant, as oneself as a reality, as oneself as nirvana—all things exist in this lake. And as we stare into it, we tend to focus on something, we tend to select something. Without thought, we're looking into the lake. But something will kind of solidify in front of our eyes. For a moment, the color combinations will join or bond in a certain way. And at that moment, if we're distracted from the continual flow of perfect mind that we're in, suddenly everything configures, everything solidifies. Suddenly a shape appears out of flux. Suddenly a world appears, karmas appear, pasts, futures, presents, time structures, yin and yang appear.

In other words, there wasn't a single day in which the world was created. It's created anew at every moment. The structures of eternity are completely fluid but they are bound together by the mind, and as the mind binds them together, forming a nexus or a point of configuration from which structures emerge, so reality comes into being.

The world wasn't created. It is created anew at every moment by mind. By your mind. As your mind reflects and perceives, so it configures past and future, good and bad, success and failure. The pairs of opposites.

Now, by the time we get down to the world, we've forgotten all about the lake, and we're sitting, living, walking, talking, sleeping; we're existing and we've forgotten about the flux of perception. We've solidified into a karmic configuration from which there is, in a way, no escape. We've gotten on a circle. It's either a circle of affirmation or negation. And we will just go around and around that circle in what we call a karmic progression.

Karmic progression implies that we are kind of alliterating steps in life. There's an alliteration, a kind of a rhyme structure. That is to say, once we're in time and space, the variable structures are somewhat limited. Once we've conceived of time and space, once we've accepted or endorsed their existence, then that implies that there is a structural order to *binding realities.*

For example, a map. If we take a map of the United States, we can see North, South, East and West. We can see Maine and California, Wisconsin, Florida. And there's a sense of order to that map. There's direction—places have names. There may be highways, mountains, cities. Looking at a map, we accept that reality exists in a certain defined way. We are admitting that what we are seeing is not just a fluid mass of moving, changing light, which does not have any particular definition or any particular structure, which is always in flux—rather we are giving a solidity to reality. We're admitting that there's a solidity. But in other states of perception, there may be no North, South, East or West.

If one is enlightened, one does not perceive life with North, South, East and West. There is no California, there is no New York. In a higher bonding state of attention, everything is fluid light. And the way that you perceive life, the way most people perceive life, doesn't exist. It's not there. The structures become fluid. The ice that's frozen on the pond, that's been there all winter, that's created a place for people to skate, a landscape, something that we drive by in a car every day and we see—suddenly spring comes and all that ice goes away, and there's water, which has no definite shape. It looks like it has a shape, visually. But if we go over there, the water's in constant movement.

The particles of the water are constantly combining with other particles of water. It is not solid. We pick it up and it slides through our fingers. That's what life is—it's not solid. But at times it appears to be solid. And it is that appearance of solidity that creates reality on basic levels, on sensorial levels, basic mental levels.

The process of meditation, the action of what we call *the tantric path to enlightenment,* is melting the ice. It is assumed right now that your entire world is frozen. The ice is very solid, it's very thick, which is your life, your mind, the way you perceive things. But through raising what we call the *kundalini* energy, which is a very hot energy that exists in a part of the mind, by raising that energy we raise the temperature and we melt—sometimes just a little, sometimes a great deal—the ice that is the solidification of life as we perceive it.

The primary solidification, of course, is always a self-objectification. That is to say, we perceive the solidification as the world around us, which appears to be relatively solid. But that solidification is just really a reflection of the solidification of one's sense of self.

So what we're seeking to do is not really melt the map—of America. We're seeking to melt the self, the solid form that we consider ourselves to be, which is relatively unchanging [in] the sense that it is a solid self. I have been thus and such a person, I was born this way or I grew up this way, I am this way, I can make minor modifications, perhaps—change a few habits even though that's somewhat challenging. But to take "me" as a structural being and melt myself down, the only time that happens that we know of is in death.

At death we all accept that the self ceases to exist. There are various theories that maybe the self continues on in another life, in another body, in another plane of consciousness, a heaven, a hell, something like that. But I think everyone would realize, or everyone could kind of feel or construe, that after death the self would not exactly be the same, even if it did continue on. The perceptual body that you are at the time of death ceases to be. It is not structured quite so tightly.

So what someone does who seeks enlightenment—deeper, clarified awareness, a finer way of perceiving life—what they're seeking to do is melt the self. This is not done in one fiery blast. It's done very gradually, a little at a time. And as we melt the self, we then—after it melts a little bit—we allow it to solidify and it solidifies in new patterns.

What we're seeking to do is become transparent. Sort of a transparent window on reality. But that takes time to do. We're starting with a very solid, objectified view of ourselves and existence. To change that around, it's necessary to gradually loosen up the glue that binds the self together. I suppose you could say you've become unglued, right? But each time we loosen the glue, we only loosen it a little bit and then we allow the self to come together again in a new structure, just as it did at birth.

Now, what makes all this work is velocity. That is to say, the theory of personality transmutation is that the self follows—is an aggregate, it's a series of formations that has a karma to it. It's going around a circle. There's a pattern to it, just like the DNA causes a growth structure pattern. So that you start out at a certain size, you grow larger, and there's an orderly pattern, there's a progression that's implicit in the DNA, which the coding of the DNA causes the body to develop in specific ways.

The self, too, has some kind of—it's like a DNA. We call it the *causal body*. There's a part of us that has a coding, and that coding follows a progression just as the growth of the body does. The progression of the self is implicit in its own structures. But normally those structures only change at the time of death. If we think of each death and each rebirth in a series of lifetimes as a day in the life of a human being in which there's growth and development and change, but that growth and development and change are following a pattern—we can say it's a logical, orderly pattern if we like that kind of language. It really doesn't matter, it just is. You may like it, you may not like it, but the DNA does what it does. It doesn't sit around waiting for your opinion.

Opinions are secondary when dealing with reality. They're subjective reflections, but they don't change the DNA—unless you get into the DNA and change it, which can be done. But who's changing the DNA? You know, it's the old thing. Is it the DNA through the person who's changing the DNA that's changing the DNA? In which case the DNA is not changing—you know what I mean. You see, you go around on one of those circles. Obviously God is changing the DNA through God as God for God by God, and all that sort of thing. See what I mean?

So in self-discovery, what one does is—the way you change is simply by liquefying the self. It's not necessary to know how to get to the next structure. It's implicit in the self that the self will automatically evolve if you can dissolve it. It repatterns itself after archetypal formations that exist deep within the mind—way back up in that lake, with that being of light that's looking into the lake of light, with the endless horizon of light that's constantly changing hue and intonation. Another image will come. Suddenly the being will be looking into the lake again and everything will have liquefied. And then another image will come up of another world, another time, another space, another body that suddenly they're in again. That's implicit in reality. Reality takes care of itself very well. Nirvana is perfect.

Our part is not to try and determine with thought, desire or aversion who or what we should be. We allow life to do that, in other words. There's an implicit faith or trust in the processes of life. Not simply the physical processes of life—you know, you can say, "Well, I trusted life and I walked out onto a freeway and I got hit by a car. So much for trusting life." OK. But we're discussing the part of life that makes us what we are, that has given existence what it is, that ultimate intelligence which everything is a reflection of.

If you were able to trust life implicitly—that which creates you, is you, changes you, dies with you, is reborn with you—if you can let go to that, then automatically the set point, the self, becomes what it should be. What we seek to do through the process of meditation and through the practices in Tantric Buddhism is simply to liquefy ourselves. And then life automatically will bring us to the next stage. You don't really have to know where you're going—it's like breathing.

In yoga what they call *pranayama* is the science of breathing. And in pranayama you don't worry about taking breaths, you focus on exhalation—because if you exhale properly, you will inhale. And the more deeply you exhale, the more deeply you will inhale. So we really don't have to worry about breathing in. It will happen, I assure you. But we focus in pranayama on exhalation. Breathing in will follow automatically.

It's not necessary to know where you're going; you just have to get out of where you are, and automatically you will be someplace else. That's how the universe works. The structures of the universe are perfect in that way. People are always thinking, "Well, I want to change." You don't have to know what you want to change into, you just have to change. You just have to get out of where you are and automatically, the next step will follow. If you pick your foot up, it's going to come down someplace, do you follow? Even if it's going to be the same place, but it won't really be the same place—it'll only look the same if you're in a state of mind that is not seeing reality, which is constantly in a state of transmutation. No place is ever the same because everything is shifting, always. Change is continuous and the aggregate of the self is constantly shifting. But on outer structural levels, which you call a personality, it can look—because of striated states of mind—very definitive, very hard.

Meditation is a process in which we are seeking to liquefy the self by raising the kundalini energy. When that happens, we experience an ecstasy. That ecstasy is the freedom of moving beyond a self that is much too structured. It's like you've chained somebody and they've been sitting in shackles. Suddenly you take the chains off and there's just an innate ecstasy to getting up and moving and being able to just get around and not being chained to a particular place.

No one likes being a slave, and the ultimate slavery is being a slave to yourself. Being stuck in who you are is the ultimate slavery. In other words, what causes pain in life is being specifically who you are. The less definitive, the less you are who you are, the more ecstasy there is. The pain in life is caused by being someone.

Now, being nebulous is not particularly ecstatic. It's a condition of light—hard to explain in words, obviously—it's a condition of light that creates ecstasy. It's being up in the world of light, looking into the lake, watching the shifting aggregate formations of existence perfectly moving without a sense of direction, constantly forming new patterns. That sense of freedom, when the mind stops and folds into itself, when thought stops, when the perception of self as separate from the rest of life ceases—at that point reality is apparent.

Naturally there are countless realities and every perception is a reality, every state of mind is a reality. But all of those realities are circles that go round and round forever. They're like rides at Disneyland. You can go to Disneyland and get on Space Mountain and it'll be the same today, tomorrow, the next day, the next day. That ride is there for you. You may like the ride, you may go on it again, you may get a kick out of it. But it's always there. So every lifetime, every state of mind, every dimension, every reality, is just a ride. And eventually what we seek to do, we realize that we can go on all the rides in the world, but we're still who we are.

In Buddhism what we seek to do is not necessarily just find a better ride, but we seek to find a better us. We seek to change ourselves into someone who's beautiful to be. The pure act of being who we are is beautiful, a beauty so overpowering that it becomes ecstasy. In other words, it isn't the action of doing something that produces ecstasy. The act of doing or engaging in something will only reflect who you are.

If you're a mean, nasty person, then whatever you do will be kind of mean and nasty. As you'd be riding on Space Mountain, you'll be mean and nasty, and you know, (Rama talks like a bully) "Well, I got ahead in the line! Ha-ha-ha-ha! Look at those people down there, they're stupid!" (Back to normal voice.) See? You'll bring that with you wherever you go.

If you're a high-minded person, right? Then you'll walk around, sort of in your self-reflection of being someone who'd always go, "Gee, everything is so wonderful. Look at those nice people down there standing in line. I let those people get ahead of me because they were in such a rush, they were so excited to be on the ride." Right? And you're stuck in that state of mind. In other words, states of mind engender reality. It doesn't matter what ride you get on, you are on the ride that is you.

What we do in Buddhism—changing rides is inevitable. That just happens, you can't avoid it in life. Life is a cyclic, changing situation. But what we seek to do is what other people don't do. We seek to change ourselves. Most people think that if I can simply get a better ride and ride it all the time, everything will be good. You know, that is the approach to life that most people take. They assume that what makes a difference is a better house, a better car, a better lover, a better job, better possessions, a better body—these are the things that make one happy. But all rides come to an end. The coach changes back to a pumpkin. You outgrow the glass slipper because your feet get fat. They don't show what happens to Cinderella ten years after—after five kids.

Buddhism, then, is the study of changing the self. Naturally, as the self changes, it will select different rides to go on because there are different tastes. You really don't have to worry about that part. In other words, today you like Space Mountain; tomorrow you'll like It's a Small World—various rides at Disneyland. Your tastes will automatically evolve as you do. So, if instead of putting all your attention into always trying to get a better ride but instead you put your attention into creating a better you, then whatever ride you go on is much more beautiful, is much more ecstatic.

Meditation is a process of liquefying the self temporarily and then allowing the self to rebond. The ice melts and then it comes back again. But when it comes back again, it comes back in a more evolved configuration. It's less dense. It's less structured. It's more lucid.

Now, why does it do that? It's because in between the liquefactions we're building up a level of power. In other words, why shouldn't it just come back in a structure that's about the same? Why not come back in a structure that is less ecstatic or more, if we can use ecstasy as a measurement. Ecstasy is a relative measurement of freedom. When we're not free, there's no ecstasy. The more free we are, the more ecstasy.

We're using gradients of light as an auric measurement, a quantified auric measurement of the ascension of consciousness from the relatively sensorial, material perceptions of existence to the more refined, spiritual perceptions of existence. And obviously there's a lot more ecstasy in the spirit than in the flesh. Flesh has its moments. But the spirit has a much, much higher processing rate. <u>The body is very low-level language. Machine language.</u>[6] The

---

6. A computer's native instruction set, at the chip level.

language of the soul, of the mind, is much more evolved. There are many languages.

What causes that change is not simply the detonation of the self. What causes the change is that in between the restructurings of the self, one is directing oneself towards light. Now we get—we must wax metaphysical. Up to now, it's been an occult discussion, which is basically the chemistry of change. We're dealing with diurnal structures, which are relatively easy to understand. This is just physics. The physics or the chemistry of the soul, kind of. The DNA structures of reality.

But the magic of life, of course, is not something that can be explained. Structures can only take us to the point where they begin or end. Beyond structures is the white light. The white light is reality in a form that cannot be apprehended or understood. It can be admired, it can be feared, it can be focused upon, it can be rejected, it can be forgotten. But it's there, just as the sun is there. You can forget it's there; you can get so involved in your thoughts as you walk around today that you forget that there's a sun up there. You never look at the sky once during the whole day. That doesn't mean it's not there. If it's not there, you're in serious trouble. The world will freeze and you will be dead.

The sun is there, whether you're aware of it or not. The white light is there. And the magic of the white light is—when we step into it, it transmutes us, it transforms us. It just does. That's mysticism. Mysticism is the acceptance that everything cannot be logically explained. I mean, everything can be logically explained, but it has nothing to do with what's really happening. Those are just appended kind of algorithms so we can discern the motion of a mathematical equation. But what does that have to do with the equation itself? The equation just exists because there's a flow in the world of mathematics.

Algorithms are not dependent upon understanding. They just exist—like pre-bonding structures of reality. In other words, the cellular structures that compose the body do not need scientific explanation. They work without it. They worked before it. They didn't come into being because somebody understood them.

Human beings like to think that, "I think, therefore everything comes after that." But that's bullshit! That's science. Science is bullshit. Interesting bullshit—nevertheless, it's still bullshit. Only because there's so much ego correlated to it. The assumption is that, "Ah! We have discovered the universe." Excuse me! I beg to interject that the universe was there before you "discovered" it. Your discovery did not give it life.

The structures of existence just are. Blame it on God, I suppose. "God did it" sort of thing. They're just there. But if one is wise, one can learn to move within those structures in ways that create ecstasy, or pain. Now, in a simple civilization like the one we're in now, they don't know too much about DNA, they're just sort of figuring it out. If you were born with a certain structure of DNA, you must live that way. In other civilizations, they have known how to take the DNA and completely manipulate it. And when you manipulate the DNA, you can change and regrow things and restructure the body.

Most people don't know what to do with their minds and their lives—they're kind of stuck in their own DNA. But Buddhists have made a study over thousands and thousands of years, of how you can change the structures of the self, how you can manipulate the DNA of being. You can't change the fact that it's there—everybody has it. But you can cause it to move into new formations, into more lucid formations in which there's ecstasy.

I don't think I have to explain why there's a desire to be ecstatic. I think that's implicit in any understanding of life. It's just there. We seek ecstasy. We seek freedom. We don't particularly seek the lack of ecstasy. We don't particularly seek the lack of freedom, although looking at the human race, one would think it does. The human race seems to go heavily out of its way to avoid ecstasy and to avoid freedom.

So if you seek ecstasy and freedom, and again those are kind of intangible words, but—if we can get beyond them—then the only recourse is the study of the dissolution and the reformation of the self. And of course, there's something beyond that, which is—complete enlightenment, in which we go beyond selves and reformations of selves and all that stuff. This is a process we go through just to build up speed, and if we get enough speed through either the path of negation or the path of creation, if we get up enough speed, we can flip beyond creation or negation to pure enlightenment, which is a structure that is not even a being up there somewhere looking in a pool of shifting light at itself shifting its light.

If we can get up far enough, then there isn't even a being looking in a pool. There's something beyond that one that's creating that. We can get back another level—that's nirvana. No way to talk about it. Not from here. Maybe if we get up to the point where the being of light is looking in the pool, maybe there's a way of understanding it from there a little more, or at least seeing the direction. From here, it's necessary just to get up to that point, then the next step will follow automatically.

It is through many lifetimes of shifting the aggregate of the self and refining it and transforming it that one finally reaches a point of maximum velocity whereby one can snap off the circle completely and move into a freedom that's not simply, "Gee, now I know how to get around the circle real well, whereas before it was kind of painful and I was stuck in it and didn't really get its motion. Now I know how to get around and get to where I want to go and avoid the places I want to avoid." But that in itself becomes another circle, which is another kind of trap. So now we know self-discovery very well, we know a system very well, and we become trapped by the system and by our knowledge of it. Ultimately one can snap beyond systems to something else that is even more free, more ecstatic—whatever words we want to use—more liberating, more enlightening.

It's by building up a kind of a momentum that that is done. But that step and all the steps are really the same. It's the transmutive power of the white light that is God, that is the central nexus of being. Not the peripheral nexus, or "nexees" maybe (Rama laughs). Not all those little guys out there, those other nexes, those other points that cause the ten thousand states of mind to come into aggregate suspension. Not those things, nah! The central nexus is the white light. Because it's a nexus, it does not have an opposite point. And when we step into it, it's like taking a shower.

You're all dirty and grungy and you go step in the shower and you come out clean. So when you enter into the white light, it does something to you. It frees you, it shifts you, it changes you. Then there will be points when one can make an ascension—one is not simply stepping into the white light, which is the equivalent of meditating each day and doing a variety of other things that give one speed in terms of energy flow.

It's sort of like—remember when you were a kid, they had the little local bank? And they had the Christmas Club. And you'd go down every week and you'd put ten bucks in and then by Christmas time, you've got a bunch of money and you go shopping. So you're saving and suddenly you get enough money and you go do something.

Remember the stamps in the supermarket and the books you used to paste them in? And you get enough stamps and then you could go get a neat thing, right? But for a while we don't have the neat thing, we only have the apprehension of it, looking at catalogues of neat things, you see. For a while we just have the licking of stamps and the placing of stamps in booklets, and shopping carts. And one day we take them down to the center—they used to have these little centers where you'd bring all your coupons and you would select from wonderful gifts—this was back in the day when they believed America was immortal and science was all, and we could do no wrong. Products were the ultimate answer to all problems. "At General Electric, progress is our most important product." See?

Now, who knows what Ronald Reagan had in common with General Electric? Do you know? What? (An inaudible audience member responds.) Well, yeah, he was the host on what? (Audience responds, "GE Theater.") "GE Theater," that's right. Now there's a nexus for you. And he spun from that to being President of the United States, from being the host of "GE Theater." So there must have been a power to it. Sorry. (Audience laughs at the pun.) Oooooohhhh!

So all yoga and meditation is essentially the accumulation of coupons. (Audience laughs.) Now, this is different than the lottery. The lottery is very different. The lottery has no certainty. Actually, it has a pretty large certainty that you won't win, because out of millions of tickets, only a few people score. And you could buy those tickets theoretically forever and never score. It's entirely possible. Forget this chance theorem. There's a chance that you could always buy a ticket forever in eternity and never win. You do realize that.

You know, when they say the odds—"Your odds at winning are one out of two million." So that means if you buy two million tickets, eventually you're going to win? Not true! Not if you know anything about probability factoring. Probability factoring implies that there is absolutely no such thing as probability. There's only luck. Unless you buy every single ticket—then there's no luck. But then, of course, if you bought every single ticket, that costs more than what you would win. That's a very, very frustrated person who wants to win very badly.

You can do that in self-discovery. I've known people who have done that. You know, people who finally get so pissed off that they're not enlightened that they just go to ridiculous extremes after thousands and millions [of lifetimes]—in other words, the fact that you're reborn does not mean that you'll ever become enlightened. You know, there's a theorem you read in some of the Far Eastern spiritual books where they say (Rama talks in a high-pitched voice), "Well, Sally or Bob, sooner or later, after you go through enough lifetimes, you will become enlightened." (Return to normal voice.) Wrong! All dogs may go to heaven, but that's—no. No, it's like the lottery. You could buy lottery tickets forever and it's possible you will never come up with a winning ticket. Obviously, I should not be the spokesperson for the New York State Lottery. They will not hire me, I can tell.

So you could go through incarnations forever and never become enlightened—unless, of course, you do something about it. But just the fact that you exist—"I exist, therefore some day I'll become enlightened." No. Some people say that though. They believe that, so therefore they don't do anything, therefore they never become enlightened and they go around the circle forever.

Sooner or later you determine that it is through self-effort that one advances, not through luck. It's through self-effort. You finally realize, "I can sit here forever, waiting for a date, waiting for someone to call, but I haven't met anybody." Now there is a possibility that the phone will ring. But it will probably be one of those terrible computer things that calls you up. Do you see what I mean? Whereas if you get out and commingle with humanity, there is a likelihood that you might meet someone who might ask you, or you might meet someone you could ask. But sitting at home with no one there, looking at the walls, the chances are slim, if you see what I mean.

It could happen, you could get a wrong number. "Gee! You have a nice voice!" "Well, so do you!" "Do you like Bingo?" "Love it." "Do you like sunrises in hell?" "Love 'em!" "Gee! What a great coincidence that we're talking to each other." "No coincidence at all!" You know, that sort of thing. So hang up the phone quickly. Disconnect it. Burn the house down. Change countries, change time zones, change anything. Somebody wants you that bad and finds you, you don't want to be around them.

The Buddhists believe that everything in life is random. There are patterns that are intrinsic to life. We don't know why, we just know they're there like the DNA. We have no idea, we just blame it on God. We believe that the universe is a series of patterns, and those patterns go on forever. They themselves change because they themselves follow. Patterns are patterns. All of life is a series of patterns that transmute and change, but the patterns follow patterns. Cycles are in a cycle themselves. Those cycles exist just by themselves. They will always be. And we're a pattern that follows a pattern, and we will always exist following that pattern. If life is a circle, we're part of it.

But the Buddhists also feel—they've discovered, observed, come to know, learned that, bothered to listen to life—that it is possible to click through different patterns and get to that which makes the patterns, even though it's not observable in the patterns. You can apprehend that there's an order to creation by the fact that it's extremely—obviously—orderly. And that implies that something has created that order. Unless, of course, you're simply mad and you're imposing your mental order upon it and there is no order whatsoever, which is entirely possible. You have to consider everything. It's the Buddhist way. We take into account every possible variation, subvariation and negation of all variations and subvariations. Let alone the negation of the self that creates and is implicit in the variation and subvariation of the various selves. So once you know everything, and you know nothing, and you know all subvariations, nonvariations, lack of variations, variegated variations, you go through all this ridiculous stuff, you're still at the same point. You're sitting in a room being stupid. (Audience laughs.)

It's like in *The Little Prince*, the guy goes up the trail in the planets and the guy's counting the stars, right? And he's very busy. Once in a while one of the stars goes out, and it pisses him off and he has to redo all his calculations, because there's a super nova, do you see what I mean? What that leaves out is the white light. In other words, without the white light, there would be no hope. It would be very bad, because you would only exist as the pattern within patterns, bound to a circle forever—Prometheus bound.

The white light is the joker in the deck. It does not have a fixed identity. It creates transmutations that are completely unpredictable, which is what makes it fun, which is why it scares the hell out of most people. All of meditation and Buddhism has to do with going into the white light. And if you go into the white light, which is a direct formation of God beyond patterns, that white light repatterns you, shifts you and transmutes you. And you don't have to know how, since God is God, and inherently God therefore does godlike things. You don't have to hassle it, you just have to get there.

You get to Hawaii, you go outside, you lie down, you get tan. Don't worry; it is Hawaii's nature to tan one. If you lie in the sun, it will happen. Stay in the sun too long, you burn. You build up to it, see? Or if you just like to be in the sun, you get, of course, a total sun block. That's what most people have—total enlightenment block.

So then, you can follow the path of negation or the path of affirmation. I'll talk about the path of negation and affirmation another time. They're two different paths. One is the easy way, one is the hard way. But either way can take you into the white light.

In the West, they're only aware of the path of affirmation. In the East, we also have the path of negation. In the West, the very concept of the path of negation taking you into the light doesn't exist. Here they believe that only through affirmation can one enter into the light. Negation, they think, is the opposite of the light. The light does not have an opposite. That's why it's the light. If it had an opposite, it couldn't be the light. Darkness is not the opposite of the light.

The light that I'm talking about, which is why we usually call it the "clear light"—I'm using white light because it's easier for Westerners—but we call it the clear light, and the clear light cannot have an opposite. White light can have an opposite—dark light. The clear light can't have an opposite, therefore it is superior to your common light. See what I mean? The light to which I refer, which we call the inner light, as opposed to the sunlight, which is perceived through the senses, the inner light does not have an opposite. Dark and light as you know them come out of the inner light. But the central nexus of the mind where the flux of the inner light is, is all you need.

Buddhism is the path that leads through affirmation or negation, or if you're really kind of techy or confused, through both, to the clear light. Once you get in the clear light, you get in the shower, you'll get washed off. You get remade. You get reborn, transmuted, purified. And if that happens enough times, in enough ways, you build up enough momentum to blast off the circle completely and go into that clear light so totally that you become it. There's no way to explain it, in other words, there's something else beyond that. Existence doesn't end with nirvana. It just—no words.

Chapter Ten

THE PATH OF AFFIRMATION

Why do we meditate? Why do we engage in practices? Why bother? Why spend hours sitting by yourself when you could be with convivial companions doing socially acceptable or unacceptable things? Why go off by yourself into a condition of solitude within your own mind, focusing on images, on chakras, on points of light for many hours, day after day, year after year, lifetime after lifetime? Why exclude a lot of experiences from your life that you might enjoy? Why include experiences that perhaps are not initially innate to your energy flow?

That's self-discovery, and self-discovery is a process of exclusion and inclusion. We exclude things that take energy from us, even though they might be enjoyable. We include things that might be difficult because they create energy. Ultimately the energy is enjoyable and the loss of energy is not, needless to say. But, since we all die at the end of a lifetime, is it really better to be an ascetic? It's like, "Wouldn't you really rather have a Buick?" That was an ad slogan some time back.

I don't know. Would I? Somebody out there wanted me to think that I would, and I guess if I heard the jingle enough times maybe I would really want a Buick. I'm not sure. So in the development of one's life, you could just party constantly and if you have a somewhat good constitution and you run a few miles a day, you could probably party hardy for a whole lifetime and die at a ripe, old, well partied-out age and have had a very good time.

On the other hand, you could not do that and lead a life of internal origination where you're meditating—probably die at about the same age, and at the end you die and it's all forgotten. Oh, there's rebirth, of course, and determination where your stateroom is going to be in the next life. Are you going to be in first class? Are you going to be in steerage? Somewhere in between? Or are you even going to get on the boat? Are you going to be working? You know, that sort of thing, on the big cruise of infinity.

OK, but aside from that reincarnation stuff, being pragmatic just about one life, why go through all the—what most people would perceive as trouble—to learn to control your thoughts, your emotions, modify your lifestyle in such a way that might seem unnatural from the point of view of many members of our society? Of course, implicit in that is what they do is what is natural. And if you do what they do, you are natural because whatever they do is somehow godlike. That's the thesis. But I don't know about all that.

Why do this? It's a lot of work! And maybe you're really not going to have a better time than the person who just has a nice family, parties, has a nice life, goes boating on Sundays. Why get involved with self-discovery? Why go through these practices? Why come to meditative sessions with mystical teachers? Why modify your life? You've already developed a lot of habits by the time you meet self-discovery. Most people don't run into self-discovery seriously until they're at least 18. In 18 years you've habituated your entire being to a certain lifestyle and the rest of your life is just an extension of that, primarily. Why change that? It's a lot of work. You've already got the thing going. Why change the direction so radically—which is what's necessary in self-discovery—to different mind fields.

In other words, is it really worth it? Why would a person do that? Why do mystics sit in caves on top of the Himalayas when they could be down where there's central heating and a nice warm couch? What drives people to do these weird religious practices? I can say ecstasy, but what does that mean? You might be able to be very ecstatic with central heating. The reason that one practices self-discovery is because we're seeking a feeling. We're seeking a feeling. And when we feel that feeling, there is nothing like that feeling. It's just a feeling.

Someone might say, "Well, wait, what's this feeling stuff? That doesn't sound like a reason to live your life." Oh yeah? What else do you do? You go to work because of a feeling, you follow a career because you have a feeling, you love someone because it gives you a feeling, you raise a family because it gives you a feeling, you raise a flag because it gives you a feeling, you die for your country because you feel something for it. Everything that we do is related to feelings. It's just that our feelings are more difficult to express in simple words because they're not simple. They're very complicated.

There's a feeling that occurs sometimes when you're standing at sunset looking out into the horizon, where you just slip away from all of this and all of that. You're at a party. You're at an office party. It's Christmas. Everybody's busy, everybody's having a good time and they're celebrating. For a moment you go out on the balcony and the sun is setting and you just look at the sky. You slip away from all the noise, all the good times, everybody looking good in their good-looking suits, all the beautiful men and women. You just go outside by yourself and you slide the glass door behind you and you just look outside, and for a moment, the noise, the excitement, the hubbub vanishes, and there's a stillness.

The stillness isn't the end of things, it's the beginning. It's always the beginning. You step into that stillness and you just go away. There's a feeling that comes up which cannot be expressed in words, and that feeling transports you beyond this world to other worlds, other realms, to different places inside your mind, maybe. And that feeling is so perfect and so complete, it's beyond all other experiences.

We could take all the pleasures that have ever been and will ever be in all of the universes that have ever been, are now or will ever be, and add them up into one experience. And if you were absorbed in nirvana, it would not be noticed. There's no way to calculate the pure and perfect stillness of absorption in nirvana. All the existences, all the creations, the manifold lives, the beings, the pageant of infinity, which always is, is unnoticeable in nirvana because its silence, its essential nothingness, is so complete and so perfect and so pure that there is no relation point. You know, holding a candle to the sun.

In the beginning there is religion, and after religion there is occultism. There are the esoteric and the exoteric stages of practice. Religion is primarily exoteric. It depends on outer symbols, on words like purity, power, goodness, evil, representative colors symbolizing things, statues, things like that. In the beginning a person is seeking to have some form of consolidation between themselves and infinity, this thing that we call life. They must feel an absence. Why else would someone be drawn to religion, unless they're just forced into it by birth and family and caste and that sort of thing?

But if a person comes to religion on their own, they come to religion because they're looking for a feeling. They're looking for something that they're not finding in other parts of their lives, clearly. So initially, religion, which is the exoteric experience of the self-discovery process, breaks it down into a very conceptual kind of viewpoint. There's purity, there's impurity. There are commandments—do this, avoid that. You see? It's very much religion by numbers. It's very simple. It's very easy for a person to hold in their mind.

But religion, of course, is the beginning of the experience of transcendence. After you've gone through religion and it's taken you as far as it can, then we move into the esoteric experiences, which is the study of meditation and enlightenment. In the beginning we read about someone else; we read about Buddha, his experiences, what he did, how he came to be enlightened, the miracles that occurred around him, the transmutations. But then a time comes when it isn't enough to read about Buddha, we wish to have that happen to ourselves. That's when we move from the exoteric to the esoteric, from religion to mysticism or occultism. I use those terms; they're the same thing.

In religion we're reading about someone else, and we might feel something because it's inevitable, if we focus on certain higher octave qualities long enough, that we find those qualities in our own mind. But in mysticism, in occultism, there's a very definitive methodology for bringing oneself into the transmutation, into the white light—the clear light—that causes one to realize that one is enlightenment, one is Buddha. And the experiences are not so much reading about somebody else but they're the practices that the person did who we're reading about.

In the beginning we talk about purity, humility. In other words, we're suggesting that there's a tonal range that's more pleasant for an individual to experience than the tonal ranges of emotions, thoughts, feelings, that most people experience and that we can pick and choose, just like we do at the supermarket between the good apples and the bad apples, between the good plums and the bad plums, the good nectarines and the bad nectarines. We can pick and choose by focusing—by feeling there's something called virtue, self-respect, truth, higher principles in life—if we think of those things and we choose to live in them, then we bring those qualities that are in our mind, as such, out.

In other words, within your mind is everything. All heavens and hells exist within your own mind. The qualities are not in some spiritual land, they're in your mind. Within you is a horror, an awful being, somebody you could just kill without thought. Within you is someone who is a savior, who could save, no matter what pain it cost them. Everything is within your mind. Your mind contains all of infinity, although you may not be aware of that yet.

Life is really a process of choosing which qualities we wish to bring into the foreground and which qualities we wish to let recede into the background of the mind. In religion they simplify it for you; they tell you what to do. They say the qualities you want in the foreground are as follows; these will make you happy if they're in your foreground. The qualities in the background are the ones that will make you unhappy; we want to push them as far back as we can. Somebody else figured this out, don't question it, just do it, and you'll feel better.

That's paint by numbers. Remember the little paint by number kits? You have paint numbers—red is one, blue is two, green is three and so on. And if you will simply paint in this little outlined area, where they have a little number there, it will say three, so you paint the green within the line. If you keep doing that, eventually you get a picture that looks pretty good. If you paint by numbers you can turn out, even at an early stage, something that at least looks like the object that you're trying to create.

But eventually we move from painting by numbers to just taking a canvas and some primary colors and seeing that we can whip up different art forms, and that's mysticism, that's occultism. That's the advanced practice of religion. We're no longer painting by numbers, just doing what somebody says. Needless to say, our mistakes can be larger, as can our successes.

Through a series of lifetimes, we paint by numbers. Then we exhaust that, and if in this lifetime conventional religion never interested you, then you've exhausted that in other lifetimes. In this lifetime, if you did conventional religion for a while, it obviously wasn't finished. Then you finished it off, and now you've done all the painting by numbers you want to do. Now you are learning how to just paint. Now we have DPaint II [software product] here, right?

We're going to paint. And our canvas is our mind. We're going to create within us a structure. We seek to create a structure without us in the practice of meditation. We want the structure of our lives to be as simple as possible. We want to set up a maximum curve for the internalization of energy. We want as little hassle in our day-to-day life as possible because hassle equals having to take our attention from that which is within, externalize it into the sensorial world and try to straighten things out. And of course, as soon as something is straightened out, the very nature of things is that they change. We can straighten things out forever and spend our whole lives straightening things out and never get a chance to take ourselves within our mind.

We seek to make our life uncomplicated, only do things which cannot be gotten out of. You have to do them. Then, those things that we must do, we set up in such a way that they actually become part of the yogic process. This is tantra, where the things we do externally actually become forms of yoga. The way we make our bed, the way we keep our condo, the way we select a car, everything we do becomes a process that enables us to utilize the mind better. We gain power from our selections and from the mere act of selection.

But what we really want to do is not be very involved in the world because the world just drains you. We seek, for those who are now beyond religion by numbers, we seek now to be able to internalize our attention. We realize that what's out there are just people and places and things. I mean, there's not much out there. All people are basically the same, within simple structural levels. All places are about the same. There are subvariations, but really, you've seen one, you've seen them all sort of thing.

On the other hand, there are things available within the mind that have much more variegation. There's a lot more variety—mental states. So we seek to take our attention and bring it within our mind and make paintings. And we really don't want to look outside too much because outside there are other people's paintings and they're usually not very good. They're very unhappy. If we spend all our time concerning ourselves with what's going on in the physical world, it's going to change anyway. We're just building castles made out of sand, which slip into the sea eventually. If you like that, go do it. There's no prohibition; you can do it, and you can learn about ineffability.

That's the path of negation. There's a path in enlightenment called the path of negation where we intentionally throw ourselves into experiences that are extremely transient for the pure purpose of seeing the transience of all experience. In other words, we do all the stuff you're supposed to normally avoid to become enlightened, intentionally. But our intention is that by going to the very essence of these experiences we can find enlightenment, nirvana. It's a path of reversal. It's more complicated, I guess, I'm not sure. I've done it, personally. I've done them both and they're interesting. It's like two different martial arts forms. Either one makes you capable of defending yourself and makes you physically fit, but they're very different approaches.

But today we're discussing the path of affirmation. In the esoteric experience, what we're doing is trying to get enough time and room to meditate and not be so caught up in the demands of daily life that we can't meditate. If all our energy is used up in the getting of a living, keeping the house clean, the dog fed, the insurance premiums paid, if that exhausts us and if at the end of the day you just come in and "Oh, God I'm exhausted" crash, you lie down—you don't have the energy to go into the mind and change the foreground and the background.

So life has to be set up in such a way that the things we do empower us; and that we must do certain things. But we're seeking to be able to meditate well. Meditation means adjusting the mind from within. Meditation is not some ineffable thing where you're just sitting in a quiescent state of nothingness. Sometimes that's meditation. But meditation really means the structural modification of the mind through the selection of mental states. And through the selection of specific mental states we can get to a point where we can go beyond mental states, but that's not going to happen until you get to very refined mental states. Then we can make that jump where we go beyond the circle to something else, to the origination of the circle or that which is simply other, which is nirvana.

For a person who is practicing mysticism, they shouldn't really think about purity and power and all these terms too much. A person who's practicing mysticism should be out doing things, not thinking philosophically so much. If you think about purity, if you think about these things, that's nice. But what a person who seeks mysticism does is they build a fire. Now, I don't know if you like—I like to build fires, OK? I have a fireplace. And I love building fires. Fire is one of the primary mystical symbols—fire, air, earth, water, ether, all that stuff. But fire is particularly interesting because it's a transmutation. You take some wood, you take some flame, and you get ashes and smoke and the wood goes away, and of course you get heat. Very interesting. It's a symbol of yoga, the building of a fire.

In order to create heat, you have to have something to burn. So what we do in yoga is, we burn ourselves up, to create light. In the exoteric religious experience, we read about other people who have done that, and we hope some of their light shines on us and some of their heat shines on us, and it makes us feel better. They must feel great, if just thinking about them, we feel better.

In mysticism, we seek to feel great. We want to build that fire. The fire is already burning. It's the inner light. But it is only by directing ourselves into that light that transmutation occurs. A mystical experience occurs because you go into the light, not because you read about others doing it. If you have the time, why not read about it because it puts you in that direction and it keeps the mind in a flow of that experience as opposed to being drawn away from it by the auric currents of the world, which are fairly low and simple and tend to lead one to sensorial experiences.

What we seek to do is, the key factor—it's like studying for a test. The most important thing is to study the material that's going to be on the test if you want to get an A. You can study and spend hours studying lots of stuff, but if the goal is to get an A, find out what the guy or the gal's going to ask, study that, learn it cold, you get the A.

If what one is seeking is ecstasy, freedom—these ineffable words suggestive of a state of mind, a condition so perfect and so beyond the conditions that are experienced by human beings in the relative world as to be almost unheard of—then we have to get the right stuff that's going to be on the test. In the world of Buddhism, there are so many things to study that you could never get the stuff that's going to be on the test. Tantric Buddhism is the school of Buddhism that is known as the "cut to the chase" school. Let's get right to the point. What's on the test? Let's do it, get it done, transmute. Whereas in other forms of Buddhism, they really enjoy studying a lot of stuff that isn't on the test because it's fun.

Some people aren't in a hurry to get a degree; they just like learning. You go to school for four years, why not take five? Why not take six? Why not have a couple of majors for a while? Learning is fun. The piece of paper is not everything. Some people, though, want the piece of paper so they can get into a specific job. School is fun, but it's a means to an end. For some people it's an end in itself. One is not right or wrong, it depends on the disposition of an individual being. For the person who wants to get to the mystical experience directly, Tantric Buddhism is the path. Zen is Tantric Buddhism, Vajrayana is Tantric Buddhism, there are various forms of it. Tantric Buddhism simply means cutting to the chase. It's a very, very extremely esoteric mystical side that takes you directly into the light. It's not a discussion, you just do it, you're there, you transmute. It's very direct, which is why it is the least practiced form of all Buddhism because most people would rather talk about it, enjoy it, but to actually transmute is heavy duty.

To actually take who you are and go into the light is, for the being that currently exists, very scary because the being is literally going to destroy themselves in the light. Granted, infinity is going to create a new and shinier form of that being. But the ego does not want to dissolve in the clear light of reality, definitely not. "No way Jose!" "Hasta manana baby!" "Don't call us…" You know. "Let's do infinity!" Right? (Audience laughs.) That's L.A. spiritual talk.

So then, the reason we do this is for a feeling. That's tantric mysticism. It's a feeling; it takes you directly to the feeling. Do not pass the feeling, right? Go directly to the feeling, that sort of thing. And the essence of all practice is to stop thought. When you stop thought, other than with a sledgehammer—that stops life—when you stop thought, the white light is all. And the more you can stop thought, or the closer you get to it, even if you can slow thought down, modify it, remove some—more kundalini is released, and as the kundalini is released, you go above the thought level, you go to that feeling. You touch other spheres of existence that most people don't know exist.

You know, the Renaissance is fun when you read Boethius and some of the Renaissance philosophers. They talk a lot—they're Christian mystics—they about the other spheres. There's a music of the spheres. There's a music that's actually in the universe, they believed, that's out there in different dimensions. They called it the music of the spheres. There are other spheres of existence. They thought and believed that there are other universes of mind and consciousness that we as human beings can raise ourselves to and touch and feel and become.

Today people don't think about that much. Don't know why. But they used to think about it. They think about it in the Far East. They believe that we can take—our mind is like a terminal, a computer terminal, and we can patch the mainframe of existence. There are billions of programs out there. Comp-U-Infinity. You know, $19.95, right? Comp-U-Infinity where you can just hook into all kinds of great programs, great graphics, all kinds of stuff that you can patch into which you don't have on your own little terminal. You've got a PC and you can plug it into a mainframe. A mainframe in a cup, you see.

That's what meditation is. But in the process of plugging in, you become that. It changes you. This is mysticism. Again, everything is empirical in mysticism until you get to the moment of the mystical experience, then we forget about all this empirical stuff and we just go into the light and dance for a while. That's why dancing is important. Shirley MacLaine wrote a book called *Dancing in the Light*. Good title. (Audience laughs). What we seek to do is to be as rich as Shirley without being as well known and picking up all the auric focus.

What you're seeking to do is to get to the mystical experience. Once you're there, it takes care of itself. It transmutes you, it translates you, you become new, you're baptized in the spirit again and again until you become an enlightened being. And the more often you can get there, I guess sooner, if you want to look at it in time and space, it happens.

Mysticism cuts through the bullshit, and it takes you right there to the experience and everything in your life is eventually set up so that your life is a pragmatic energy flow into the light as continuously and as constantly as possible. We play with the foreground and background, obviously, because it makes it easier to get to the mystical experience. We get rid of the parts of ourselves, not that we ethically think are not correct because we don't necessarily believe that—we believe in ethics, but we believe that ultimately it's a matter of speed. If there's a part of yourself that hangs you up and brings you down, you get rid of it, not because there's a moral base to that part that says it's a good part or a bad part but because it hangs you up.

It's a structural question. In other words, you get rid of evil, whatever that means to you, not because it's intrinsically evil because evil is intrinsically God also, since God is everything, but you get rid of evil because it slows you down. It interferes with the transmutation process. So our view becomes very different. We're not operating out of a moral philosophical base, we're operating out of a base of maximum efficiency. But maximum efficiency does not preclude the experience of perfect emotion. Do not think of it in a cold way because the maximum efficiency is the purest emotion. That's why we do it.

Purity means maximum efficiency in self-discovery. Purity doesn't mean whether you have sex or not, or how. Purity means that there is no self, or less and less all the time, meaning that there's a perfect flow of energy; there's a translation of all of infinity through itself without interruption. In mysticism we really don't worry about commandments. We just notice, as we go along through our practice, what causes us pain, what limits us and structures us, and we eliminate that from our lives. We don't try to become a good person or a bad person. That's religion. We did that already in other lives, obviously, if we're at the point where we're interested in this, and that seems simplistic to us or just doesn't feel good. That means we've already passed the course.

Why take it again?

When you're interested in mysticism, when you want the pure experience and the thou shall's and the thou shall not's seem restrictive, that means you've already done them. Third grade would be very restrictive at this point for us. At the time it wasn't and for third graders it's not. It's not restriction, it's an opening into new worlds and new realities. In mysticism, we simply use the empirical flow of consciousness as our only dialectical guide to infinity and the divinization of our own awareness, the movement into ecstasy. If it works, do it.

Tantric Buddhism is just a collection of things that work by doing them. And sometimes we add new things. We have electronic music; we did not have it in Tibet. So if we can use electronic music to hit new keys, new notes, new sounds, new resonances that we couldn't get with the musical instruments we had—we had the mind to compose, but now we have stuff that we can do with synthesizers we couldn't do—then we can open up new doorways for transmutation using music as a vehicle, which we always do in Tantric Buddhism for entering into the light.

So there's new stuff. Technology is great that way, but it only helps us do what we were doing before in new ways. When you use a microphone, it simply enables the sound waves to travel further through an amplification and speaker system, but you're not saying anything different. But it gets it further. That's what technology does; it just gets it further, but it doesn't change anything.

It's the mind that is—what you're seeking is a conceptual leap. Don't forget that, in practice, beyond practice. In other words, all these words are great and these erudite phrases I and other teachers use, but the point of them is so you can blow away from all the erudite phrases into a pure ecstasy, a feeling of completion. Communion with infinity is what we seek because in that communion we lose and find ourselves in ways that cannot be described in words. That's mysticism.

A teacher of mysticism is not someone who simply employs words cleverly, but they're an individual who actually has gone in and out of the white light countless times and even observed that there's a systemization to the white light in its motions—not in itself, intrinsically no one can systematize it because it's beyond systems. But if there's a continent someplace and it's always changing and shifting and the conditions are strange but kind of exciting, a guy who goes there and can obviously deal with it himself can get others in and out. You might go there and get very confused and very disoriented and get lost. A teacher of mysticism is someone who is actually able to flip in and out of the light at will, and they understand the transmutations. They can't tell you why they occur; no one knows that but the light itself and obviously, it's not talking. But they know how it's all done.

A teacher of mysticism is someone who does it themselves all the time, and they're just showing you some of the moves they've learned that work and are helping you avoid the ones that tend to slow you down or create something that's not sought. Whereas a teacher of religion is someone who knows words and concepts. They may be a moral person, they may be a good person; they've adjusted the foreground and the background of their mind to suit the philosophical base they're operating from. But that doesn't mean they can snap into the light and pivot through the vortexes of ecstasy that occur within the ten thousand states of mind and the other dimensional planes and realities, let alone make it clear, beyond self, into what they would call the absolute holiness of divinity, the Godhead, or whatever you want to call it. I just call it nirvana, or Sam. (Audience laughs.)

That's the teacher. Mysticism is the adventure of religion. Occultism is the adventure part where you're out going and doing it and you're becoming a Buddha, quickly. Consequently you have to go through all the pitfalls one goes through in becoming a Buddha, which are many and varied—various illusory bardos where you can get hung up for periods of time, like thousands of lives, or whatever it is. But hey, it's like Tyresius told Odysseus, right? "You don't get through hell in a hurry." You don't. You don't get through the samsara in a hurry. It goes on forever, and so do you.

But what you should be doing is seeking the white light. In other words, don't try and change yourself. Oh, obviously you have to adjust the foreground and background; you do that every time you turn the terminal on. You adjust the foreground and background so you can see what's on the screen according to the light in the room and your own eyesight. Naturally you get rid of all the things inside yourself that bring you down and do all the things that bring you up. But ultimately that will only bring you to a certain point in your advancement and then you'll stay there and you'll be stuck. Once you've maximized the background and the foreground, it's done. Where do we go from there?

We're only maximizing the background and the foreground so we can take another step, which is into the light. Once you go into the light, then don't worry about it, you're there. We just set up the background and foreground for maximum efficiency for accessing the light. Then we go into the mystical experience of ecstasy. We unleash the kundalini. We direct it towards the light, foot on the accelerator, hands on the steering wheel, aiming towards the light. Then we just go into it at warp speed, and we come out in some other part of the universe of mind as someone else—a more refined, higher tech version of ourselves that's much more in tune with the essential spirit of the universe on a higher plane level, which we obviously find enjoyable, which is why we do it. At this point words break down, and it's a good time to stop recording.

CHAPTER ELEVEN

BUDDHISM

The thing about Buddhism is that it stresses attainment of something ineffable, and I think this is where it differs from other religions in that it's more correct. We live in a world with promises of paradise. Everyone is telling us that if we will only have a certain experience, amass a certain amount of belongings, become rich and famous, whatever it is, we will be happy. And there are people who tell us that just the opposite is true—if we give up all that and we live a life of chastity, simplicity, poverty—sort of doing penance—that creates happiness. Those two schools of thought are very prevalent. But Buddhism endorses both of those schools and says, sure, you can go through that path of giving things up, and it will create a certain momentum and discipline for you to go beyond the limited perceptions that you currently have or, you can have it all and go beyond the limited perceptions that you now have.

Buddhism's stress, in other words, if it's advanced Buddhism, is really not on how to live. Basic Buddhism has all the little scriptural thoughts on right thought, right action, right conduct; it tells you everything, for a person who is trying to rise above being completely possessed by their desires and senses and just get some intrinsic purity going. But once you're past that stage, Buddhism suggests that the only thing worth attaining is that which is ineffable. And this is really the question that you have to ask yourself. Theoretically, you are in this room because you are interested in something that's ineffable. And at the same time, we all have a side that is very, very materialistic. We want personal gain above all else. And sometimes it just gets extreme; we get out of control with it. We want something and we will do anything to get it. We'll even do something illicit, that we know is intrinsically wrong. We would kill somebody if it would profit us, and not even think about it.

So in Buddhism, we feel that whatever you attain is a loss. Whatever you lose is kind of a plus. This is intermediate Buddhism. Because when you lose something it makes you aware of the transience of all samskaric existence, of all the existences of all the worlds. The worst thing you can do is be in comfort and luxury and paradise and have everything working for you. Because it totally blinds you to the reality of existence, and that is that everything is transient. You get into a very relaxed and comfortable state until the bottom drops out from under you, whether it's your death or change of some type. You get into kind of a blinded state.

So we feel that when you lose something, when there's disaster, what most people would not seek in their life—when it occurs to you, we consider that a very good thing because it keeps you on your toes. It awakens you to the fact that you are in a dream world, that the very nature of life is continual change.

So when something goes wrong, we love it, because it says, "Wait a minute. Time to saddle up, buckaroos." We have lost touch. And this is life's gentle way, or not so gentle way, or downright ornery way of reminding us that this is the nature of life, and what we should be doing is establishing a solidity in ineffability. Since nothing in the material world lasts and all material things ultimately cause pain, because all material things are eventually lost or they lose their luster, it is best to develop a solidity in something that does last.

It's like a career. You know, you can get a career where there's no solidity. You're a performer. This season they like you, you get a lot of work; next season they don't, you're out of work. On the other hand, if you're a computer scientist and there's a demand for good programmers because there's a shortage, then you can be assured of work all the time. So one looks around at life—most people, of course, don't, they don't really awaken enough—and you kind of dope it out and you realize that everything here is transient and no matter what you attain, it will pass, and that all happiness, personal happiness, is based upon things that are temporary—and that's all well and good, but temporary happiness is followed by absence, by pain, by depression, by alienation, then there will be temporary happiness again. That's just how life is.

So in Buddhism, we seek to go to something that is ineffable because it's more solid. We feel that there's a world, we see it, we experience it—there's a world of light from which all these material worlds come, from which we come, all the things we love come, all the things we don't like come—and if we can meld our mind with the essence of that, then we will live in a perpetual state of newness, renewal, and ecstasy and happiness. And our happiness is no longer dependent upon whether they like us this season and want us or not.

Buddhism is essentially the establishment of one's mind in that which is ineffable. Ineffable meaning it does not appear to be solid, but actually it's much more solid than that which appears to be solid, which is actually much more ineffable. The world that we say is solid—knock on wood—is transient. Nothing here lasts. The wood doesn't last; the whole planet won't last forever. But on the other hand, that which is ineffable, which is the world of light—meaning it's hard to see at first, can't perceive it through the senses—that lasts forever; it's always been and it will always be. And its very nature is happiness, ecstasy. So if we take our time and, rather than building up some huge fortune which then is swept away, we take our time and instead invest in stocks that are infinite, as opposed to finite, then we get to enjoy that forever.

Now, Christ said that, like most teachers of any caliber say that. They say, don't get so stuck in life and living, don't be so caught up in the getting of life, possessions and families, because it's all going to cause you pain eventually. And even if it's a very pleasant ride, the ride is going to end and where are you going to be then?

So the general advice of the awakened one in your neighborhood is to unhook a little bit from the very big system of the material world and consider wisely that all this is transient. And if your teacher is even a little more awake, then we're apt to say, don't hate the world, don't hate things that are transient, don't feel that there's something intrinsically wrong with them. What's transient is transient, and why should it bother you? Pleasure will be pleasant for a while, then it will pass. Pain will be painful for a while and it will pass. Since everything is transient, then there is no eternal pain because that passes too. Everything is transient. Your mind is transient. You're transient in this body. You're transient in this life. You're just passing through and it's passing through you.

As you're passing through this life, as you're passing through this body, as you're passing through this moment, you may run into one who's awakened. And if you run into one who's awakened, then if it just is—we believe it's coincidence if it happens because we believe everything in the universe is coincidence. And so, if by coincidence you happen to run into somebody who's awakened—out of the billions and infinite billions of beings in the samsara, there's not very many awakened beings—if you happen to run into one who is awakened, if for some reason, by some coincidence—call it karma, call it fate, call it what you will—you end up in front of a being that is awakened, they are aware of how this works, this thing called life and eternity, and you are not.

You are just pushed and pulled around. You don't know why you're in this life, why you're on this planet, why you're in the type of body or the type of mind that you're in. You're not quite sure who you are, who is in this body and in this mind, what your beginning was, where you're going, where you come from. You don't know what will happen tomorrow. There's no surety in anything. So if you happen to end up in front of someone who's awakened and you're a basic consumer, then you make inquiries, because consumers are interested in progressing. As a consumer you're interested in bettering yourself and having a better experience.

Now, I assume that all species wish to evolve. I mean, that's intrinsic in being a species—that one wants to do better. And sometimes we get confused and frustrated and end up not doing so or causing ourselves or others pain, but that's not necessarily our intention. That's just confusion. So if you happen to end up in front of an awakened one, the question that you ask is, "How do I get out of here?" See what I mean? "How does this work? Where am I? Where am I going to? Is there any order to any of this? Should I bother to look around or will I just—is it a waste of time? Am I just going to be counting numbers that go on forever and have no meaning?"

Buddhism suggests there is something ineffable that you cannot see with your physical eyes or feel with your hands, and that it can be reached, that it can be known and that it is ecstatic. There's a lasting, perfect happiness that lies beyond all of that which is apparent to your senses—and it is infinite—and one can take an inner journey from the awareness, it's merely a shift in awareness. You can shift your awareness from where you are now to that. But if your awareness is completely bound up in the things of this world, which it would be if you felt that they had the most validity and solidity, then, of course, your awareness won't shift.

We focus upon what we feel is most important. That's just how the mind works. The mind follows a prioritization system; it's coded that way. Whatever is most operative is in our mind the most. When that's taken care of, our mind automatically moves to the next most operative situation.

So when we feel the illusion of the transitory, that it's not transitory, that it's real—when we feel that this world, these peoples, these experiences, are in some way ultimate, that reality is here in the sensorial worlds—then that's where we place all our attention. But of course, it's a terrible mistake because the sensorial worlds are only a band of perception. They are just a way of seeing life and there are so many different ways. If you place all your attention in the sensorial worlds, it's painful, ultimately. Whereas beyond the sensorial worlds are worlds of light, the limitless structures of infinity. They're just there. They're like the stars. You may not be aware of them tonight, but they're out there—billions of them.

Now, we might feel, what relevance do the stars have to me? I mean, they're way out there and we've got one that's close enough and it takes care of the earth, so what do we really need to know about all those stars for? Well, that may be true in case of the stars but in case of the inner light, the inner light is the most relevant thing there is—because without it, you're stuck in very limited planes of awareness and you don't see life very well and you pass from experience to experience without knowing why and without control and without knowing that there are other options that are much more interesting than the ones that you are currently accessing.

Buddhism is the study, then, of other options and how we access them, essentially. But it's difficult for the beginner sometimes because we discuss the ineffable in very pragmatic terms. And when one isn't used to that, when you haven't experienced a lot of ineffable consciousness, it's difficult initially to see that it is more solid than that which appears to be solid. So the best thing to do is to get experiences. You need experiences, both in daily living and in ineffable consciousness. And then you can make a comparison and determine which is worthy of most of your focus.

Now, tantra is a little bit different than other forms of Buddhism because in tantra what we do is we use the sensorial worlds as access points or pathways to ineffability. Normally, since the ineffable is most easily discerned and experienced and focused on and become through the practice of meditation, one leaves the physical world—goes off to the monastery or cave or the desert, or whatever it is—and just devotes all one's time to meditation. But to be quite honest with you, if you're interested in establishing your consciousness in the immortal light, it is easier to do it directly through the process of meditation, of course, but also through the access points that are already present in the physical world. A kind of Catch-22 of enlightenment is that since enlightenment is all things, whatever is physical contains enlightenment too. But, while that is true in a sense, it doesn't mean you can get to it, unless you know how, otherwise we wouldn't be having this conversation.

So then, tantra is a process in which we are using aspects of mind in the material planes to transcend mind as we know it in the physical planes and mental planes and the material world. At the same time, in addition, of course we do meditation whereby we move directly into ineffability. The funny part is that ineffability is not ineffable at all. There is nothing more real and more solid than nirvana. It is the most real and the most solid thing there is, and all of these things that we see here are its creations, which it spins forth for a while, sustains for a while, and then it dissolves them. Whereas that which we're so used to thinking, "Well, you know, the spiritual realms are sort of vague," they are not vague. They are the only things that are certain and solid, and the things that we think are solid are not solid at all—they're transient, they change, they're simply the byproducts of immortality. Yet they have their own luster. Yet they are immortality. Immortality is contained in all things, since it is all things.

So in your quest for certainty or enlightenment, the most important thing is to try and get beyond … desire, because desire causes hate. If it were not for desire, there would be very little happening in the world. Desire is inevitable. Desire is intrinsic to a body and a mind. But when you identify too much with your desires, which means you just don't let them go by but you get stuck in them, they pull you places. And when they pull you someplace—there you are.

We seek absolute neutrality in Buddhism. Complete neutrality. We don't want to be drawn to anything in particular; we don't want to be pushed away from anything in particular. We want life itself to select where we should be and what we should be at any given moment, knowing that life will always make the ultimate choice in the matter—the best choice—whereas we with our limited perception will probably make all kinds of mistakes. But since life created us and created all of this, obviously it knows what it's doing and it knows how the system works.

We try and reach a point of complete neutrality where we can face life and death with an equal eye, success and failure with an equal eye, loss and gain with an equal eye. But that neutrality is only found in the clear light. It's an interesting idea, but on a pragmatic day-to-day level, as soon as you really want something, you'll forget all about that philosophy and you'll get totally wrapped by it. And that desire will just overcome you, and you're willing to do anything to get that, even if it means destroying yourself or others. You lose your balance if you get caught in desire. The same is true of aversion. When you're afraid, you'll do anything to get away from that which you fear. You go crazy. Fear can overpower your better judgment, in other words. So can desire, aversion and attraction.

The way you overcome attraction and aversion is by going to another condition which has little to do with both, which is wakefulness. In that wakefulness, you see beyond attraction and aversion. You can see that they're just operative forces in the universe that you can sidestep. It's like an opponent in martial arts who's rushing towards you; you can just get out of the way. You just take a quick step back, and they keep rushing by you rather than getting entangled. Once you're entangled, it's messy.

The best way to deal with desire and aversion is to push them away. To cut to the chase, if I may here, we all know what we should be—I believe that—we just don't listen. But we know that we should be terribly humble, completely consistent, and that we should strive to enter the light. There's no reason for that, it just is how it works, just like the fact that we're alive. We know we should be completely humble, we should stop thinking that we're very marvelous—we're not. We're interesting at best because we're part of life and all of life is interesting. But we're not marvelous. We'll come and we'll go.

What's necessary is a very integrated humility, wherein we just are who we are and we do what we do and there's a sense of peace to it, a stillness. It's not necessary to impress others or to impress ourselves. Rather, what's most important is to integrate ourselves with the light, to lead a type of life that does that. And some people may understand it or not, it really doesn't matter. It's not an audience participation situation. Rather what we're doing is just seeking to find the still point in the middle of all the turning worlds, simply because we like that, we know that that's where we belong. If a person doesn't feel that, then it's not necessary, obviously. But if we get hooked up with people who do feel that [it's not necessary], we can pick up their desires, their consciousness, and they distract us from that which is most important to us and that which is real, for us. Reality is personal.

I think that you know whether you are a person who is interested, ultimately, if you really searched your being, in finding stillness and dissolving in the light. No one has to explain to you what that is—you know. If you don't know what that is or what I mean by that, then it will not draw you. There are certain things in life you just don't need to explain. You either are at that level or you're not.

In Buddhism we don't really seek to explain things or convince people per se. We talk about things a lot, but we don't believe that it changes anything. We just talk about it because we like it—we like the way it sounds. We like to talk about the light, hear about it, see it, because we just get such a kick out of it. But we don't believe that you can explain Buddhism or life to anyone. We just do it because we get off on it. But a person either has the understanding or they don't. So, OK, I'm a teacher, great. OK, I'm a teacher of the clear light, great. I've been a teacher in thousands of lives. Great, big deal, so what? It's a job. It's an occupation. I've done other things before that.

I can go around the world teaching and teaching and teaching, and people will come and see me and hear what I have to say—big deal, so what, doesn't mean a thing. It's just what I do. But if someone ends up in a room by coincidence some day with me, and they have some level of awareness, I will not have to explain anything to them, meaning—of course I'll explain things to them—but there's no convincing necessary. I don't have to say to a person, "Gee, look at the benefits of our program. You get this, this—buy now. Buy. Try this! New improved, with the extra additive, clear light plus."

We feel that this knowledge of enlightenment is not something that you can convince someone that they need. They are either at a point where they are wakeful enough to know that that's their path or they're not. And if they're wakeful enough to know that's their path, then they should get on it, learn it, do it properly and attain that which can be attained and lose that which can be lost, and so on and so forth.

So we feel—in other words, Buddhism is the most private club in the universe. And we're not looking for members. We feel, actually, we have enough old members from other lives to keep us going forever. But it's a club that meets on regularly scheduled days and regularly scheduled hours where we all get together and do the same thing we do in every life. And there's no reason for it, it's just what we do. A person is either drawn to it or they're not. And if they're drawn to it, they've got to work their ass off, otherwise they don't belong there. Because that's what we get a kick out of; we get a kick out of working—really hard, all the time—to the point where we work so much that we just enter into the light because all our work is directed at bringing us into the light. Because we feel there's nothing here on this earth that we want. We'll take anything, sure, why not? You know. Toys are great. Toys R Us. But we don't feel that anything really matters, ultimately. In a transient sense all kinds of things matter, sure. But in the ultimate sense—and we go back and forth between the two— nothing matters here.

So we don't tend to get so caught up if we don't get something today. We don't have to destroy everybody because we're pissed off. If you have to do that, then it means you're very much in the transient world and you're not in the world of enlightenment at all. We don't have to off somebody or destroy them because they have something we want or because they stand in our way. Because we know that everything we need is within us, not within someone else. At best someone else can show us how to get that, but we even have to do that ourselves.

So we're very self-reliant in a kind of Emersonian sense, the Buddhists. And we can accept very quietly incredible suffering—and incredible ecstasy. But our life is not really bound up in suffering or ecstasy; we're seeking something else and we seek it in every life, and we seek it throughout every eternity. And that's the perfect quiescent absorption in the clear light of eternity. Because once you've seen it and experienced it, nothing else can ever move you again. You can enjoy all things, but they can't possibly be ultimate. Because what can compare to that? How are you going to keep them down on the farm after they've seen Padmasambhava? It just doesn't do it any more. You know, MTV has its moments, and that's all I put it on for. Well, it's fun. But the clear light is much more appealing, ultimately. The power of MTV is nothing as is the power of this whole world and all of its fantastical beings and mind states. It's nothing compared to the clear light.

So we just feel that we do what we do. In each lifetime we try and get back to who we are. And if we're back there, then that's all we had to do. Then from there we just have to be that and that's our lives. We don't seek to gain, we don't seek to lose. But we definitely like to play games because we feel that the world is a big game that God has designed for us to play. And so, since we happen to have very big minds, we like to play with them, and we play games. Just to see if we can win. We don't really care if we do, but it's fun to try—because you've got to do something with eternity.

We play games that tend to just bring us more and more into the light, more into the ineffable. And we avoid games that do the opposite. A lot of people play those, and that's what they need to do now because they need to experience the transience of pain and frustration. But since we've already figured that out in other lives and we know about it, we don't feel it's necessary.

Nothing burns or hurts you like desire. It destroys everything beautiful in your life. You're sitting, perfectly happy at home, staring at a flower and suddenly you've just got a desire, you've got to go do something. You have to have something. You have to get something. You have to be something. And you can't just enjoy the perfect clarity of life.

The Buddhist world, as I said, is the ultimate private club. We don't seek members—we just try and find our old members. And then we just do what we do in every lifetime. And it would sound boring to some people, I guess, except that it is the ultimate ecstasy and infinity, which doesn't really lend to boredom.

Chapter Twelve

COMPUTER SCIENCE

I like computers. I've got a few of them, and I keep them around the house. Sometimes they're turned on, sometimes they're turned off. I like them as much when they're off as when they're on. I just like computers. They're like pets—but you don't have to feed them too much, a little electricity once in a while. But they're nice. Sometimes I get different ones just because I like the way they look. They're just fun to have around the house. I like their aura. I like their energy. I like the energy of computers.

Computer science is very interesting from an occultist's point of view because it has to do with zeros and ones—it has to do with analysis. In order to experience enlightenment, in order to be enlightened, to be enlightenment, in order to raise into upper gradients of pure celestial light, it is necessary to refine the mind completely. The issue is style.

There is style in fashion, but there is style in states of mind. Some people are connoisseurs of states of mind, just as some people are connoisseurs of wine, food, countries, lovers. Buddhists are connoisseurs of states of mind. We savor certain states of mind. States of mind always exist. They're always there, unlike the old Beaujolais, which this is the last bottle of. The state of mind will always be there. And when you've been around the universe for lots and lots of incarnations and experienced lots of states of mind, there are certain states of mind you learn to particularly appreciate.

The trick is getting to them. There may be some wonderful wine but it's very expensive and you don't have the money. So there are certain states of mind—the most beautiful ones are very hard to get to. They're like places on earth that are beautiful. You have to travel a long way these days because the earth is very populated and the most beautiful places are very inaccessible these days. So, if you are a true lover of natural beauty, you have to travel a long way.

The states of mind that we seek are inside ourselves. They're inside our mind. Our mind is a databank—not the brain, but the mind, the consciousness principle that we are. That which is the existence in us, is infinite. It contains many things, as it does infinity, as it is infinity. But in particular it contains what we call the ten thousand states of mind. Ten thousand is a symbolic number in Buddhism which just suggests that there's a lot—a tremendous amount, more than ten thousand, more than ten billion, beyond counting is what ten thousand symbolizes.

That's good, and it's nice those states of mind are there, and it's wonderful that there are enlightened states of mind and ecstasy and knowledge that human beings don't know about. But how does one get there? How does one get to this paradise of mind?

It's through refinement. It's by developing a sense of style. I would say that style is the opposite of mediocrity. Mediocrity implies a lack of exactness—colors run together and get kind of gray, you see? Style, on the other hand, implicit in it is a certain awareness of not only what style is, but an ability to extract from the vast multitude of things, those things which are brightest.

So what becomes necessary is a process of extraction. How can we extract from all of infinity, and the various infinite states of mind, those that are the most bright? In order to do that, we have to become very exact. We have to make our minds very sharp so that out of millions of possible states of mind, we can feel intuitively and select those states of mind which are the most bright and the most beautiful. Buddhists spend a great deal of time working on and refining their minds. Because once the mind is properly refined, it will automatically select the right states of mind. It just happens by itself. What's necessary is just to refine the mind.

In the West, people work. They get up in the morning and they go to work and they spend the day working. The primary energy that they have in their lives is directed towards their work. The work that most people do in the world tends to deaden them, deadens their mind, uses up their energy and they get a paycheck and old age—and not much energy, not much aliveness. They're paying you for your energy. You get the check and they get your energy. That energy is translated into corporate dollars. Your energy causes things to occur which someone wants done, which they reap a profit from. You're trading energy for dollars, and that's all you're getting—exhaustion, very often deadness. You're being put in situations that your body would normally wish to veer away from because it feels the auras in those situations are not good for you. You go sit in a situation doing things that you normally wouldn't do—because it's not your vibratory level—because you're getting paid. This is not a good situation if you're trying to refine your mind. You can't be deadening it eight hours a day and losing all your energy and life force; you're never going to get to anything enlightened at all.

Computer programming is a field in which you use, particularly in its intermediate and advanced states, certain analytic techniques that are very similar to techniques that Buddhists have used for thousands and thousands of years to refine the mind. As a computer programmer, particularly working with higher level topics—artificial intelligence, relational database and things like that—one tends to use certain interactive skills, methods of logical analysis that refine the mind. Essentially, if you're a computer programmer, you're getting paid to refine your mind. Even though that's not someone's intention, it's happening.

Computer science is interesting for a lot of reasons. It's electronic. What you focus on you become. You're tapping the electronic network. You're dealing with a higher level, more volatile energy than is present. Whenever we're dealing with anything that's electronic, we're tuning into a different spectrum. It's a faster spectrum, and it has a higher and faster aura. That's why I like the stock exchange. The stock exchange is a real interesting place because it's a fast energy. Currency exchanges also—very quick energy. It's a faster processing. And we process very, very quickly as we move into upper gradient states of mind. It's natural for a person who meditates to want to be around something fast.

Fast is not frenetic. When I say fast, I don't mean rushed, in a mess, chaotic. That's not what I mean by fast. Electricity is fast; it's faster than steam—the aura is more rapid. We try and put ourselves in conjunction with as many fast auras as possible since that's the nature of our own aura, so we experience less coefficient auric drag.

The world of computer science and data processing is a very fast field, even the way it's growing. It's probably the fastest growing field in the world. Data processing, for example, also generates America's largest volumes of dollars of any industry now, more than automotive, more than steel, more than oil—the big three. And it's clean energy; it's nonpolluting basically. You're dealing with high-process-curve informational accesses, the distribution of information and its analysis. As you engage your mind in computer programming, you're moving into a high auric field that has a very low coefficient drag in terms of energy output.

When you deal with people, it tends to drag your energy down, if those people are in a lower auric state than you. If you meditate and they don't, then by the end of the day you tend to be more drained. On the other hand, when you deal with a terminal, when you're dealing with programming and using your mind in very challenging ways, at the end of the day you do not tend to have picked up a lot of people's auras. Consequently, you have not polluted yourself as much and it's much easier to meditate and to get into higher levels of attention. In other words, it's a job in which you can actually gain energy, not lose it.

There's a normal physical exhaustion that occurs when we work, always. But [with computer science] our mental energy can increase and we don't really get as involved in other people's auras as we do in a lot of other jobs. Also, economically, there's a very high-curve economic situation, and if one practices meditation, it's necessary to create a level of insulation from the world. If you don't live in a Buddhist monastery in the Far East, then the next best thing in the West is to have enough money to insulate yourself from those aspects of life that drain your energy—energy you'd rather keep to bring into your mind to move yourself into higher mental states. You need a lot of energy to move into higher mental states. And while we access energy in the process of meditation by meditating on the chakras and raising the kundalini, in addition to that, we need to not lose energy.

It isn't even just a question about—it's a kind of energy. In other words, you can talk with one person for five minutes and be sick afterwards. You can be totally physically drained because their aura was so low. You can talk to someone else for an hour and just feel fine. You can talk to somebody who's very advanced and after just a few minutes you'll glow. It's aura.

When we deal with programming, we're dealing essentially with our own aura. A project—sometimes there are other people on the project, the team leaders, but mainly we're working with a screen and with a discipline that develops the mind in a very specific way, which lends itself to furthering our ability to meditate and live in higher mind states. You are able to make a lot of money in a very clean way, in a way that doesn't injure anyone, in a way that, as a matter of fact, often helps others. So it's a very clean field to be in. It enables you to conserve energy and at the same time develop your analytic tools and abilities so that you can select different mind states.

Programming, initially for most people, is a real bitch. When you start to program it's just really hard because you don't think that way, which is logically. But after you've programmed for—initially there's a tremendous resistance to programming, but as you get into it further and further, once you develop your muscles a little bit, it's really fun. And people who are drawn to meditation innately make excellent programmers, often exquisite programmers. You might say it's just an innate ability that people who meditate have. The kind of person who would be drawn to meditation is the kind of person who, in most situations, makes an excellent programmer because the two skills are very similar, the natures are very similar.

A person who meditates, who becomes a programmer, is like a duck in a happy pond. You're in the right situation for many, many reasons. But the reason I like computer programming the most is that it has to do with visualization and creation. When we're programming, we're extending ourselves into a series of planes of mind in which we have to, in a very creative way, interact with data and create pathways through things, particularly when we get into the world of complicated relational databases and mainframe systems. We're creating, kind of, neural pathways. We're mirroring the mind as best we can. It's necessary in complex programming to make jumps that are nonlinear—to get to a point of understanding as to how the data pathways should flow. I mean, data pathways are God in advanced programming, essentially.

In order to create data pathways, we have to get to them before they exist, in our mind. That's the real secret. In other words, there's a place for a data pathway that cannot be directly seen because it's nonlinear, it's not logical. And in meditation we develop an intuitive skill whereby we enter into nothingness, the voidness of existence. And within that voidness are all possibilities, but they're not necessarily built upon human logic. In other words, it's intuitive.

We learn to use the nothingness of infinity to create things that we could not get to in a straight line. In other words, the shortest distance between two points is your mind. It's not a straight line, it's your mind. If we go into the mind, we can see data structures in other worlds, in other universes, in other infinities. We can bring those data structures into this world, and then we create data pathways that we could not have conceived of in a logical linear sequence, but we can just assess their there-ness. Then those data structures become binding realities in which we entwine data pathways, and so on and so forth. That's computer programming at a higher level—other than AI, which is a little different, it's not that different.

That's kind of what we do in advanced meditation. We are going into nonsequential universes of mind and creating pathways between the parts of us that exist. And we interphase different parts of ourself and our being in different time/space structures and beyond time/space structures in different gradients of auric light in order to transmute our consciousness.

Advanced meditation is not just stopping your thought. It's very technical. The process of eliminating the samskaras and reaching complete enlightenment is a very technical, wonderful—mystical of course—process. As you do very advanced queries in computer science, as you create data structures and data pathways in a more advanced way, what you're doing is pushing the envelope of mind significantly in a way that will then assist you later on when you do more advanced meditation.

So I suggest that people become programmers, even though they may be initially bored by programming and the initial phases of programming, just to create a logical discipline of the mind, which is a helpful and necessary stepping stone later. But later, when you start to get up there, as you advance, you will find if you meditate that you will probably be an outstanding programmer further up. It's like you have to learn the grammar of the language and you might even learn the grammar more slowly than somebody else. But once you get into the language, you may be very fluent. You may do well with the literature. Whereas the person, maybe, who learned the grammar quickly, that's as far as they could get. But when it comes to the ideas within literature, they don't have the mind-state to really deal with them.

People who meditate have the mind-state to deal with advanced concepts. Sometimes it takes them, if they were raised without a lot of mental discipline, a while to pick up those disciplines. But once you get those disciplines down and you get up there, your mind will take over. And if you're willing to be patient enough to get yourself through the basics of computer science, even though it may take you three times as long as someone else, once you've done that, if you're patient, once you start to get up into higher level programming, then you rock and roll—a person who meditates.

Your mind and the abilities you developed in past lives—you will access those states of mind to create advanced data structures and advanced data pathways. And it works really well, and it's a wonderful workout, basically, for the mind, which is what we're looking for in preparation for the enlightenment experience.

CHAPTER THIRTEEN

THE AWARENESS OF MEDITATION

Meditation is the art of breathing—breathing out and breathing in. The universe, which is beyond understanding and description, is always breathing out and breathing in. It breathes in our lives and then it breathes them out. It breathes in dimensions, beings, feelings, understandings, mind itself. It breathes it in and breathes it out. We could say that life is a cycle, but that implies there's something that is observing it or that's outside of the cycle. There's really only breathing. It's very simple, really.

Meditation is a process in which we're essentially, at first, breathing out. We're exhaling. We're taking all the thoughts, impressions, feelings, vibrations, understandings, all the self-importance, attitudes, desires, loves, hates, passions, dispassions, meanings, lack of meanings, confused states, illumined states, bored states. We're taking everything—the concept of everything; that which perceives everything, that which is beyond perception, that which is beyond perceiving—everything must go. We're exhaling existence, taking it out of the mind, and the mind out of the mind.

After meditation, we inhale. We experience life. But we've changed. We're different because in the purification process of meditation we have touched a deeper threshold within ourselves, of eternity. Mind appears to exist because of the diverse attributes of existence that it perceives as itself. Mind by itself is nothing. It's colorless. It doesn't have a substance or a form. Mind only comes into apparent existence through the action of perception. Mind appears to exist because it perceives. It perceives the perfection of existence. As it perceives it, it is that. But by and of itself, mind not separated from mind is qualityless.

The action of perception is inhalation. The action of perception is mind perceiving something as other than itself. The qualityless mind cannot perceive itself in that there's nothing to perceive. Mind is an essence. It doesn't take a formation. In other words, we tend to think of mind as who we are, "My mind, it's what I think with, it's what I experience with, it is my mind." Some people are a little further in their understanding of mind, and they think, "Well no, mind isn't a tool, it isn't a CASE tool.[7] Mind isn't something that I think with. It's not like my foot that I walk with. Mind isn't just an appendage, it's not brain, but I am mind. I am the mind. I who can think or perceive or even construe that a mind exists, that is mind. All that can be said to be existent is mind. There's nothing else but mind."

Someone a little further along in their cosmology would say, "Well, there is only mind. But truly, mind is qualityless." This is the Tibetan Buddhist realization, that mind does not have any particular qualities or attributes of its own. It's clear. We say that the mind is composed of clear light, "clear" indicating that it doesn't have a definite shape, color or destination or point of origination. It is always existent. It is beyond cycles of existence. It will always exist. There's only one mind, and that is infinity.

The perception of mind in its variegated states, the perception of mind as different roses—yellow rose, red rose, black rose, primrose, various roses—variegation, coloration shifts, subtle or great changes in intonation—that is mind perceiving other than mind. Mind, if it were only perceiving itself, cannot do so since there's nothing there to perceive. It's qualityless.

Now, this is hard to begin with; this is not easy. You've got to strain yourself a little bit to understand what I'm saying. This is not the easy course in meditation that gives you mediocre results. This is the hard course in meditation that gives you outstanding results. You have to follow along with me.

Now your mind has to follow my mind, which is qualityless. Your mind has qualities because in its apparent perception, it's involved with a differentiation process that is not yet completed and it still perceives itself as

---

7. Computer-Aided Software Engineering, popular software tools in the 1990s.

other, whereas my mind does not perceive itself as other. It doesn't perceive itself at all because it's clear light. Intrinsically they're the same. But in the act of working out perception—which we call structural being, or living, taking a body, incarnation, existence, multiplicity, duality—we perceive mind as separate and as having qualities.

One person's mind is different than another's. Bob and Sally are different because their minds are different. Their bodies may be different, but their minds are real different. But if mind is truly perceived as mind, it is qualityless; it doesn't have form or shape. There's no difference between anybody's minds because there's only one mind.

But yet we all have a sense of having a different mind. Your mind is different than somebody else's mind. It isn't really different. We are perceiving it as being different because the mind is perceiving qualities. It's identifying with things that are not mind. And in doing so it makes a mistake; there's an error in judgment. It perceives separativity, the mind as separate, and qualities appear to have a validity that they really don't.

Now, we could get into a discussion, I guess, of the difference between that which can be perceived—in other words, if there is mind, and mind is qualityless, what the heck is that which we're perceiving, which has qualities? If there is only mind, then how can there be anything out there to perceive? You see? But that really is tangential to our discussion. We just take it for granted that the universe is complicated and we're not going to get it all in one night or one incarnation or one infinity. The universe doesn't have to be sensible and doesn't have to work out to our pleasing. It's complicated; it has variant sides. And to try and think that in one unified field theorem of mind you can get it all is ridiculous, because it's just not that way.

So we try and perceive it a section at a time—the section that we need, by necessity, is the section that we're in. That's karma. Karma relegates us to the reality that is currently extant for us because that's where we are in our perception. In other words, we're born into a world that's suitable for where our mind is at, for what we're working on. That's the assignment that we've gotten.

So we perceive that action, an orientation of reality that is self-sufficient for us at any given moment. To go worrying about what we're going to do next month when it's not next month yet is kind of stupid. We stick with one thing at a time. We're not going to worry about the qualities that are beyond perception or that are perceivable and confusing. Our aim is to have mind in its primordial, basic, perfect, pristine state, which is meditation.

Meditation, in other words, is mind perceiving itself as mind, without qualities. That's perfect meditation. It's simply perfect mind. Meditation is not an action. It isn't something that you go and do. Rather, what it is, is just mind in its perfect state, without qualities, without confusion. You don't have to go and meditate. That is mind. Mind is meditation.

Meditation is a word that we're using to suggest something other than our normal perception, which is confusion. Confusion is the mind confusing itself and thinking that it's something at all. It can only do that through the function of ego, the sense of "I am." "I am" is the confusion. "I am" implies a quality or series of qualities, which we call self or being. That suggests that being and self are separate from qualityless mind, and this is where you get all screwed up.

So to start with, as I said, this is the hard course. To start with, to understand mind directly and meditation directly is to see that meditation is not something that we do. It's not an action. "Susie meditated," OK. Meditation is in that sentence a ____? (Rama asks audience. Audience responds.) It's a verb. Right. OK. Meditation can never be a verb because meditation is qualityless. It is mind in its primordial state, and there's no grammar in nonexistence. Grammar has qualities, shapes and forms. As a former English professor, I can assure you that grammar is the qualitative interpolation of language. Adjectives, pronouns, predicates, past pluperfect indicative ridiculous. It has to do with qualities, shadings, differentiations, rhythmic structures of symbolic meaning. Curiouser and curiouser, if you will.

So then, mind has nothing to do with any of this. Mind is the world of *Alice In Wonderland*. Alice is sitting up on the bank and she's learning her lessons and she's bored, and this little rabbit goes whipping by and down the hole and Alice says to herself, "Hmmm, wonder where the rabbit's going?" So she slips down the hole and she ends up in Wonderland. Now in Wonderland, if you've read the book or seen the film, you know that nothing is the way it appears to be or it certainly wasn't like it was before you fell down the hole following the rabbit. Caterpillars talk, Mad Hatters have tea parties, all kinds of things go on that don't make a whole lot of sense to the rational mind that likes to work in the field of qualities.

The study of meditation is the entrance into the world of Wonderland. It has nothing to do with how you'd like it. You want a nice neat little study that's easily understandable, that can be laid out with start, middle and end. But the end might be the start, the middle is all the time and there's hardly ever anything but a beginning in meditation. You're in Wonderland and it's just not going to make sense. It's just not going to do it. So you will either reject it, or you'll go study TM.[8] TM is logical, scientific, and will do very little for your complexion. It's watered down meditation; it's designed to pacify the mind. In other words, it's very sensible, scientific—it makes sense. If it's that, how can it be profound? Profundity suggests that the simple mind is immediately excluded from the audience.

Meditation is profound. It is mind and it is essence. So then, meditation is not a verb. It is the way mind is. That's why in Zen they call it the natural state, which means that you don't have to go and do anything to meditate. In effect, a person who is trying to meditate is doing something that's impossible since meditation is not an action. Yet at the same time, if you don't do something, you know you're not going to be meditating. That's the Catch-22 of meditation.

In the Zen monastery we used to pound people on a regular basis whenever they thought they understood anything. Because if you think you understand, obviously you don't, since mind is by its very essence qualityless. In qualityless, things are not understood. You can't understand. You can't understand since there's nothing to understand and no one to understand, and understanding itself is a quality principle that is invalid. This is why not too many people meditate. Or if they do, they do TM, which is simply

---

8. Transcendental Meditation

repeating a mantra over and over that has nothing to do with meditation.

In other words, they practice some form of meditation which is simplistic and not really meditation. It might someday lead to the awareness of meditation. Ah! There's a key phrase—the awareness of meditation, the awareness of mind. We're in Wonderland and sometimes a thing is the way it appears to be for a few minutes, and then it changes into something else. Nothing is the same in the world of mind.

At best we can say that mind does not have qualities. And what it appears to have as qualities—it's confused, it's identifying itself with something other than mind. And that's not up for debate, it just is. If you debate the issues and the principles, that's great, but you just get caught up in more qualities and there's no meditation.

So then, in order to meditate, all we have to do is stop. If we stop, it's perfect meditation because it's perfect mind. That's it. We just have to stop. Now what do we stop? Thought. Impressions, desires, aversions, states of consciousness, ideas of being, essence, substance, predicate adjectives—everything has to go. Final clearance, everything must go. Exhalation—we're going to exhale everything, all qualities, all perceptions from mind until there's only the perfect, pristine, clear light, which does not perceive itself as other.

Since we're in Wonderland, that doesn't imply that it doesn't perceive. Just because it's qualityless doesn't mean that it doesn't have qualities. This is Wonderland where anything can happen. Because it's the essence of the void doesn't imply it's a vacuum. That's just an idea that a person has.

Qualityless simply means that there's no way to discuss it. There's no way to pin it down. It could be anything at any given moment since infinity is not bound even by itself, nor by the words that human beings choose to try and talk around it. We're dealing with something that's very big here. It's mind. It goes on forever. It's endless. It's perfect. It's radiant. It's enlightenment. Mind is enlightenment.

There are numerous ways to get into Wonderland. Once you're in, it's very hard to get out, fortunately. That's the good news. Once you've become enlightened, it's almost impossible to become unenlightened. There are as

THE AWARENESS OF MEDITATION

many ways to become enlightened as there are many roads that lead to McDonald's. Once you get there, there's the drive-up window or you can go in for the full experience. So meditation comes in many and variegated forms. The product is the same—when you go to the drive-up window at McDonald's or whether you go inside, the product is the same. The double cheeseburger is going to be the same, the shake is going to be the same, but you might feel different in your car or in the McDonald's. That's a whole different issue. It doesn't have much to do with what we're talking about, but I just thought I'd point that out to you. You can get real lined-out in the McDonald's—I mean the aura of the people who have been there before you, well, you understand. Of course your car, who knows? It's hard to say.

So then, if you perceive meditation as something that you don't have to do, it's easier. It's breathing out. What you have to do is simply breathe out everything in your mind. When everything is gone and there's only mind, that's meditation. See how easy that was? Whereas if we had done it any other way, you wouldn't have arrived at this understanding. That's why I had to go through all of that. It's not that I don't understand, it's just that I'm qualityless, immaculate, perfect mind.

This is not easy. You want it to be easy. You're Western. You want it to all fit in the microwave. You just want to mic it up and it's done. No effort! Kick back. Sure, meditate. Sure, nothing to it. That's why TM was such a big seller. They said it was effortless meditation. That doesn't—I mean there's no connection—effortless meditation! Effortlessness is a quality. Meditation is qualityless. You think I'm just fucking with you. You're right! (Audience laughs.)

But we're also discussing perfect meditation. It's Wonderland; we can do both simultaneously. That's the good news. We only have good news in Wonderland. We don't print anything else.

All you need to do to meditate perfectly is to eliminate everything from mind that has a quality, and when there's only mind, it falls back on itself and there's no perception of other—which is why in true meditation there's no perception. There can't be perception. If you're meditating and there's a sense of the passage of time, if there's the sense of otherness, of self—even if there's no thought and there's a sense of anything—you're not meditating perfectly. There are still some qualities in the mind and you've got to get rid of them. You've got to breathe out more. When there's no perception, mind is perfect—in its perfect state. It's not confused. So meditation is simply the elimination of everything—in mind, in your mind. Everything that is in your mind goes.

Every time one thing leaves the mind, mind is more pure. It has one less quality and it's more correct. So it isn't really a hard thing to do, to meditate. It isn't really something that we do. Rather, what we do is sit, and we allow the mind to fold into itself and to become perfectly still. Then, as the kundalini energy increases, as the energy of the psyche becomes more pronounced, which it does as thought becomes eclipsed by silence, all the variant mind states and all the stuff burns away. It just goes away, it breathes out.

In other words, we don't even have to force it out. It'll go by itself. All we have to do is to make the mind completely silent. If we stop thought, then everything will go away. The breathing out will be done for us by the stoppage of thought.

What meditation really is, is the science of stopping thought. When there's no thought, it's meditation. When meditation is meditation, then there's only pure mind. Pure mind, of course, is ecstasy. All pain, suffering, difficulties and general life problems come from the confusion that occurs in mind, of perception, where mind is perceiving itself as something other than pure mind—of itself as a body, a person, a state, a plane, a being, a rock, frog, cosmic deity. This is all confusion. This is the duality of existence where we believe that we have a separate existence other than pure and perfect, immaculate mind.

Pure and perfect, immaculate mind, which is also referred to as nirvana, is not something, by the way, that's cold, unfriendly or in any way related to what you call death. Death is simply a doorway that we go through in our experiences. In other words, mind is still confused. If you can die, you're confused because death is a perception of something ending and something else obviously beginning, which means we're still hung up in the qualities.

The wonder of immaculate, perfect, pure mind is that when it is in its perfect, extant state without confusion, it can be anything it wants to be. In other words, the riddle is that mind can still manifest itself forth in qualities but remain qualityless. Mind can perceive itself as qualityless in the middle of the qualities. But if you're perceiving yourself as qualities, that's the difference.

So the enlightened person, or whatever they are, enlightened shrew or anything, perceives itself as immaculate mind in the valley of qualities and can move through the qualities and even experience the qualities, but knows that it is not of them. Whereas nonenlightened simply means that you perceive yourself as qualities and enlightenment as something other than qualities. Enlightened mind simply means that you are enlightened mind. That's all there is, and that's all there could ever be. But you can be in the valley of qualities—in the Valley of the Jolly Green Qualities, right? And that's fine, that's not a problem.

In other words, to be pure, immaculate mind does not mean that you don't exist. It doesn't mean that you're in a can somewhere on a shelf with some big guy who is green on the label. It has nothing to do with green giants and green valleys or anything that's green whatsoever. It's qualityless. Green is a quality.

You're very serious people. I noticed that right away. I can tell that you're people because I can see that you're identifying with the body and the mind of humans. If you weren't doing that, then you'd be enlightened, you see? Or you'd be asleep, dreaming. That's different, of course. Then you're simply seeing the qualities and identifying with the qualities in the astral as opposed to in the physical and the awakened mental.

When you're enlightened or when the mind is void, vacuous and perfect, it doesn't mean that you can't sort of zip around, drive your car, read a newspaper, walk and have experiences. You can. Void, immaculate mind is all there is, so obviously it can do all those things. In other words, there's an objective correlative to infinity that is a good trick, which suggests that (Rama talks like a nervous person), "Oh God, if I, if I was just void, immaculate mind, I wouldn't be any more, Harold! It would be awful! Oh, I don't want that! I just want, like, better everything! Who wants to get involved with all that cold nirvana? Oh, not good. I won't be anymore. And who will feed the cat?" (Back to normal voice.) Well, since the cat is truly void, qualityless mind, free of all catness, I'm sure the cat is capable of finding a mouse. This is the peril of mice. This is why it is good not to incarnate as a mouse. Exactly. That's the truth. You can choose these things.

So then, the key perception that we're getting to here is that meditation is not what you think. Meditation is not an action; it's not necessarily difficult. You just have to be very patient. It's something that's natural to all of us because we all are that. But it's not easy to understand. You have to work at it. Meditation is coming back to your original self, if we can use self without a sense of self. It's perfect, clear light; radiant, infinite mind of the universe, as it is, without identifying with qualities. That's something that you already are.

It's like amnesia. A person has amnesia and they walk around and they think that they're somebody other than they are. They've forgotten who they were and they take on a new identity. They wake up one morning in the hospital, they just can't remember. Somebody gives them a new name, they go out to get a job, pretty soon they have family, friends, and they've forgotten that before that hospital they were somebody else. That's what birth is. Birth is a forgetting—not death. As Wordsworth said, birth is the forgetting. We forget who we were before birth, that we were in another body in this world or another world with another identity. Life is eternal.

Meditation is remembering. Meditation is not void. It's not empty. It's simply perfect, qualityless, clear light, which is the essence of all existence, and the substance, perceiving itself as such without anything else. That realization, when the clear light perceives itself as such, without qualities, which isn't really a perception—it's a way of trying to talk around it—then that existence always is and it can do whatever it wants. So really, what we're just saying is that enlightenment, meditation, is really a shift in perception. It's not a thing that you go and do or become, since you're already that. But rather, what you are doing is becoming aware of something that you're unaware of.

You're waking up from the amnesia of birth, the forgetting of life, and you're remembering. And remembering is a flood. Suddenly you remember billions of lifetimes. Suddenly you remember the perfect, immaculate nature of the clear light of mind. That's what meditation really is. It's not a state, it's not a condition, it's not an ecstasy, it's not peace. Those are things you go through as you eliminate qualities, as you eliminate qualities from mind. It's the identification. You experience ecstasy, peace, perfections, bliss, naturally, pain, and all those frustrations, desires. Everything goes away. All the things that are negative go away and then all the things that are positive go away until there is just clear light.

But don't think that clear light is just clear light. In other words, you have a mental concept of what that is and it has nothing to do with it. That's just a mental concept. Clear light is the extant, radiant, perfect knowledge that is reality. It takes all forms, which are all of us and all things that are extant in any universe, in any reality, in any dimension, in any samsara. And yet it's beyond and above all these things, what you would call God, I guess, unless you think of God as having qualities—masculine, feminine, mean, friendly. But if God does not have qualities, if God just is beyond all consideration of the mind—God's really big, you see, and your mind can't quite—God does not have qualities. That's the clear light. But that's what we are.

That's the message of all enlightened beings to all unenlightened beings, that we are God. We are the clear light and you really don't have much to worry about. You just don't know that right now. Someone who is enlightened has shifted their perception so that the clear light is aware of itself as such, without qualities. Yet it acts and exists and takes form. And that's what you already are, but you just forget that.

Meditation is a remembering. And each time we meditate, we are remembering that simple thing. But it's not a remembrance in the sense that it's an intellectualization. It's an actual experience. You the experiencer meld yourself with the qualityless, perfect light until there's only the qualityless, perfect light, and you do that as much as you can, and that determines your advancement in meditation—how much you can melt into the light.

So meditation is melting into the light but what I'm suggesting is, the confusion is—you think that you are the person that is melting into the light. That's what this whole explanation was about. Whereas truly, you are the light that is being melted into, but you don't know that now, and I do. I don't just mean "know" as a phrase meaning, "I accept that idea, I believe in it." I mean it as an actual, visceral experience. You know it. Not just as a thought that, "Yes, I agree with that concept" or, "No, I don't." But knowing implies reality in Buddhism.

CHAPTER FOURTEEN

FOCUS AND MEDITATION

The practice of meditation is emptying the mind. When the mind is empty, completely empty, it's perfect meditation. It's really that simple. There are a variety of different approaches to emptying the mind. All of them work equally well. We can just stay with one; we can use a number of them. It really doesn't matter; it's a question of personal choice. What we're doing is stopping thought. But really, before that, we're learning to control thought. And really, before that, we're learning just to sit down and focus on something.

I have a simple prescription method for learning how to meditate, which, if you do it, works very, very well. The main thing that you need is not really creativity but consistency. Creativity is a nice quality but it doesn't have much to do with learning to stop thought. Consistency does. Consistency really involves just doing something once, each time, and not thinking about time or space or repetition. You just live it once. Forever. And that's consistency. That's perfect consistency.

To meditate, what I suggest a person does is, of course, they sit in an upright position—if you lie down you relax too much and you don't really have the focus of concentration necessary to meditate. You can sit in a cross-legged position on a rug, you can sit in a chair. All that matters is that the back is relatively straight, the spine is straight. What I suggest a person do for their practice is to focus on something with their eyes open for half the meditation, and for the second half of the meditation to focus on something with their eyes closed. The length of time depends upon how long a person has been meditating. If a person wants to start meditating, I recommend that they meditate for fifteen minutes a day, once a day. After they've been meditating perhaps for a few weeks, then I would suggest that they double the time and go to half an hour. After several months, I would suggest that they increase the time to 45 minutes and then, that they stay at 45 minutes for a while, until they've been meditating about a year, every day consistently. After a year, if a person chooses to, they can increase the time, perhaps to an hour—maybe for another six months or a year. Then maybe after two years, go up to an hour and a half, ninety minutes.

The primary meditation, which is done in the early part of the day, after waking, is the meditation I'm discussing. It is nice to have a second meditation in the early evening, or about halfway or two thirds of the way through the day. It renews the initial meditation. It renews our contact with the divine, with the infinite light. That meditation should be of fairly short duration unless you're just very inspired—maybe 30 minutes, 15 minutes if you're new. But the important meditation is the meditation that you do to start the day because when you wake up from sleep, the mind is relaxed and you've not yet set it into motion. It has the motion of the astral dream experiences, but they're slight. Whereas, after you've started to have conversations, act in the world, perceive things in a sensorial way, the mind gets very stimulated; it picks up a lot of impressions and it's harder to move into the qualityless state of no thought.

The best time to meditate is when you first get up, whether it's morning, evening or afternoon, depending upon your schedule. It's nice to be clean; it wakes you up and just takes a lot of the energies off. Water neutralizes strange energy, unpleasant energy. So if you can take a shower before your—we'll call it the morning meditation, regardless of when you do it—that's a good idea. Or at least wash your hands and face. But water takes a lot of the strange energies that you've picked up in dreaming and the human aura of the planet Earth and washes it away and it makes it easier to meditate.

Then sit down. If you're terribly hungry, you should have just a little something to eat. If you're terribly sleepy, you should have some coffee or some tea or some kind of stimulant that will keep you awake. But if you eat too much, you'll be too aware of your body and you won't meditate very well, and if you use too much of a stimulant, too much caffeine, caffeine makes you think and it makes it harder to meditate. Ideally, I suppose we'd wake up in the morning and take a shower and just meditate. But sometimes a little bit of food or something with some sugar in it is helpful, just because there's so much impure aura on the planet Earth and it raises the blood sugar and kind of gets us going, and sometimes some caffeine or whatever you use might be helpful. You don't want to fall asleep, and you don't want to sit there being hungry; it'll interfere with your meditation. Nor do you wish to satiate your body with too much food because you'll just get very sleepy, and too much of a stimulant, too much caffeine, does the same thing—your palms sweat, your adrenaline starts to rush a little bit and you don't meditate well.

Then you want to sit down and for whatever period of time is apropos for your level of study, you want to practice concentration—focus. All meditation involves focus until we enter into the qualityless, thoughtless essence, when we perceive ourselves as the that-ness. So really all you're doing is learning to focus. Let's say you're going to be meditating for 30 minutes. I would suggest for 15 minutes that you meditate with your eyes open, focusing on an object of some type, hopefully an object that's beautiful or powerful. You could find a pretty colored stone that you just feel good about. It's a little rock that you found somewhere, life drew you and the rock together—your karma. It has a nice energy, and you could place that in front of you on the ground or on a table at eye level, if that's more comfortable. And you could focus on that. You could use a flower, a candle flame, anything you want that's bright and suggestive of beauty and eternity. Then with your eyes open, you'll focus on that to the exclusion of all thought.

Naturally in the beginning, if you're undisciplined, which everyone is mentally when they start meditation, you'll think a million thoughts, a lot of images will come through your mind. But if you focus on the object and you keep focusing, gradually the thoughts will become quieter and quieter, gradually the images will disappear from the mind. What's happening is, through the power of focus, as you look at something and concentrate on it, the kundalini energy which is situated in the base of the spine, in the astral, begins its long journey up through what we call the *shushumna,* which is an astral nerve tube that goes from the bottom of the spine up to between the eyebrows and a little bit above, which is the *agni chakra*. And as that energy begins to radiate and raise, it causes the mind to become quiet, and the further that energy goes up, the higher we go into different planes of consciousness.

The planes of consciousness are correlated to what we call the chakras, which are located along the shushumna. There are six of them. Then there's one other chakra of the primary chakras, which is not directly connected to the other six, that is located approximately at the very top of the head or an inch or two above it in the astral body, and that's the seventh [chakra].

Each of those chakras really are dimensions. We think of them as objects, but they're not really. They're dimensional access points whereby we can enter into different levels of mind, and that happens automatically. It's kind of like the mercury in the thermometer rises as it gets hotter. As that mercury goes up, it hits little plateaus and when we hit those plateaus, everything shifts. We pop into a different dimension where we perceive ourselves, the universe and mind completely differently. When we get to the top one, if we do, we're in very high planes of attention. And the higher we go, the less physical things are, the less time and space exists. But there's a big transition from the sixth chakra, or the agni chakra, to the seventh, because it isn't exactly a pathway—we do it another way. And that's the chakra of illumination, the planes of enlightenment. That's a little more complicated.

But for now, we're back in the first chakra again. We are in the earth plane, very much in time and space, very much in a body, very much identifying with all kinds of qualities, and we have no sense of the mind as being pure light. If anything, it seems like it's the opposite. So we sit down and we focus. And as we focus on something, the more intently we focus for longer and longer periods of time, the kundalini rises and the kundalini is hot, it's a hot energy. Sometimes you feel it cascading up your spine, and it's kind of searing or it's tingling. It almost feels sexual, but it doesn't arouse. Sexuality arouses, and it causes a physical arousal with the glands in the body. This feels sort of like that, but there's no arousal of the sexual organs. It's that same sort of tingly energy, but it goes up the spine in the astral body. It goes up the shushumna. You don't have to be aware of this, it just happens. You're not necessarily aware that your blood is flowing, but if you go running, your blood flows a lot more rapidly, even though you don't feel it coursing through your veins—but it's happening. There's no need for it to flow rapidly unless there's an escalation of the heartbeat, which occurs in motion.

Normally, kundalini is always flowing through all your chakras, through your subtle body, subtle physical body, what we call your astral body. Kundalini is the blood of the astral. And it's doing everything it needs to, but it doesn't need to flow much more than it is, unless there's reason, unless there's demand, unless there's activity. So in human life, unless there's something very major that happens of an emotional nature, there's very rarely an elevation in, kind of, the seratonin level of kundalini. It doesn't change much. But when you seek to enter into other states of consciousness, that requires more energy, and so the kundalini flows. Of course the more complete your concentration is and the less thought, awareness of self in the mind, the more the kundalini flows and the higher you go beyond body, mind, time and space and so on. It's hard to talk about some of these things; you have to really experience them.

When we meditate, then, what we're doing is not just simply concentrating. We're raising the kundalini through focus, through concentration. There's a metaphysical astral process that's taking place. What I would recommend is, if you're meditating for half an hour, sit down with the eyes open, look at your little power rock or flower or candle flame or anything—yantra, geometrical design. Focus on one point and hold your attention there. The mind will waiver, you'll think a million thoughts, but each time you do, bring your mind back to the point of concentration, seeing it visually. If one were blind, one can simply focus on a feeling.

Sight is not absolutely essential for this process, but we use sight because sight is the dominant sense. We can use hearing and do the same thing. We can listen to a tone. We can feel something physically. We could smell something and do it. But sight is the dominant sense. It takes precedence over all other senses unless one is blind or has been trained otherwise. So it's easiest to interrupt the flow of thought in sense perception and move the mind beyond sense perception with sight. That's why we do something visually to start with.

What we're seeking to do is internalize perception. Perception is very much involved with the senses and the mental processes and the emotional processes. That's what 100 percent of our perception is usually engaged in. But what we're going to do is gradually remove our perception from the sense world—seeing, smelling, tasting, touching, all those sort of things. We're going to remove our awareness from our thoughts, the thinking cognitive process. We're going to remove our awareness from feeling emotions and we're going to take all of our awareness and take it someplace else—into luminous realms, into inner light, into the very thing that we are that perceives. We're going to take perception into itself, into the perceiver, and see that what's there is perfect, qualityless, endless radiant light, which is a way of talking about something. It's not really just qualityless light; those are human abstractions. But it's nirvana; perfect perfection, beyond comprehension—ecstasy.

What we're learning to do is really change a lifetime of habits of taking our perception and having it go into the senses or into thoughts or into emotions, and we're retraining our perception to go into the void. It sounds a little nebulous at first, so what we do is, rather than just focus on the void, which would just be an intellectualization and wouldn't really occur, what we're doing is changing the course of a mighty river, and we do it in steps. We're creating a new pathway for it. And we do that first by focusing on something physical.

By disciplining and training the mind to focus on one thing, we gain control of our perception; we learn to grab it and put it someplace we want it to be rather than just in any sense that happens to be operating, or in any thought that happens to be passing through, or in any feeling that just happens to be going through us—who knows why, or even if we do know why.

We're learning to take our perception and place it in one place. By focusing on something, we do that. And be not discouraged. Everyone goes through the process you're going through. Takes a while to do it. Takes a number of years to learn to hold the mind perfectly in one place. But each day we do a little better, and in the doing of it we're releasing energy that is taking our mind into higher, diffuse planes of attention in which we're seeing life more as it really is. And if we do that every day, there is an add-up process. It's kind of like—as we release more kundalini, we use a little bit of it but we also save it; we store it; it resides in our awareness field, so that as we meditate; it isn't just that we go up and come back down, we come down a little bit less each time.

"Come down" isn't really the right phrase because that implies we're getting high; high implies that it's an abnormal state and low is the regular state. The opposite is true. Our current perception is very cloudy and all screwed up and as our perception increases through meditation, we're seeing life more correctly. The higher our perception, the more kundalini that's active and being properly focused, the more correct our perception is.

So, really we're in the darkest darkness now and we're moving towards light. And light frees us and the mind is perfect and we feel ecstasy, and we don't have any suffering and any mental aberrations; we're not in weird planes of consciousness perceiving ourselves as a self that's in some kind of pain or struggle or whatever it is. We see that we're the perfect light of existence that has always been and will always be. And we live that. It's not just an ideation.

Meditation is the freeing of ourselves from all mental states and concepts of self. But it really begins with a focus, with a retraining of the life force or the life energy. So you look at your object of concentration for, say, 15 minutes. Put a watch there, take out a clock, time yourself. Then, after you've done it for, let's say, 15 minutes, if your time period is half an hour, and you've really tried just to see that one thing, to look at it—you can blink, you can shift your position a little bit if you need to—but then after you've done it for half your meditation, close your eyes and now do the same thing focusing on one of the three charkas, either the navel center, around the navel; the median center, which is in the center of the chest around the heart, or the third eye, which is between the eyebrows and a little bit above.

You focus on one of those three centers, focusing on the physical area in the body that's near where it is in the astral. And if you focus around the navel center, or around the center of the chest by the heart, or between the eyebrows and slightly above, you will elevate the kundalini and you'll be releasing different types of energy into the astral nerve system. I recommend that you focus on these three centers in rotation. So Monday morning, do your navel center; Tuesday, the center of the chest; Wednesday the third eye; Thursday go back to the navel center. Rotate them because they take in the three basic meridians.

There are three lower centers. There are two intermediate centers, the throat center and the chest center; and then there are really two higher centers, the third eye and the crown center. You're accessing all three meridians, which creates the development of a balanced being, if you rotate them that way. If you just always meditate on the navel center, you get too heavy, you get too into certain energies relating to the lower three centers and you don't have enough will, you don't have enough power to deal with life and the world and the forces you have to deal with as you go through different dimensional planes and access points, in more advanced meditative states.

If you just meditate on the intermediate states, they're beautiful and pleasant, but you develop the psychic chakras a lot, a lot of the emotional body develops—but without the other centers there's a lack of balance. The upper centers are wisdom; the central centers are feeling, emotion, identification, beauty, the perception of life as beauty and truth; the lower centers are the power centers. So we put power, wisdom and feeling together and we have a good package in development. Otherwise, we're just developing without balance, and without balance our meditative practice will not continue to escalate.

Balance is the most important of all qualities. We don't want a little bit of rapid growth and then to stagnate. We want continual growth, continual development, which implies balance, always.

To begin with, you would focus for fifteen minutes, if you're doing half an hour a day, on a physical object; then you'd close your eyes and focus on one of the three centers, chakras, for the same period of time. If you've never focused on chakras before, the first few times you can actually put your finger around the navel center and apply a little bit of pressure until you get used to a feeling there, the same with the center of the chest or the third eye. After you've done it a few times, you'll find that you can just feel that area.

Now, interestingly enough, as you practice, you'll begin to feel the centers more. You'll actually feel that part of the astral body and you'll feel the energy releasing, and you'll notice that meditating on the navel or the center of the chest or the third eye really brings you into different mental states, to different planes of mind. Each one makes you feel very different after meditating. They're quite profound.

What we're really trying to do, then, with practice, is to spend more time in a complete focus. We do reach a point, however, when, while we are focusing, if we focus very completely, thought will stop. And when that happens, it's no longer necessary to focus—we can just let go. It's not as if in an hour and a half of meditation you're going to be sitting there, straining to focus on one thing the whole time. Rather what will occur is you will perhaps meditate for ten or fifteen minutes very intensely with a focus, then you'll find that your energy will raise sufficiently so that thought will stop for a while, and then you don't have to focus—you can just kind of let go. And then, when you start to think again, you go back to focusing again and releasing energy.

It's kind of like getting away from gravity. They develop a lot of momentum [for rockets] to get beyond the gravitational pull of the earth and then go into outer space. Then they shut off the rockets. They don't have to keep them on. Then you just float, in the light. Then, as you continue to travel, there may be some other great object, there may be a gravitational force that starts to pull on you, so you put on the rockets again until you're floating free again.

When you're floating free, of course, you are in the light. There are less qualities that you're apprehending, and then the transmutation takes place. Then the magic takes place. When you go in the light, and the longer you stay in the light, the more you transmute. The light washes out all the impurities of mind; it clarifies why we are, who we are, what we are, and it evolves us. It makes us more complete. It makes us more like the light and less like other.

You don't have to do anything when you get into the light. When you stop thought, it's not necessary to go anyplace or do anything. You've arrived. Nor is it static; it won't stay the same. But you've just gotten to a country where everything is done for you. You don't have to know, you don't have to not know. When you've gotten up that far, you just let go. There's complete consciousness, but then at that point the light does what is necessary for you. If you get in a shower, you just have to stand there and once in a while you turn around. If you get in a shower where it's hitting you from every angle, you're all set. So the light hits you from every angle. You just have to get there.

At the end of meditation, at the end of the period, we always bow and we touch our head to the floor—"Buddha's name be praised." That's our way of acknowledging our contact with all of life, thanking the universe, and it's just a letting go. It's realizing that there is something higher and deeper and more profound than our current self, and we're just acknowledging that and thanking it. We know that that is us. We know that we're not fully aware of that as "us" yet and that we hope to be some day. And we will be. Even though we already are, we don't know it. We have amnesia.

CHAPTER FIFTEEN

PROFESSIONAL MEDITATION

When a person has become used to meditating on a regular basis and the practice has become a part of your life, we reach a kind of threshold which some people don't cross. Initially, when you begin to meditate, it's challenging, it's difficult just to get yourself to sit down once or twice a day to do it. Then you begin to see results. There's more energy in your life, your mind works better, your body feels better, things appear to be brighter, you have more enthusiasm, your awareness shifts, you start to become a little bit clairvoyant, you can see inside people, see inside yourself and you just see there's a rise of your power. Everything in your life begins to come together.

Then what happens is the practice becomes a practice. It becomes something that is a routine, and each meditation may be fulfilling and you don't stop because if you did, you'll notice the days are not as bright. So meditation becomes something that we have to do because the loss of it reduces our energy level. But it's not something that we do because we are making continuous breakthroughs. It develops a kind of functional autonomy.

There was a time we didn't meditate, and we obviously got by. Now we start to meditate and there's a brightness and an addition, but now the reason we meditate is not because we seek a greater brightness but simply because the loss of meditation will bring us to a lifestyle, an energy level, an awareness level that we find unacceptable.

So then, once we're meditating on a regular basis and that's become part of our life, if not the main focal point of our life—the meditation and all that implies—the issue is how to continually make breakthroughs in meditation. How never to let meditation become just a routine in our lives, something that we have to keep because we fear the loss of it as opposed to something that is each day taking us into realities of mind, taking us into warp drive, taking us through dimensions, changes, dissolutions of the self and so on that are each day more amazing than any day before.

Now that's realistic when you get into advanced practice. In the beginning, that's not realistic. You can't say, well, each meditation is going to be five times stronger than the day before, because you have not yet developed the consistency of reaching a singular level. One day you'll do well, one day you won't. It's sort of like in sports, there's amateur and professional. An amateur is someone who one day is brilliant, the next day they're not. A professional is someone who demonstrates a consistency in brilliance. And their worst day will be about the best day of the amateur. They have their off days and their off seasons. But even when they're bad, they're consistently good. They're just not amazing.

Meditation is similar to that. In the beginning you're an amateur. This is once you're consistent and meditate once or twice a day for an hour, hour and a half a day. You're meditating consistently, but one day you'll have a great meditation, and then maybe for three days it'll just be so-so. And what I mean by that is not how you'll feel during the period of meditation, but how you will feel after you've meditated. During the period of meditation, it's not a good idea to evaluate your meditation. When you're running, you don't say, "Gee, this is a great run" or "This is a bad run." You just run.

When you meditate, you just focus. And if you're evaluating, that means you're not doing a good meditation because you're not focusing or dissolving, depending upon your level of ability in meditation.

So then, we'll have one great meditation, then four or five that are just so-so. Meaning that afterwards, one day after we've done what we would call a great meditation, we know it's great because everything shines. The whole world shines, everything is bright, we're flooded with optimism, new ideas, enthusiasm, or maybe there's just a perfect peace and stillness, a sense of self-transcendence, and it's a day like no other day.

It's kind of like a perfect spring day, when winter fades, and there is such a thing as a perfect spring day when the whole world is awake and alive after winter. And the breezes that blow, these just kind of gentle little breezes, when they touch your body, your body is alive in a way that normally it isn't. There's an energy present on certain days in spring that's not available at other times. Each season has its special days. We call them days of power when certain energies are available in our locale or on the earth that are not available all the time.

So when we do meditate well, when we're able to stop our thoughts for a long period of time—or if you're not at the point where you stop thought, yet you are able to concentrate intensively on one point and you really hold to it, you really just put a lot of effort into it—then the day will be very good because you've released a lot of kundalini energy in that process. That energy will flow through you all day and all evening. Your personal power is up; you'll just zig when you should zig and zag when you should zag. When your personal power level is up, you see better. So you'll know, "Oh gosh, I'm not going to take that exit today, I'm going to take this exit," and get a whole different day. Everything works out. The days that our personal power level is low because we haven't done a good meditation, we don't see well. Then we don't meet the right person, we don't attract the right energies to us. Things don't work as well in life.

So the trick in life, of course, is keeping your personal power level as high as possible, and that's what meditation does. But in the beginning, we don't necessarily have the consistency to make that happen no matter what. You may wake up one morning and you feel kind of sick, and you can't necessarily meditate very, very well. You may wake up one morning, and you're just nervous or you're depressed or something's bothering you, and it's just hard to bring the full power of concentration into your mind. One day you just—your thoughts won't stop; they're incessant. And every time you try and concentrate, you forget that you're supposed to concentrate and you get caught up in your thoughts.

A professional is someone who is able, no matter what the state of their mind or the state of their life, to sit down, meditate, stop thought, enter into a state of deep concentration and shut the world off, bring their mind back from the senses, back from the thoughts and back from the feelings, and enter into a quiescent state. When we stop thought, when we don't feel the senses or ignore them, when we don't feel feelings, per se, when we shut off the emotions and the thought processes and the sensorial processes, all of our awareness is free. And then, if we don't direct it, it directs itself. That's when we really begin to meditate. At that point, the mind enters into deeper spheres of its own being and we start to touch the radiant spheres. And of course, there's no way to talk about it at this point because we go beyond words into actual, occult, metaphysical, meditative, enlightening experiences.

The trick, then, to keeping your meditation practice alive—not simply consistent but wonderful—is you need to bring a certain will or force into every meditation. For the person just starting, I wouldn't be concerned. It's just enough to get yourself to the point where you meditate every day and then you see meditation as indispensable. That's a good place to get to, where it's just, it's like breathing, when you just get up in the morning and you meditate. You can't conceive of a day when you don't do that because the day would just be horrible. It wouldn't be a day; it would be a nightmare. And it's not that you've become addicted to meditation, it simply means that you want to be in touch with eternity and life at every moment. It's just an intelligent way to live.

I suppose we could say a person is addicted to food, and maybe they should give up eating for six months or a year. I don't think we get addicted to meditation. I think we just realize that it's an innate, natural process. To not meditate is very unnatural for a person who's evolved.

So then, once you're meditating every day and you see it as something that's indispensable, it usually becomes a routine. You sit down, you focus, you go through the usual states of mind that you go through. You may have pleasant experiences. But you're just driving down the highway at 55 [miles per hour]. You don't even have to pay much attention to your driving. You're fairly reflexive and usually nothing unusual occurs, so you just kind of drive. You get to where you're going, but it's not remarkable. That's not meditation. That's just a boring state of mind. But a lot of people call it meditation.

Or you have a certain power of concentration, you do increase your energy levels so you have more energy during the day, but there's no white light, there's no ecstasy, there's no smile on your face that's so big while you're meditating that it hurts after a while. There's no sense of brilliance, the world flooding into a thousand lights, your mind cascading through a billion dimensions and then going completely clear and entering back into the qualityless state—that's a hard word to say, "qualityless." That'd be a good tongue twister.

And—so you're not meditating. If it's not ecstasy, you're not meditating. I don't know what you're doing. Ecstasy comes in many forms, in many shapes and colorations. But you're not meditating if you're not experiencing ecstasy. You may be learning how to meditate but once you're meditating, once you're a meditator—one who meditates daily and who sees it as indispensable, as part of their life—you should be experiencing ecstasy every time you meditate. Not necessarily during the meditation—maybe at the end, maybe afterwards. But you can't be satisfied with anything less.

You concentrate so intensely, you bring your will to such a singular point that you break through all the limited mind states. You bring in so much kundalini because your focus is so intense that you snap out of the limited mental states into higher mental states, and then, of course, you experience the pure, shining void in whatever form you're capable of experiencing it and seeing it as, from your sentient mind state, and that in itself is ecstasy.

In other words, the universe is ecstasy. Now that doesn't mean much; that's just a phrase. What does it mean, "the universe is ecstasy"? I mean, you experience the universe and you do not necessarily experience ecstasy. How could plants, trees, stars, quasars, black holes—what does that have to do with ecstasy? Ecstasy is a personal experience. Those are—the universe is filled with things. Not true! That's how the universe appears through the senses.

But if you rise above the sense level, if you don't view life just through the senses, if you view life through the emotions, then the universe is made up of feelings. If you view the universe through the mind, it's made up of understandings. If you go beyond the mind that thinks and analyzes and understands, if you go beyond the senses that see, smell, feel, touch and hear, if you go beyond the feelings of pleasant, unpleasant, love, hate, I like it, I don't like it, attraction and repulsion—there are other levels of perception within us.

Meditation is a process by which we go beyond the senses, the mind and the feelings, and we engage the other levels of perception, other forms of perception. It's like sense perception, or mental or emotional perception. We have many other ways of perceiving infinity. But most people, of course, are completely unaware of them. And when you perceive life through those other modes, that's when you see that the universe is ecstasy. That's when you experience its ecstasy.

There is physical ecstasy, something sensorial. A great food or a great lay, or whatever it is. There is emotional ecstasy, the feeling of oneness, of love, of kindness, euphoria, joy. There are feelings of mental ecstasy where we just understand something, we just grasp something, we intuit something—a higher beauty, an intelligent understanding of life, of ourselves or of a project.

There is ecstasy in the body a little bit, in the mind a little bit and in the emotions a little bit. But there is also pain in the emotions—unhappiness, depression, disillusionment. There's pain in the mind, in the thoughts; there's a lot of pain, discouragement, confusion. There's pain in the body, physical pain. But in the other modalities for perceiving infinity, there's no pain. There's only ecstasy. And the mere fact that most human beings—out of the five billion people that are currently extant on the planet Earth, maybe several hundred, maybe several dozen, maybe a dozen, experience life in its true pure state—maybe a dozen. Maybe there are several dozen who experience it on and off in its pure state. Maybe there are several hundred who touch the pure state once a day. Maybe there are several thousand who touch it once a week, and then the rest only have heard about it or don't even know it exists. Or don't believe it if they hear it.

Maybe there are just a dozen people who live in the pure state all the time, a dozen fully enlightened people on the planet Earth. Maybe that's all. But because there are only a dozen, doesn't mean, because the number is few, that their perception isn't much more correct than the billions who don't perceive that way. There were very few men who framed the Constitution of the United States. A lot of people couldn't read and write back then. More couldn't read and write than could. Hamilton, Madison, Jay, Jefferson, these people—there were very few well-educated people—they put together a Constitution which has created a framework for millions. Just because they were a minority doesn't mean that they didn't see much more clearly than anyone else.

So there are very few people who are actually enlightened, who live in the higher spheres, in this particular world. There are worlds where everyone is enlightened, where everyone is in touch with that qualityless essence of existence, mind perceiving itself without coloration, and that's normal and natural. In this world it's normal and natural that most people perceive life through the three primary bands of attention. And when someone perceives life through the senses, that's a correct form of perception. It's not incorrect; it's just limited, limited to the senses. When someone perceives life through the emotions or through the mind, they're not perceiving life poorly. But let's say you're looking at life through a glass darkly. You don't see much through the senses, you don't see much through the emotions and you don't see much through the mind. They're very distorted levels of perception—distorted in that they don't show you the whole picture. They show you only a fragment. But the illusion is that when you see life through those three modes, you see life completely.

When you go beyond those three modes into the other levels of attention, perceiving life through other aspects of what we would generally call mind, you realize that all your life you've lived in a tiny village, maybe three tiny villages. And you would visit them. But there was a vast world with continents, oceans, mountains, things you never knew about, cities, that were outside of that. And it's only when you leave your three-village area that you go and see the universe. It's fun to live in a three-village area. I like it. But sometimes you need to leave to get a proper perspective, and there's pain there, and suffering, but there's no pain and suffering beyond the senses and the mind and the emotions. There's only ecstasy in variant shapes and forms.

So then, we would say that your meditation is quite excellent when you are able to, each time you meditate, go beyond the senses, the emotions and the thoughts. Not into a sleeplike state where you're just kind of unaware, but into states of complete awareness where you're perceiving life in other modalities, other than the three I've alluded to.

The way you do that, the way you become consistent, I think personally, is unexplainable. I mean, it can be explained but I don't think the explanation will change anything. I can say that, "Well, when you've suffered enough, and you see that the mind is wonderful and the senses are wonderful and the emotions are wonderful, but yet you've had enough suffering in them and you realize that they can never fulfill you completely and you seek that—then you'll go beyond them." Sure, I can say that, and it's true. But it doesn't really explain anything. I don't think you can explain life. It just is.

So if a person were to say to me, "Rama, how can I become consistent? I mean, I meditate every day, but I want that ecstasy level, that deep understanding of life, the dissolution of the selves, and you know, all the things that happen in the upper gradients." In other words, 99 percent of meditation occurs in the upper gradients, one percent is just getting started and getting above those three things and that may occupy a few years of a person's time, but real meditation occurs beyond thought, beyond emotion and beyond sensorial perception. So how do you get up there, how do you do that? Well, I would say, "What really has to occur is a kind of magic. It can't be explained. I can explain why or why not, but that won't make you do it. Sometimes your life just puts your back against the wall and you've experienced so much unpleasantness in those three realms that it drives you further. That may happen."

You can explain that to someone but if that circumstance comes along, it'll happen; if not, it won't. The closest I can come to saying this is—meditate. Meditate and realize that when you meditate, no matter how high you go, no matter how deeply you perceive, that you're only touching the bare surface of infinity. Just hold in mind the fact that beyond your perception is ecstasy. Not far beyond. Just with the stoppage of thought there's ecstasy—power, understanding, in limitless amounts. And no matter how far you go, you can never experience all of it. And if you dissolve the self completely, it doesn't end. The self is just a filter that prevents us from seeing completely. It has its place. Sometimes we need that filter, but sometimes we don't.

So I would simply say—meditate. Sit and meditate as deeply as you can. But when you meditate, don't get so caught up in doing it that it's kind of like the vitamin pill you take every day. You take it just because you assume it's doing a good thing, and maybe you didn't take it for a week and you noticed your energy was low, so you went back to it. That's not meditation. Meditation is about ecstasy. It's about the understanding of truth. It's about us changing ourselves and making ourselves God-like. Our mind melds with the mind of infinity and we become infinity. And we become perfect by virtue of the fact that the universe is perfect in its nonphysical aspect. It's perfect in its physical aspect, but it's transient, it changes. But the light itself is perfect.

So I would just say meditate on the light and merge with it. And always remember that you're only touching the surface of infinity. That it goes on forever, and that you have before you limitless ecstasy. Even the sage who's going into samadhi, and he's got all his terminology for nirvikalpa, salvakalpa, sahaja—you know, they divide it into a system, and maybe some of that's true. Maybe you can systematize a little of it. But even the sage who's doing sahaja samadhi, the great guru, I'd say, "Hey buddy, you know, I like the robes and everything, but remember, you're only touching infinity. And if you claim to be doing more, I think you're pretty much in the senses and the body and the mind, because infinity is endless. None of us can compromise it or understand it."

But we can swim in it. It's like the ocean. You can go swim in that ocean. That ocean is big. It connects to other oceans and it changes all the time. And there are tides and currents, and even the very water that's before you today will be someplace else in the world tomorrow, and there'll be different water in your section of the ocean. And it's deep! The mountains under the ocean are higher than the Himalayas. But we don't even see them. There are many worlds there.

So when we meditate, we're going swimming in the ocean—the ocean of bliss, the ocean of ecstasy, the ocean of transmutation and personal refinement. Just remember that it's big and that every part of it is perfect and it's fulfilling beyond imagination. And if you do that, I think you'll find that you will be more likely to touch more of it, just with that simple understanding.

CHAPTER SIXTEEN

THE BEST MEDITATION I EVER HAD

The best meditation I ever had, I haven't had yet. It's in the future, which as anyone knows doesn't exist—anyone who meditates knows. But yet, I'll have it some day.

The best lifetime I've ever experienced hasn't occurred yet. I've had billions of lives. I've been around the universe almost as long as the universe, I think. I remember my lives; you don't. Or you remember a few. I remember a billion. And I've had wonderful lives. I've had wonderful lives, beautiful lives, lives of struggle, lives of battle, lives of ecstasy. I've had beautiful lives, and this is a beautiful life I'm in now. It's a hard life, as they go, but it's a beautiful life.

But I haven't had the best lifetime yet. It's around the corner, I know it is. It hasn't occurred yet because things get better in infinity as we get better. And in each lifetime we get better.

The universe is always ecstasy and it's always perfect. But we don't perceive it that well. And if we keep doing our yoga in every lifetime, we perceive it more correctly. It isn't that infinity gets better—I have no doubt that it could if it were in the mood, and maybe it does—but the real issue is perception in meditation. Meditation is the study of perception. What we seek to do in meditation is refine, which means, simply, make more accurate our perception of things. So I haven't had the best meditation I can have because there's no end to the refinement of perception.

Yes, I say that I am enlightened. What does that mean? It means I live in a condition of light. After many years of meditating, practicing, I've reached a point that can't be described or discussed—but one is always in a condition of light. There is really no primary self anymore. It [enlightenment] comes back in every life without me seeking it. One has to refine it, but it just comes back unsought. I live in a condition of light inside my mind. Nice. But that condition of light can be refined. There's no end to it because we perceive the universe through the universe. We perceive light through light, and there's no end to the gradients of perfect light.

So I believe that the best lifetime hasn't occurred. I don't think the most beautiful sunrise to be seen in the world has been seen on this earth. It isn't that the sunrise will grow more beautiful, it's that we will. And we'll perceive it more completely than anyone before. You might say, "Well, God, the universe is filled with a lot of slimy stuff. There are pollutants in the air, there hasn't been much aura on the earth from the time of Atlantis, and you could really see then." And I'd say, "Well, that's true, but you know, those chemicals create beautiful sunsets."

You see, Buddhists are optimists. We never saw sunsets in Atlantis like we do now. We didn't have all those great chemicals in the air. So what is beauty? Is beauty the acknowledgment that chemicals in the air create beauty or would beauty be to bitch about it and say, "Well, God, back in Atlantis it was much nicer!" And what does it mean? I would think it would mean you're further along in your perception of beauty if you can see beauty in things that other people wouldn't consider beauty.

It's the refinement of our nature that is perfection. It's not a thing that we go and do. You're seeking a perfect town, a perfect car, a perfect wife or husband, a perfect teacher. You're missing it. The perfection is in your apprehension, not in the thing. It's in your apprehension, in your perception of things. You want a perfect job? Create a perfect mind and whatever your job is, it will be perfect. You want a perfect life? Create a perfect mind and whatever your life is, it will be perfect. You want to see a perfect sunset? Create a perfect mind and look at the sunset, any sunset, and you'll see a perfect sunset.

I've lived in worlds where there are three or four suns. We had incredible sunsets, beautiful. But they weren't more beautiful than here, if my mind is more beautiful in each life. Eternity becomes more beautiful as we age, if we age well—and I mean age not just within a lifetime but in a multi-life sequence. If we age poorly, then we don't improve our minds, we don't refine all the aspects of our being.

In other words, enlightenment is not static. You know, there's this sense of, "The Buddha was enlightened"—great, good for him, and that's like some absolute—meaning that's the highest enlightenment. Or once you're there, that's it. It's sort of like a Ph.D.—you got your Ph.D. But what does that mean, when you get one? I've got one. It means that you've passed some comprehensive exams, taken classes, written a dissertation and done a lot of classwork and research and now you have a vague understanding of your field. And now your job is—now that you have your Ph.D.—you're going to go out and actually learn something about it. All the Ph.D. ensures is that you have some vague understanding of how large the field is, and you have some methods to approach it with.

So enlightenment simply means that you've gotten above the body-mind complex. You've refined the self, dissolved it in the white light of eternity and gone through all the gradient shifts. I mean, it's technical. But it doesn't end there. In other words, we have this view that enlightenment is, once you're enlightened, that's sort of it. That's the end of the show. You just kind of hang out in this quiescent state. You don't know that the quiescent state changes and moves all the time. It's never the same. If you become the quiescent state, which is what enlightenment means, it means that you're never the same. You move and shift as the quiescent state, in a body or out of it. And since the quiescent state is perpetual and endless ecstasy, therefore you are endless. You're not finite; you're infinite.

So the end of all meditation is the beginning of all meditation. It's the refinement of one's nature. The refinement—ultimately in advanced meditation—of enlightenment itself. Enlightenment can be refined, which may seem like a strange concept, but who cares about concepts? The reality of the issue is there's no end to it. Since infinity is by its very nature infinite, then enlightenment by its very nature is infinite and thus can be experienced in infinite ways, by itself or without itself.

So the most beautiful day hasn't dawned, the most beautiful lifetime has not been experienced. The most beautiful meditation has not been had, even by the enlightened. I guess that's the good news—it doesn't end. Enlightenment is not an end. Nor is it a beginning. It's just—there's no separation between the quiescent perfect state and anything else, inside your mind. Everything's inside your mind. Enlightenment isn't out there; it's just inside your mind. But it's not an intellectual understanding. It's not a knowledge that can be taught.

You can't teach someone to be enlightened. It's something you have to go and do. You can't teach someone to meditate well. It's something you have to go and do. You can explain, "Well, do this, focus on this, dissolve the ego this way"—there's a lot of technical material that you learn as you advance. A lot of it is very technical, as you go in and out of the different samadhis, as you learn to dissolve the self in a variety of ways—things that we don't teach to people unless they're very far along—[they] wouldn't make any sense, they wouldn't be understood—the motions of infinity. You have to learn the motions of infinity with your mind. Your mind becomes a perfect mirror to the motions of infinity.

Sometimes—you watch the Olympics and you see one of these people who are on the bars, you know the parallel bars, the uneven bars? They start to do these wonderful flips, spins. I mean they're moving so fast that you can barely see what they're doing, and unless you know their art very well, you wouldn't know the names for the ten different spins and shifts they just did. But each of those spins is quite technical. And of course they are judged on how well they technically execute very refined motions. But they're all put together so quickly that to you it's just, "Wow, look at that guy spinning around, that's amazing!" But it's even more amazing if you knew how many motions are in each spin.

In advanced meditation, we learn to do something like that with our minds. There are methods and formations of joining the mind with the various aggregate aspects of the universe, with the universal mind. Fusing it, dissolving it, things like that, that are done sometimes thousands of times in a microsecond, or outside of time. That's the tech of advanced meditation. But it's really all the same. Infinity is really all the same. Mind is really all the same. There's only one infinity, even though there are countless infinities. It's really all the same.

All of life is colored by your perceptual field. And whenever you're in a perceptual field, it seems like it's ultimate. It's a self-wrapping consciousness. There doesn't seem or appear to be anything else other than the attention field you're in. It's an ultimate view. So it's important to remember that there are countless views in infinity. If someone says, "Well, I am enlightened," that means they have a particular view. Maybe their view is above everyone else they've ever met, but that doesn't mean that it's ultimate because it can't be ultimate. Infinity is the ultimate view. And to have it, you can't exist. You can't be in finite form. No one could ever be said to have the ultimate view because all views ultimately are beyond perception, if they're at all advanced.

The study of advanced meditation, then, is the ability to undo the most impressive views there are. In other words, what you try and do in beginning meditation is to become consistent—meditate every day. In intermediate meditation, you try and always reach ecstasy—and deeper and deeper forms of ecstasy. But in advanced meditation, what you're really learning to do is to undo the most perfect perceptual states because every perfect perceptual state is seen as a trap. There's nothing wrong with it, but it's limited. And the game is, the more perfect the perceptual state, the less real it can be, the more you're drawn to the latest nirvana.

It's like restaurants. You know, you find the new wonderful restaurant in the city and it's just the best restaurant there is. You have to immediately leave it—after you've had dinner, by the way, and tried the dessert and gone through the whole experience. Then you have to leave it because the mere fact that it seems ultimate tells you that it's not, since there can't be any ultimate in infinity. You immediately have to leave it. But then you have to find the next ultimate. You're always looking for the ultimate. It's kind of like journeying to Ixtlan. You're never going to get there, but that's no reason not to try. You're never going to eat the best food—somebody must be hungry, I'm feeling all this hunger psychically—you're never going to eat the best food that there is because maybe it hasn't even been discovered yet. But that's no reason not to try, you see?

In advanced meditation, what we're always trying to do is avoid illusions.

In intermediate meditation, we're trying to create illusions, the illusion of perfect meditation. But once we've achieved perfect meditation, we're terribly trapped because that's an illusion. There's no such thing. It's necessary to first reach the point of perfect meditation so that you can see beyond that. But ultimately, enlightenment is an illusion. Enlightenment, of course, is real. But what I'm suggesting is any enlightenment that seems ultimate is an illusion. There can't be anything ultimate.

So advanced meditation is a process of constantly undoing perfection. Because as soon as it seems to be perfect, we're trapped. We're stuck in an idea-form of perfection and all these idea-forms, of course, come out of the seamless void.

Advanced meditation is the study of the simple. That is to say, we come back to the most basic things and we see them as far more infinite than the most infinite things. So I can go shopping and pick up some Bounty Towels. Paper towels? The three-pack? You know the one. I can go home and open those up and look at them and see more infinity in them than in the Buddha's best meditation—in the three-pack. If I can't do that, that means I'm wrapped by the Buddha's best meditation. That means I see it as ultimate. And if I see it as ultimate, of course, that means I'm stuck in a view that can't possibly be, since nothing can be ultimate in the universe. There can't be anything ultimate in infinity because infinity is boundless.

So, advanced meditation is a continual process where we come back to the beginning. In the beginning we reject the senses, we reject the mind, we reject feeling—meaning, we feel that they're limited. We don't reject them, but we just don't spend all our time in them. In intermediate meditation, we hardly ever utilize those forms anymore. But in advanced meditation, if we happen to be in a body, we come back to those most basic things and we see infinity in thoughts, in physical things and in emotions.

It seems very strange to see—you see a very advanced master who's got a girlfriend, who listens to rock and roll, who thinks about things that are very earthy. And you say, "Well, how can this be?" Yet they glow. You say, "Why would they be interested in these things?" You don't understand, the advanced course has to do with coming back to everything that you had to reject in the beginning and seeing it as a far greater infiniteness than everything that you've attained.

But what you see is not the same as what everyone else sees, of course, because you've already mastered samadhi or been mastered by it. You've already mastered all the quiescent states in the universe and infinity, or enough, anyway, and you've refined the being out of existence. So it's perfectly possible to come back to the most sensorial level of perception and see all the infiniteness of all the endless, quiescent states in breadcrumbs—what are those things? Croutons! You see croutons, Pepperidge Farm Cheese and Garlic. Yeah, I go to the supermarket, I buy the pack and in one of those croutons is all of nirvana. In that physical, sensorial apprehension is infinity plus.

You come back to the beginning. That's why in the "Searching for the Ox" sequence, at the very end of that sequence of the Zen paintings, we're back in the world again. We go around the circle. We go back to where we started, and we're back in the marketplace—in the picture, the block print, in the "Searching for the Ox" sequence where they're depicting the enlightenment experience in Zen. And we're right back where we started. We're hanging out again. We're in our Levi's and doing or going to work, but the thing is, we're doing something different with our mind than we were at the start. We've already become enlightened. But now we're seeing if enlightenment really exists in everything like they say it does in the books.

We've gone back to being very common. But not really. We're in different infinites all the time. So, consumer goods become enlightenment. Relationships—anything! It doesn't really matter because infinity exists in everything. "Greater than the greatest, smaller than the smallest, the self dwells in the hearts of all." That's in the *Upanishads*. If that's really true, then infinity is everywhere, but of course, you have to develop the mindlessness to perceive it in its infinite perfection, in all forms and formlessness.

Advanced enlightenment is really the apprehension that we have not seen the most beautiful sunset or the most beautiful sunrise or the most beautiful life or death. Then, in all things, in everything and in nothing, there's God. There's nirvana. There's infinity. While we have to leave a lot of things originally to purify our perception, in the end we just realize there's no end. It just goes on forever, in countless new forms. That's what's wonderful about the universe. It's not finite; it's infinite.

Chapter Seventeen
METAPHYSICS

As objective perceivers, we have a sense of who we are. We have a sense that we are a person with ideas, history—we are who we are. You know who you are; you are whoever you happen to be. However you see yourself is how you are. That's all it is.

And we have a sense—unless you've been involved with metaphysics for a long time, unless you've been practicing Buddhism for a long time, and not just in time, but I mean you've done something with the practice, you've evolved—until that has happened, we have a sense that we choose to do what we do in life. We have a definitive sense that, "Well, I've chosen to do this. That's why I'm doing it. I'm meditating, I'm involved with the spiritual quest, I'm exploring other dimensional realities, I'm exploring enlightenment, I'm trying to become happy and free from pain or guilt or depression or various ailments of the psyche, I want endless ecstasy," whatever it might be.

But we have a sense that we are participating in metaphysics and the metaphysical experience voluntarily. We're doing it because we're doing it. We've chosen to do it.

As you go much further in metaphysics, you discover that that's not true at all. The reason that you're engaged in metaphysics is—there's no reason, you just don't have any choice. You couldn't stop, no matter what you did. You're held by power. Now, this is a very different view of life. In other words, we believe that we are all—people are created equal and we have free choice and all that sort of thing. It's very big these days—on the earth—the idea that you can just go get yourself a four-wheel drive and a cute guy or girl and a house and a job and you can kind of do what you want to. This is very American, but—very egotistical, very centered around self.

I like independence and I like that idea, but to be honest with you, in metaphysics, we see as metaphysicians, we perceive that it isn't really we who ever decide anything. It's power that decides things. It's power, if I can enter into the world of the American Indians for just a little bit here, who believe that there's a force that binds life together. There's something that makes everything what it is, and we call it power. In Buddhism, I guess we'd call it karma. But let's be American Indians for a minute, since we're in America. They were here first.

Power. Power binds us to something. You see two people together. They're in a relationship. They don't like each other; they're bored with each other. Why do they stay together? "Well," they'll say, "because, God, I wouldn't know what else to do. I really don't want to meet someone else; it's inconvenient. We have children," whatever it is.

But it's really power that holds those people together. And when the designs of power change, those people will separate and there's nothing they can do in the meantime about it. There's not a thing they can do. Nothing. Zero.

Now this goes, again, contrary to the grain of the American and pretty much the common 20th, 21st century view of life where we can all just do what we want to. We can start a factory, we can drive a car, we can make our life what we would like it to be. But the ancients believed that that isn't true. Within a certain framework, within certain parameters, there is free choice. But the parameters, we have no choice about. Where we're born, the conditions—we don't choose that, it just happens. Beyond that, we just think we're choosing.

But there's a power that brings us to things, and there's a power that lets us move away from things, from people, places, experiences. And what you learn to do in metaphysics is to accept. That's a tough one. Because everybody is convinced that they can just go do whatever they want. Yeah, you can shop in any supermarket coast to coast. You have that choice. You can shop in Arkansas, you can shop in California, you can shop in New York, New Mexico. You can shop anywhere you want. Major choice. They're all about the same, needless to say, the supermarkets.

What we learn to do is to accept where we are and what we're doing and we learn to try and understand that there is something to be gained from experiences, be they pleasant or unpleasant. You're in a pleasant experience, you want it to last forever, and it doesn't—naturally. You're in an unpleasant experience, and you want it to go away, and it lasts forever. That's how it is, right? So we believe that experiences are inescapable, that power holds us; it binds us, just like it makes us who we are.

In other words, why are you? That's like, why a duck, you know? Why not? Why are you? No, why are you? Why? I mean that's the first metaphysical question you're supposed to ask the great guru if you ever meet him. You go, "Oh great guru"—that's the B.C. syndrome, you know, B.C. Comics? They have these little great guru comics once in a while? And they climb to the top of the mountain, and the guru's up there—they always call him "great guru," you see. "Oh great guru, what is the meaning of life?"—that sort of thing.

The first question you're supposed to ask anybody if you ever meet anybody who's far up is, "Why am I?" Not who. You know who you are; you are who you are. You already know, I mean, no one can tell you who you are. You might discover that there are parts of yourself that heretofore you have not encountered. But "why?" That's the question that everybody wants to know in this little span between life and death—why?

Some people are pissed off and they say, "Well, why is there death? Why are babies born only to die and why are people crippled and why is life unpleasant? And what kind of a God can it be…?" complain, complain, bitch, bitch, bitch. We send them to the complaint department. You know, there's a complaint department you can go to and you can complain and someone will listen and say, "Well, gee that's too bad. Uh, we're sorry."

But in reality, the question that you first ask the great guru, you say, "Oh great guru, why am I?" It's a reasonable question. "Why am I? Why? How did this happen? How did I come to be? How do I have awareness—this thing that is called life? How can this be?" And the great guru will kind of laughingly look at you, because you're used to this kind of question in the guru biz, and depending upon the sense of humor of the teacher, they will give you various answers. But basically what they will tell you is, "Well, it just couldn't be any other way. That's just how it is!" It's like the people in the complaint department. It's the same answer. There's nothing you can do about it. This is how it is; this is how life is.

It's power that made you this way—you see, always blame it on someone. Blame it on power, blame it on God, blame it on creation, blame it on a past life. Well, your past lives made you this way. But the American Indians, the ancient Indians would say, the metaphysical ones would say, "Power binds us together." Power, for a while, makes us what we are—perceivers—luminous perceivers of reality. Perceivers of being, perceivers of states of consciousness. And perception is a reflection of self. All we are able to perceive is a reflection of our perceptual field. There isn't anything else; there can't be anything else.

All perception is self-reflective. What we see is a mirror. Eternity is a mirror, and we're seeing ourselves wherever we look. If we are unhappy, we'll see an unhappy universe. If we're happy, we'll see a happy universe. If we're very sexual, we'll see things in sexual terms. If we're metaphysical, we'll see things in metaphysical terms. If we're physical, we'll see things in physical terms. But what is the universe really? I mean what is life?

In other words, if our only method of perception is self-reflection, then we can never know what life really is because we always see it as a reflection of ourselves. You look in the mirror and all you can see is the person who's looking in the mirror. That's the nature of the mirror, it just reflects. Life reflects, just like a mirror. It reflects your mind. You don't think of it that way since life doesn't happen to take the form of a mirror; it's not visible.

Life is invisible. The illusion is that what we're perceiving is in some way not a reflection of self. We don't see the mirror. What would it be like to be looking into an invisible mirror that reflected things, but you couldn't perceive that the mirror itself was there? Do you see what I mean? That's what life is. Life reflects the field of attention that we're in. The field of attention is the software, and therefore it quantifies everything in its own terms.

In self-discovery, what the teacher does is allow the apprentice to get outside of the field of self-reflection and see life directly. We call this awakening. And what we see is that there are endless planes of attention. Endless realities. Endless mind states. They're like collections of atoms and protons and neutrons, nuclei. They just go on forever. They're plasma, they're fluid, they're alive.

And what we see is that the universe is made up of an endless ocean of life itself. It is an endless ocean of itself. And for a time it binds itself together in particularized forms, and those forms have perception and they perceive themselves as being separate. They think, "Oh, I'm separate from this because I perceive it." If you can perceive something, you're separate from it. That's how perception works. "I am perception. What I perceive is separate." You can't really perceive self. Oh, you can perceive your physical body or something, but you can't perceive essence of self; it can't be done because you are the one who's perceiving.

You can look in a mirror—that's all you can do, is look in a mirror. There is nothing else you can do but look in the mirror of self, in the mirror of karma we'd say in the Far East. Because karma is the sum total of who you are from everywhere you've been. The mind state you are in is karmic. Meaning, it's related by a causal chain of existences, of moments, of particles of timelessness, if you will. It's hard to put these things into words. It's impossible, in a way.

So existence creates itself in any way that it chooses to—for no particular reason. No reason that we could assign to the world of human reason, logic, deductive and analytical "let's find out, ask Mr. Wizard", that sort of thing. There's no way we can possibly understand anything. But we can see things. We can perceive things. And we can wonder. We can just be in a world of awe and wonder. That's the best we can do.

Most people are not in the world of awe and wonder. They're in the world of deadness. Their perceptual fields and bodies are completely self-reflective, and all they see is themselves wherever they go, and the universe revolves around their self-reflection.

But someone who is a Buddhist, someone who is a metaphysician, someone who is an Indian, a mystical Indian, is aware that there are many mysteries, and mysteries are not riddles. Mysteries are places to go with your mind. You go into the mysteries. And in the mysteries everything turns inside out, everything flips. You step into the mystery of the mind, and there are billions of minds, there are billions of selves, there are billions of worlds and dimensions. You go into them and you become them, and you're never who you were. You never were who you thought you were anyway, so there's no loss.

There are endless realities. William Blake wrote a poem called "The Mental Traveler," and that's really kind of what we are. We're just a mind that travels. We travel through perception. And we just perceive ourselves in variant forms and variant conditions forever—unless the perceiver can awaken to that fact, realize that everything that they're seeing is a self-reflection. Therefore, it's sort of like an endless jigsaw puzzle that you can put together in endless ways but it always comes out the same way, because you're the one who puts it together and you can only put it together in the way that you know, and there's a limited number of ways that you know.

You will put this puzzle together in every lifetime. But you can only put it together in the way you know. And the way you know a thousand lives from now won't be intrinsically different. It may have a slight different order, coloration. This puzzle, in other words, the grooves in the puzzle, you make them what they are; you fit them together. And eventually you create a picture of yourself. Your life is a reflection of your perception of yourself. Everything you do is predicated upon that.

As a person matures, and we say they "get their life together," that simply means that their self-reflection has become more complete, to the point where it strangles you. You get your life together, so you've got the house you want, you've got the car you want, you've got the job, you've got the family, you've got the body, the money. When you've got it all you're completely fucked. Because what you've done is mirror yourself in physical form. You've trapped yourself in your self-reflection which is why it's boring, you see?

In other words, life is just masturbation in a sense, mentally. What people do is they just create a world out of their self-reflection. Then they wonder why they're not happy. The illusion of happiness is that, "if I can only create my self-reflection, I'll be happy." But anyone who's really done it, anyone

METAPHYSICS   199

who's able to create a self-reflection, knows that it doesn't make you happy. It's terrible because once you've done it, once you get everything you want and it doesn't make you happy, the illusion that happiness will come when you pull it all together fades and you are left with a situation of unhappiness.

In other words, what keeps us going is the belief that tomorrow will be different, but suppose it won't be? Well, it won't be. No life will be different; eternity isn't different if it's always just a self-reflection. Death does not end self-reflection, it just changes it in an incremental way. But in the next life, the aggregate of the self reassembles and we are pretty much who we were.

So, metaphysics is the study of how to shift the self. How to get outside of the self-reflection and to just gaze with awe and wonder at the countless universes, the countless celestial radiances of mind, of life, of enlightenment, nirvana, or God—whatever you want to call it. Power.

All the universes are bound together by a web, a matrix, which is our perception. And our perception actually has colors; it has bands. We call them bands of attention. As we go deeper and deeper into the world of meditation, we are able to travel along the luminous bands, just like you travel along a highway or a road. We're able to follow them into far-flung realities of mind. I don't mean cellular constructs of the human brain, but I mean the dimensional realities of infinity, which are endless and numberless. The days of infinity are endless. Its hours cannot be counted or found on a clock. There is no direction. There is no north, south, east or west. These are just concepts. Infinity is forever, everywhere, all at once. And that's all there is.

So we climb outside of the field of self-reflection. Just a little—if you go too far it'll blow your mind. I mean it's strong out there. If you go out too far beyond the bounds of attention, there are things in the universe, in the universes of mind in the inner worlds that it's best sometimes not to deal with unless you're very, very far along. In other words, you can go into the flux of the universe, we would call it parinirvana, where things become what they are like this moment that we're sharing together right now. There's a place this moment comes from, where it's made. Actually, it's like a big factory where they make moments, where they make realities, where they make infinities. You can go in there and you can turn into the flux and throw yourself back into it and come out somewhere else. It's like warp drive, you know? "Star Trek." You just snap it through warp drive and you come out in a different part of the universe.

But that's too much for some people. It's too strong for the perceiver. The mind has to be very luminous to be able to do that. The sights of infinity can be too strong. They can scorch the soul. It's best to take infinity on a little at a time. So metaphysics is a process where a teacher shows you how to gradually step outside of the self-reflective bubble of attention.

That's how the American Indians refer to it. They say that there's a bubble of perception and all of our lives we're looking into that bubble thinking that we're seeing life, and we're just seeing our own mental self-reflections. But it's possible to open the bubble, to step outside of it and for a brief moment, the luminous perceiver who's within the bubble, who always thought they've been seeing life directly and not realizing everything is a self-reflection, steps outside of the bubble.

They look outside and they see forever. And that reorders us. It so changes us, it's startling. That causes the luminous perceiver to run like hell back into the bubble and close it up and batten the hatches down and seal it with super glue and anything you can get your hands on, and say, "No way, Jose! I want everything that's familiar! My life, my world, my body, time, space, I need these things! Aaaa! Aaaa! Aaaa! I don't exist, I'm not even an anything."

You know when you get out there real far, boy, and what the luminous perceiver thought was far was like, two inches. It's like in *Beetlejuice*, when they open the door and they step outside, and suddenly they're in the world of the sandworms? They've stepped outside maybe a foot and a half past the door. But in this other dimensional reality it appears that they're going on forever, and they think they've been out there for maybe several hours and they've only been gone a few seconds. So when you go into the other worlds, when you go into the luminous dimensions, it's very different than here. You really have to have your act wired. You have to be very strong. Your mind has to be in the right shape. Because otherwise when you get out there, what you see will drive you mad, just make you crazy. I mean, I don't know if it's crazy, you're just seeing other orders of perception, but no one around here will understand what you have to say. And it'll be tough getting a job. Because you'll be babbling about, "There were 50 billion universes walking through my mind," and it'll sound like you're on LSD or something but you're not. LSD's a drug. This is reality. This is the reality of what existence is.

When you step beyond the boundaries of human perception, what is there? There's infinity. The trap of words is that we believe them. The trap of words is that we say something and the thing that we say we believe—is. We say something, we say a word, and we're convinced that the meaning of that word is the reality. A word is a symbol. So the word "infinity"—the trap of the word "infinity"—is that when I say infinity you already know what that means, therefore you'll never know what it means because you will let it go at the understanding of the word that you currently have. See what I mean? Because you know what that word means. You have a concept all worked out. You have a file inside your mind for that word. And when I say the word, you just look at the file. I could say the word now, I could say it a year from now, you'll just look at the file. The only thing that can happen is, experience can change that.

I can say the word "Africa." And if you've not been there, you've got a file for Africa. So you will look at the Africa file. Jungle, seen some movies—Tarzan, elephants, South Africa, you know different ideas might come to mind. You've got a file with various data on South Africa, East Africa, North Africa, West Africa. But if you got on a plane tomorrow and you actually went to Africa and you spent several months trekking around Africa, and you came back and I said the word "Africa" to you, you would pull out a different file.

The trap of words is that we're content with them. Words are the death of metaphysics. But the funny thing is, we use words in the teaching of metaphysics. It's one of those weird contradictions. The trap of words is when someone says "meditation, let's have a great meditation," or the word "enlightenment;" we have already preconceived what that means. We're very certain we know what enlightenment is. Therefore, there's no need to go any further.

So when I say, "Well, God, there are countless dimensions and universes and infinities," you go, "Oh, right, OK, got it." You just—real quickly we whip out all those files for those words, we look at them and go, "Got it, got the reference point, check the map, yep, OK. Infinities, worlds, sure." And you don't have any idea what I'm talking about. You haven't been to Africa. I mean, I'm talking about existent reality beyond your self-reflection. Beyond your self-reflection. It's not a physical place you have to go to. Beyond your self-reflection is eternity.

In other words, it is the mind that weaves the dream of life, that convinces us that what we see is what is apparent and what is real, and that there's nothing else outside of our perception. But I can assure you, as a practitioner of Buddhism, that there are ten thousand states of mind, at least, give or take a few billion, which can be seen and experienced and known, and each one goes on forever, and in each one you're something else forever.

So metaphysics is a process where we go on journeys. We travel. We're mental travelers. We travel step by step. Not too far too fast. Step by step we travel into other dimensions of mind and gradually we gain new orders, new understandings of what life is and what we are. We have an awakening where we see that we are, oh gosh, I couldn't tell you; there are no words for it. If I give you words, you'll be satisfied with those words, and you'll think, "Oh, well, I understand that now, I don't have to go do that, I understand, I can appreciate intellectually what he said." (Rama laughs.)

You have no idea what I'm talking about. It's like the desert. We were talking about the desert earlier, and I was describing metaphysical adventures in the desert that we have when we go to the desert to meditate. Immediately, if you haven't been there, you pull up the word "desert" and look it up, "Oh yes, cactus and shrubs and (Rama laughs) that sort of thing." And you don't know what I'm talking about—the occult experiences that are had in the desert where the universe collapses in upon itself and billions of realities spill out through a giant hole called reality. It changes your awareness of things.

Metaphysics is a process whereby we awaken, step by step, to larger understandings of existence. And those larger understandings of existence change our self-reflection. This is the key. They change our self-reflection.

And that self-reflection is important because the self-reflection is sanity. The self-reflection is the ability to function in time and space. It is the function of memory; it is the function of choice. But the thing that creates that self-reflection, the thing that holds it together is power. Power makes it that way, the power of the universe.

The reason the man and the woman are together is because they fit each other's self-reflections. But power is the thing that holds the self-reflection. Things change when the self-reflection changes. So when I say that power causes something to be or power causes something not to be, what I mean is power causes the self-reflection in which the self binds. The only way to change the way we put together the puzzle, let alone to throw it away, is to completely change the self-reflection. And to change the self-reflection is a very complicated thing. It's a very complicated thing because even the concept of changing the self-reflection is bound by one's self-reflection. We can only conceive of changing the self-reflection in response to our concept of self-reflection, which is predicated on our concept of self, which is a self-reflection.

You're in the funhouse with all those different mirrors. You've been walking around in it so long that you've forgotten what you look like. Or suppose you grew up in a house like that where all the mirrors were distorted? Suppose every time you've looked at yourself, it's been in one of those funny mirrors and you have no idea of what you really look like, or if the mirrored reflection is what you really look like, you see?

So, "Is there a substantial reality that's constant?" That's the second question. If you say, "Oh great guru, why a duck? Why me? Who did this? How? Why?"—you know, how now brown milkshake, or whatever it is—the next question is, "Well, what can I do about all this? I mean is there anything to do?"

OK, we exist forever; there are countless infinities; infinity has bound me together for a while in this situation, in this life. There is no free choice, but I can enjoy the ride or bitch and complain depending upon whether I want to make myself miserable or happy. But my self-reflection has trapped me in the life that I'm in. And as long as it's constant, I can't change my life.

Well, the obvious answer is to change one's self-reflection. If you change your self-reflection, you change. You become someone else, and reality changes since reality is only your self-reflection. But you can't change your self-reflection because you'll try to change it in such a way that is a self-reflection. You see? That's the trap. So that's why the teacher comes in and says, "You've got to be kidding, you're a mess!" The teacher comes in because the teacher is outside of self-reflections but can see them and steps in and out of them because they're interesting sometimes. But a teacher is someone who has taken their mind much further than you have. They've gone into the void further. They've seen the luminous realities. No one has seen them all. No one has seen them all. But they've seen more than you have and they understand the trap of self-reflection.

What the teacher does is gradually—over a period of time, really over a period of years—enable the being to change their self-reflection by compacting their life, strengthening it, getting all the junk out of it, learning to be happy, free and strong, and then gradually, again I use the word "gradually," stepping into other dimensional realities—very specific ones, where for a while we will stand and gaze with awe and wonder at the universe.

It's like looking at the sun. You can glance up at it, but if you look too long, you'll go blind, even though it gives us light and we couldn't see without it; it's one of those funny contradictions. Look at the thing that allows you to see and you'll go blind. That's how infinity is. You can't look at it for too long or you dissolve. The bands of your attention break. But if you look at it in specific ways, as you become stronger and stronger by changing your life a little at a time, you're able to step in and out between the realities of mind and you can become something or someone much more conscious.

It is possible, in other words, to become someone else. This is what all metaphysics teaches us. Otherwise why get involved? Metaphysics is not religion. Religion is the complaint department, where you go and complain and someone says to you, "That's too bad." That's religion. Or they tell you what you want to hear: "There is hope; there is anything you want; you can put some money in the basket and we'll tell you anything you want to hear."

All our complaints and all our hopes are based upon who we are. But if we can change who we are—not just to being another human being or in another crappy situation, and we're just exchanging one crappy situation for another—but if we can change who we are as a perceiver, if we can go beyond the human level to the divine, if we can have a mind like God's, you see, that's worth doing. God's mind is endless. It reflects all realities. It is all realities—and beyond them.

So enlightenment means having a mind like God's. It means your mind is God's mind. It doesn't mean you are God, that's rather an objectification of the file word "God" where you just become the president of the company as opposed to somebody who works on the line stacking boxes—you become the CEO. You're God. You can tell people what to do. You make more money, live in a bigger house. That's [the file word] God.

The mind of God is reality without limitations—perception not limited to its own field. That's what we call enlightenment. And to have that mind, to be the perfect mind of the universe, that's the only thing really worth doing because all other self-reflections trap us and cause us pain. In other words, self-reflection is painful because it's a condition of limitation and any condition of limitation vis-a-vis the experience of endless freedom is painful.

Personality is painful, be it good or bad. Bad is more painful than good but even good, even the religious seeker, the person who's kind and doesn't eat squirrels and stuff, you know, particularly raw, while they're still moving, "A good person, he hasn't eaten a squirrel in a week; he's changed." A religious person is trapped by religion. A perfect person is trapped by perfection. An occultist is trapped by the occult. A human is trapped by the human. A squirrel is trapped by squirrel traps. You know? There's always something trying to eat you; that's what I figure.

The mind of God is our topic always, in the world of Buddhist mind. The world of Buddhist mind, in its more advanced stages, as we like to call them—because we like to think well of ourselves and consider ourselves to be advanced—in the advanced stages, we go beyond time, space, life, death and *Newsweek*. We experience. We play in the infinities of mind. We gain a level of control of our mind so we can dissolve the mind and bring it back and forth between different dimensional realities, reshaping the mind from moment to moment, not as a subjective thing that's out there; it's not a carving that we're making.

We ourselves are transmuting the reality of our perceptual field, and there are endless, beautiful and perfect universes—and there are some that are also pretty gross—that you can spin your mind through and your mind becomes those universes. Or you can go beyond universes to parinirvana, to the dissolution, where there's no beginning, end or field of perception other than the universal field of perception, which again, is one of those words, file words, that you're going to get trapped in.

Now you think you can understand what I mean, when in fact all you understand are what the words mean. What I mean has nothing to do with words. I'm talking about experiences. Hard core, hands-on reality. You're talking about words and they're two different things. The trap of words is that we're convinced that we understand. If we're convinced that we understand, we'll stop with understanding. There's no need to go further. Why go further? "Well, I understand what you've said. That implies that I don't have to do any more since I've understood."

So you go and see the great Buddhist teacher, and the great Buddhist teacher or the not-so-great Buddhist teacher or downright lousy Buddhist teacher—that's me, the downright lousy Buddhist teacher—says something and now, "Oh yes, I've understood." So now you are morally obliged to do absolutely nothing since you've understood. The lesson is complete. All you've understood are some words, which have nothing to do with what the man was alluding to, which is that there are countless infinities that exist forever inside your mind and that your mind is countless infinities, but you're trapped in a tiny little self-reflection.

You're standing in a closet, and you've been in it so long that you can't remember that there's anything else, that there's a huge house with lots of rooms and there are lands outside the house and planets and universes and creations, and there are all kinds of things. But your self-reflection is a little closet, and you've been in it for a long time. You explore the closet over and over, and there's a sense of newness when you turn from one wall to another since you haven't seen that wall for a little while, and you call that the new. But you're just going around and around in the same old closet, and in every life it's the same old closet, a few different things hanging in it but it's really the same old closet, sometimes a little bigger, because your self-reflection brings you into the same incarnation.

What is incarnation? Incarnation is self-reflection. The way that the universe we're in is constructed is a reflection of ourselves. We picked the dimension according to our self-reflection. Why is all this? Why a duck? It's just because it's that way. But in other words, I can't give you a very good answer. I could give you an answer that will placate you and then you'll look no further. I'd rather frustrate you. Then maybe you'll inquire beyond words. None of this has anything to do with words. There are only experiences. But words can buoy up experiences and words are part of reality that we deal with.

Chapter Eighteen

A Clean Room

From time to time I read *Walden* by Henry David Thoreau. I didn't read *Walden* as a teenager, I didn't read it in high school; it was never assigned in the school I went to. I didn't really read it in college. I didn't read it till I got to graduate school, and in graduate school I was doing a course in American Lit, the first half—they divided it into halves. They were doing a seminar with a professor, and it was in—I think I was getting my Master's—and I encountered *Walden* by Henry David Thoreau and I read it, and it had a great effect on me. I immediately got in my car and took a friend and drove up to the lake, to Walden Pond, and it was about this time of year, March. It was very cold. I brought a sleeping bag and I hiked in after dark, which you're not supposed to do, to approximately where Henry's house had stood. They've located the foundation. If you've been up there, you might know the little sign and some stones marking where his little house once stood, and I spent the night there. It was freezing cold, and you could hear the traffic from 2A or whatever that is. But anyway, I woke up in the morning and of course Henry made this big deal about jumping into Walden Pond and how invigorating it was.

So here it is, it's early March in Massachusetts, which is colder than early March in New York by about ten degrees. I think the ice had just thawed the day before I got there. But I was young and impressionable as I am now, and so I always wanted to try things. Having successfully evaded the security forces of the Massachusetts Police Department and spent the night there, I, at sunrise, got out of my freezing sleeping bag and went down and jumped into the water—because Henry talked about it and he made it sound really great. Obviously. He got me to do it. And it was very cold, as you might expect.

Freezing I think is the word. I'll never join one of those Polar Bear Clubs where people go bathing in arctic waters. And I stayed in for a second or two, and being, you know, a foolish individual, swam around a little bit, got out of the pond and went home after walking around the area a bit and things like that.

I read *Walden* once in a while. I don't tend to go up to the pond. I go up once in a while. Once in a while life drags me up to that little hole in the ground called Walden Pond where you can see the boys and girls in the fall come to hang out there and neck, and in the summer they use one end of it as a beach, and in the winter it's pretty quiet, pretty quiet. But I read the book once in a while—maybe less travel, mental travel. I read the book once in a while because it brings me back to an interesting place. I see things a little bit differently. I think we all see things a little bit differently, but it brings me back to a certain place, and it's a place that I think of as keeping my room clean.

Henry Thoreau was very influenced by Emerson. Emerson was very verbose, a lot of ideas. Henry went out and did things. Emerson did too—a couple of Harvard boys. But Henry just reminds me of a place that I call keeping my room clean. It's very important to keep your room clean. It's a central theme for living, and it's something that we can get away from, and the consciousness I feel that emanates from Thoreau, through his writings, is that consciousness. It's a very pure, simple, extremely intelligent and intellectual awareness of how to keep one's room clean.

The way you keep your room clean, the way you keep your life clean, is by not letting a lot of clutter in. You keep it simple. The more complicated you make it, the less clean it is. So Henry built a very small house because it was his belief that if you built a big house, you spent half your life cleaning it and maintaining it instead of enjoying it. And I think maybe that's a good way to look at life sometimes. It's necessary to keep our room very clean, and we get involved with a lot of ideas about everything that's going to make life wonderful. But I think really, what's necessary is just to keep one's room clean.

I do that from time to time. I clean my room. I go through everything in the closets and throw most things away. If I'm not wearing it, why keep it? Throw it away. I go through books and throw things away. I throw away everything on a fairly regular basis that I'm not using. And then, every once in a while, I throw my room away and move to a different room.

Life is a room that we live in. Our minds are occupied with the moments that we spend in that room. And really, as Buddhists, our only task is to keep our room clean. If we do that, we've done everything. You can forget that, so that's why I keep Henry—keep the book out and once in a while I pick it up, maybe once every two weeks, once a month, I read a couple pages, and it brings me back to that place. And then I look around at the complexity of what appears to be one's life and I just look at it and realize that it could all be done a lot more simply, with a lot less "us" in it and a lot more life in it.

The Buddhist mindset seeks to eliminate the self. That is to say, what we want to experience is life, not self. And when there's less self and more life, we're very content, and when there's more self and less life we're quite unhappy. So we want to experience life, not self.

What prevents us from experiencing life is self, but what self is, essentially, is clutter. Self is clutter. Self is just a great deal of clutter, and the clutter in our lives is a reflection of the clutter in our minds. What else could it possibly be?

Buddhist monks, when they live in ashrams and in monasteries, Buddhist monasteries, they live in rooms. It depends on the monastery. You might share a room with a couple of monks, you might have one by yourself. I always got one by myself because I couldn't stand the other monks. And well, I just, I have trouble with another person's mind. If you don't have one, if you've purified yourself to the point where you don't think and you're in a room with somebody else who still thinks, you think all their thoughts. And so, having gone through all the trouble to get rid of my thoughts, I didn't see any point in sitting in a room with somebody else's thoughts, particularly since I liked my thoughts better when I had thoughts.

So I always got a room in a monastery that was private. Sometimes, you know, you're in a dormitory situation. That was fun, I liked all the guys, they were a lot of fun. They're funny. Buddhist monks are funny people. All the ones I knew anyway in Tibet, Japan. And as a Buddhist monk, you don't have a lot of possessions. You have a couple of things you wear, a few books, some writing materials, that's about it. You might have a couple images of the Buddha. You might have a thangka—unless you're a teaching monk. If you're a teaching monk, you have all the paraphernalia of teaching, but you really don't have a lot. But it's amazing how you could still get your room completely cluttered. The lack of possessions does not imply a lack of clutter.

You can fill your room up with all your ideas. I mean, I walked into some rooms in the monastery that were so full, even though there was nothing in them—I'd walk in there, and there was a solitary Buddhist monk sitting in front of a meditation table. Not much of a table, actually—a little incense burning. Some of them didn't even have writing materials. And there was nothing in the room, but the room was so crowded I had to get out right away for fear of being crushed to death by all the thoughts, all the people in that room. Everybody he knew or had ever met was in that room with him. He was carrying them around inside his mind—there were men in there, women in there, his parents, relatives. And there were all kinds of monsters in there. Whatever he feared was in the room. I could feel all these monsters. And there were all kinds of wonderful, beautiful things that he was seeking in his meditation, in his life, and they were all in the room too. Between the monsters and the angels and the relatives—I just couldn't, you know, it's like I was never good at parties.

I can throw a great party, but I don't know how to go to one. I can throw a party because when you throw a party you just work all the time to make it a great party. But I could never go to a party because I wouldn't know what to do. If I'd go to a party I'd immediately find the kitchen and start to serve food because I wouldn't know what else to do. I'm never good at socializing. It doesn't—I don't understand it because, I don't know, it's just not my way. But I observe that most people do it and enjoy it and it's a good thing. It just doesn't happen to be an option on the menu that I was born with. So I tend to go to the kitchen. You also get to eat more there too—which seems to me the best part of a party anyway. Say what you will, if the food is good it's a good party, and if it's not, the party sucks.

So when I read *Walden,* it reminds me of a clean room. Because as I go through his thoughts, as I experience his mind, his mind is very clean, very clean. And I think it's good to pay a lot of attention to cleaning our room. It's something that we forget. Our room, the place we sleep, is really ourselves. The posters that we have up, the pictures, reflect us. Everything in that room is a part of us. We're the ones who put it there. There are the things we see and there are the things we feel. And our rooms are always too cluttered. We have our whole past in our room. We have our whole future in our room. We have our whole present in our room. I just don't know how we fit it all—so many things to fit in a room.

It's good to clean your room and I like to do that. I like to clean my room. I like to simplify it because then I can see eternity. Whereas with all that clutter, there are so many guests at the party that after a while all you do is—it's just smoky and noisy and people are talking about things that are consequential to them, I guess, but sometimes I would just—after serving food I would just go outside and look at the sky for a while because I like the way that feels. Again, I like parties. I throw great parties. Boy, do I throw a great party. No, really, I throw a really great party. I like having parties. But I don't like having people in my mind. I don't like having thoughts in my mind. If they're there, I don't know what to do, I mean, I don't know how to talk to them.

So it seems to me that what Henry creates is a very simple house. His entire idea is that a simple house creates a simple life. A complex house, which we have to spend a lot of money on, causes us to go make a lot of money. And then we spend our whole life making money. Then we have to spend the money, and then we have to get things that have to be taken care of. What he is saying, in other words, is that everything is a reflection of one's mind, which is, of course, a very Buddhist thought, Emersonian thought, Henry David Thoreau-ian thought. And it's true. Everything's a reflection of your mind.

The answer is not necessarily to get a small house or not to make a lot of money. The answer is to clean your room. And if your room is clean, that's about that. We seek to do that as Buddhists when we meditate and when we breathe and when we live and when we talk and when we interact and when we're alone. Because we like the way it feels when the room is very simple and very clean because there's no clutter. It isn't that we appreciate that there's no clutter. No clutter opens the window so we can see outside and see eternity, which is very full and very beautiful. But if there's too much clutter in your room, you can't see the room anymore. You see the clutter, you see. If you've ever seen the mind in its immaculate state, in its perfect state, you really don't want to have it all cluttered up because you just see all the clutter.

Now, I ask you, do you see your minds? I don't think you see your minds. I think you see your thoughts, you see your desires, you see your relatives, friends, lovers, enemies, you see the monsters in your life, your fears, you see the beauty, the hope, your desires or what you hope the desires will bring. But I don't think you see your mind. You think of the mind as the clutter. The mind is not the clutter. The clutter's the posters on the wall. It's the crowds that are in that room every day and every night. Wherever you go, your room is there. Your room is your mind. And you need to clean it on a regular basis.

I forget that sometimes, because, I don't know, I just do. But when I pick up Henry, I'm reminded because it's so obvious that his mind is so clean that it reminds me to just check and see how clean it is. How good it feels when you can see the stars, I mean, feel the stars. Oh, you can go outside and look at the stars. But you don't see the stars. You probably haven't seen the stars since you were quite young. Because when you see the stars you see them through your relatives and through your friends and through your hopes and through your fears and your ambitions and your desires and your frustrations. You see everything through that. It's what we call *aura*. It's your aura. You see everything through the aura. And after a while, after you've lived for a while, God, you pick up so many objects from your travels and you bring them back, you get so many things in your room after a while that you're like the lady who had a thousand cats who stayed in her house. I can't give you the punch line, it's obscene. But—anyway. (Rama laughs.) I'll let your imagination wander.

Your mind can get cluttered up by all kinds of things. You could be like that lady. Anyway, so yes—Henry David Thoreau kept a clean house.

Wherever he went, it was clean. And you can see that that mind state he found, which is inside all of us—all mind states are inside all of us—you can find it. *Walden* is an advertisement, essentially, for that mindstate. He's recommending it to you. That's why he wrote the book. He's saying, "Look at how I live, it's very pleasant. You might enjoy this." It's like a review of a Club Med somewhere. Somebody said, "This is really great, I had a fabulous time, it was a great weekend. I go and come, I recommend it, and here are some thoughts I had on it." Travel review. So Henry's reviewing a place that he found. It's not Walden Pond.

I went up there, and it's a nice place. It's a beach in the summer now, and there are a lot of people who hang out there in the fall when all the pretty autumnal colors are filling the trees. You see a lot of couples walking hand in hand, enjoying each other's bodies. But it's just a place. The water was cold and refreshing. Then I went home because I realized that he wasn't writing about Walden Pond, he was writing about having a clean room. He was writing about when your mind is empty.

And once I was young and impressionable as I am now, and I went to Walden Pond and threw myself into the water because it seemed like a good thing to do. And it was cold. Like the mind. The mind is cold. It's clear. It's perfect. It has no background or foreground. It has no perception. It's always been as it is. The mind has always existed. It's eternal. Redwood trees mean nothing to the mind. They're not that old. Mind is eternal. Your mind has always existed in one form or another. But you don't see it because of the clutter.

The stars in the sky last for billions of years. That's nothing to the mind, nothing. It's an instant, a millisecond. The mind doesn't even know time because it's deathless and birthless. It shines radiantly forever. But we don't see the shine because of the clutter. What a pity. Now of course we could say, "Well, who are we? I mean, I thought I was the mind. But if I can't see the mind because of the clutter, am I someone else?" No, you're the mind. The mind can't see itself—isn't that strange? Because of the clutter.

The mind can't see itself. No, you're the mind. Today, anyway, you're the mind. In this conversation you're the mind. So it's necessary to get rid of the clutter. And anybody can do it if they want to.

I used to live in Buddhist monasteries and I finally had to leave them because they were just too cluttered for me. They were cluttered up with too many thoughts about Buddhism, too many thoughts, too many plans, dreams and schemes. They're nice. I like those thoughts. I mean, I could spend eons in Buddhist monasteries. I love those types of thoughts. They're very noble—spreading the dharma, sharing enlightenment with everyone, young monks, new monks, new middle-aged monks, old monks, talking about enlightenment, the samsara, the sangha. I love that stuff. That's my world, it's great. I love the guys. Guys are great. But it's crowded. It's filled with all these ideas about enlightenment, and those are nice ideas as they go—I'll take them above all others—but ultimately there's not much enlightenment in the monastery any more than a clean room exists at Walden Pond. It's not the place, it's the mind. That's what you learn.

After a while we learn that the trappings of the monastery are not necessary. They're good if you like trappings. It's just decorator colors. If you like the decorator motif of the Buddhist mindset, then monasteries are great because that's what you get. It's like Disneyland; there are different rides. A monastery is just a ride, and there are different ones and they vary. But the better they are, the less they are. The better they are, the less self, the less crowded they are. It's hard to find ones that are empty. I've been to a few that are empty. Actually I've been to some abandoned monasteries that were still quite crowded. They're very filled with all the ideas of the beings that were once there. I guess they come back, maybe because they liked it so much. They come back—the souls come back and wander around there in between incarnations because they liked it there, they had good moments. There are good moments.

No, it doesn't really matter where one is, as long as one is in a place that is happy for you, where the energy is optimum. What matters is life. It's like Number 5 says [in the film *Short Circuit*], "Life is not a malfunction." People begin to think after a while that life is a malfunction—"Oh, it's painful, it's difficult." Not at all, not at all. That's only because there's too much clutter in the mind. Life is not a malfunction. Life is all there is and it exists forever.

You can't get away from it. If you run away from it, you're running to it because that's all that exists, and you're—what's running is life also. Life is not a malfunction. It's beautiful. But if you do not see it that way, it's simply because your room needs cleaning. If you clean up your room, it'll look beautiful again.

I would say that in the practice of Buddhism you shouldn't get too caught up in anything that isn't fun. Enjoy it. But once in a while, even Buddhists clean their rooms. If they're good Buddhists. They even clean Buddhism out sometimes. We go directly to life without "isms" and words and names. No thought. Clean mind. Clean room.

CHAPTER NINETEEN

THE BHAGAVAD-GITA

In the *Bhagavad-Gita* is a discussion-conversation between enlightenment and that which unknowingly seeks enlightenment. Enlightenment is represented by Sri Krishna who is said to be an avatar, which is a human way of trying to define "very big." That is to say that Sri Krishna is not from the local area network, but he has come from a world that is different because his mind is different. He glows. He doesn't experience the normal round of circumstances inwardly that most people do. He doesn't experience depression. He doesn't really experience elation as human beings would know it. He doesn't experience the kind of grayness and deadness of the human condition. Instead he lives in a perpetual sunrise. He's self-effulgent. The light that he seeks is not external. He doesn't have to turn to the sun for light, or towards another being or towards a God, because he is self-effulgent radiance.

Arjuna, who is the fearless warrior in the story, on the other hand is a very worldly individual, we assume with high past lives, who's engaged in a battle, a kind of a civil war, the battle of Kurukshetra. And a conversation, a dialogue, ensues in the middle of a battlefield, symbolizing the battlefield of life in which we are fighting through our illusions. The illusions that are most dear to us are Arjuna's illusions. His illusions are the people he must fight against. It's a civil war, and he knows a lot of people who are on the opposite side of the battlefield. They've been his friends. But simply because of a political difference, which was not necessarily their doing or his doing, suddenly they have to face each other down. You've got to kill your friends.

Arjuna is a warrior of great renown. Says he won't fight. He tells Krishna, I can't fight because I love these people. It's immoral, it's unjust. I can't—what will it prove? Where is the success in battle to kill those you care about?

There's no winning. So he says, I won't fight.

Now what this represents—of course, this was an actual battle—but symbolically what this represents is a place we get to inside our mind. We get to a certain place inside our mind where we're slaying illusions in the practice of yoga and Buddhism. And we're doing a pretty good job, and it's going well. And we get to be a pretty good warrior, like Arjuna. But there comes a point where we reach certain attachments, certain illusions that we have to dispel. And we don't want to. We see no reason; we'd rather not gain the benefits of enlightenment than slay those illusions. We're so attached to them; it's illogical, of course, but it happens.

The ensuing dialogue is a pep talk from Sri Krishna, who represents enlightened mind, to Arjuna, who represents mind that seeks enlightenment, unconsciously. And he explains to him the nature of that which is and that which is not. He talks to him about reality. In other words, Arjuna is so—his mind has been so eclipsed by his attachments and his illusions, he's not seeing things well, that he doesn't want to do what he does best. He doesn't want to fight.

Krishna's message, which is definitely not a pacifist message—I know pacifism is associated sometimes in the world of yoga and Buddhism, but not always. Not always. Buddhists make great warriors. And Krishna says, fight. He says, go out in the battlefield and kill those people whom it's your job to kill. And whether they were your friends or not, you have to look at the big picture. In the big picture, you can't go kill anybody, you can't be killed.

In the big picture, we're all eternal. Yet, strangely enough, even though we are all made up of light and we are all one light, life is a game and in that game we find ourselves cast in certain roles. We call that *lila* —when the light takes forms. And when the light takes forms, we get cast into a certain role. Now *maya* —which is illusion—means that we believe that we are the forms. We get so caught up in the formations of life that we perceive through the senses that we actually believe that we are the forms and we forget that we are really essence, not forms.

Lots of analogies, of course, are made in the world of enlightened study about this. They say, "Well, you see the surface waves of the ocean and you think that's the ocean, but 99 percent of the ocean is below the surface. But if you just see the waves which are turbulent, you forget that the ocean beneath may be very calm." You know, this sort of thing.

What he's saying, what Sri Krishna is saying, is that it's a terrible mistake to believe that this life we lead is real. Obviously it's real, but it doesn't last very long in its realness. It's very ephemeral. And to mistake the forms of life—the shapes that life takes—for reality, is not wise. In other words, if you can stand back—let's say that we have a lot of clay, a huge amount of clay. And let's say we're going to take that clay today and take cookie cutters and cut shapes. So we cut a bunch of shapes and we have these shapes, and then let's say we take one of the shapes and we start throwing the shapes against the wall and breaking them. And you've made these shapes, or you've just been around them for a while and you like them so much that you get all upset about it. But what we're going to do when we're done with the shapes is—they're not going to be destroyed, they're still clay—we're going to take the clay and kind of make them molten again and then cast new shapes.

Now, what a fool to get upset, to go crazy, to pound your head against the wall or to try and kill the person who's throwing the shapes against the wall, when they're just going to go back and come out again in new shapes. It's a process. So our lives are a process in which we take form for a while. We have a shape. And life itself, the world we perceive, the earth, the stars, the moon, the things of life—plants, animals, our careers, our relationships, our emotions, all the things that we perceive—are just shapes that the light has temporarily assumed. To feel then, that there's anything you can't do is absurd, that you have to hold onto anything because any shape that you hold onto will fade eventually. It goes back into light. And it will come out of light again in another form, as will you.

Yoga, then, is the study, not of the shapes but of the substrata form of the light which the shapes come out of. And we learn to see, in a larger picture of existence, the light, and therefore we're not so concerned about the shapes.

Lao Tsu says the sound man is immune to the passing of human generations as to the "sacrifice of straw dogs." If you're Western, that doesn't necessarily mean a whole lot because you're not used to—at harvest time in the villages in the Far East, they used to have a sacrifice. To propitiate and thank at the end of the harvest or at the sowing of the seeds in the spring, they would have a sacrifice. They wouldn't sacrifice real animals, they would make a dog out of straw and then they would burn it. Now, why get upset about the burning of a straw dog? It's not a real dog; it's just made of straw. It was straw, and then we whipped it into a shape and now we're burning it. So the sound man is immune to the passing of human generations.

All that we love, all that we count on, all that we want is transient. And to care about it and to be upset when someone dies, to be upset when we die, to be upset when things don't go our way, is to attach ourselves to straw dogs—to be upset about things that don't matter. Because whatever happens is inevitable. To attach much importance to it is to hook ourselves to the forms, the transient forms of life, and this creates unhappiness that is unnecessary, unwarranted and certainly does nothing to change anything that is.

If you could see further into the process, you would understand that the transient forms—which go back into the light—are unharmed. The light cannot be created or destroyed. The intelligence of the universe—that makes things beautiful, that makes the things we love, that makes the things we fear, that makes the things we care about or don't—cannot be altered. The intelligent, perfect consciousness of God, of the God-mind of infinity, cannot be tampered with by you or I or anyone. And we are all part of that.

So then, Sri Krishna says to Arjuna—through the form of the *Bhagavad-Gita*—don't worry about all this. What you should do is, you should find what matters. Find that which takes you from the shore of the transient, where we just see endless pain and endless suffering and we see the most beautiful creations wither. The beautiful young maiden becomes the old woman and she hates her body because it isn't what it used to be. The man with his dreams and plans and ambitions becomes the old doddard who has trouble remembering where he was going to go later in the afternoon. And he remembers all the wonderful experiences he had, and all the women he had and now all that's gone, and he's bitter, you see? This is inevitable. This is normal and natural; it's a process.

If you live in the land of the senses, that is all you see. You see one thing after another destroyed. War destroys things, disease, or you just see the unconscionable misery of everyday existence where just through unkindness, which is really an outgrowth of lack of awareness, in their unconsciousness, human beings just hurt each other or they hurt themselves with their unknowingness. To be bothered by any of this is ridiculous. But if it's all you see, if it's all you know, if it's how you perceive the world to be, then of course it makes one unhappy—because, of course, you have affixed yourself to that which you see and perceive because it's all you know.

So Sri Krishna says, Meditate. Go within and you will find that there are other universes, that there are other dimensions, countless dimensions and universes, which are also transient. Some last longer than these worlds, some not as long as where we are. And you'll see they all go through the same process, even the world of the gods, of godlike beings. The heaven-paradise realms don't last. And the beings there don't last. Everything goes back into the fire. Everything is straw for the fire. But that's not the end. The fire transmutes and purifies the forms; it cleans them off. And then, the moon rolls round again and a new phase begins. Everything is born anew. Universes are born anew, creations and infinities.

So Krishna says, Arjuna, don't be so concerned with all this. There's a pathway that leads beyond this, that takes us to the place where all of this comes from. Obviously, if universes are coming out and going in, they're coming in and going out of something. Obviously, we have come forth from something and we are returning to something. He says, you can go through the cycle forever and always be on the outer peripheries of attention, of consciousness, and only see the surface, and of course you'll be filled with dread and apprehension at the loss of your own life because if you feel that your life is terminated by death, that could be very frightening—or very relieving if you have a horrible, horrible life. But still we don't know what lies after death. So he says, meditate and you'll see these various ephemeral worlds, or various ephemeral beings, all of them going through the same thing—some are rich, some are poor, some are more knowledgeable, some are less knowledgeable—in countless myriad universes forever.

But there's a source, there's a perennial source from which all things come forth. We call it the Godhead, nirvana, the tao, enlightenment. It's big, it's bright, it's perfect, as are all of its children, as are we. He says, know that if you meditate more deeply you will come, in your meditation, in the stilling of your mind, you will come to enter into that. Sounds sort of nebulous, but it's not. It's just like giving somebody directions. Sometimes I'm out running on the street and a car pulls up and they ask me how to get someplace, and I tell them, well, you go a mile down here and turn left, and go another half a mile and then make a right, and you'll find the street you're looking for.

So the directions for meditation that Sri Krishna gives are very exacting. He tells him exactly how to get past all of the things that cause suffering and transient pleasure, to something that is perpetual ecstasy. His directions are that exact. He just goes, it's down here a mile or two, and take a left, and go past the old gnarly tree and turn right, and pay no attention to those people on your left and right that are shouting at you—just keep going, and you'll get there. Pay no attention to all of the people who are inviting you into their houses for a wonderful dinner or something in addition, a little bit more, dessert, just keep going, just keep going and you'll get there. Just keep meditating and ignore these transient forms. Because they're all aggregate manifestations of your mind—meaning, the way you see them is incorrect.

We're all the same; we're all one. It isn't that you have to get away from them—how can you get away from life? You can't get away from people, places and things. And even if you managed to get away from people, you're still with yourself. What he's saying is that you want to see beyond all this, and running away from the world and from jobs and homes doesn't accomplish anything. You can sit out in the forest and meditate, but you've still got the squirrels to deal with and the trees and the sound of the wind and the bugs. It really isn't much different.

He says to bring your mind into the center of being. Meditate. When you make the mind still, when you stop thought, at that time a doorway opens that you go through. Then you go into the land of perceptual perfection. And the more you do that, the less you leave it. Till eventually, while your outer form may be in this world experiencing pleasures and pains, ups and downs, growth, maturation and decay of the cycle, your mind will not be here. Your mind will be absorbed in perfect light. Then he explains how to do that, how to hold the mind one-pointedly by concentrating on a singular object and so on and so forth.

And then he answers a lot of philosophical questions that Arjuna has, and he explains what we call the *dharma,* meaning the road to truth beyond the transient. He says, what you really need to do is get yourself a teacher, that's number one. Because there's absolutely no way you can understand any of this without a teacher, or you may fool yourself and think that you are meditating when you're not. He says, follow explicitly the teacher's instructions because the teacher will show you, step by step, how to become free, how to free yourself from the *samsara,* from the wheel, as Buddhists describe it, of birth and death, of these transient forms that we've become so attached to. We've become attached to them because we don't see what else there is.

Sri Krishna's message is the message of anyone who comes from far away, anyone who's come from that world, anyone who has been to, seen and melded their mind with the eternal light. His message is the same as Buddha, Lao Tsu, Bodhidharma, Milarepa, Padmasambhava—Eastern famous spiritual sorts and people whose names we don't know. Anyone who has gone deeply into the world of light experiences the same thing, light. And the experience of that light teaches us, changes us, nurtures us, modifies us, rearranges us and makes us of it. The more time we spend in it, the more we are of it. When we are of it perpetually, all the time, when the light can't be separated from us, we say that one is enlightened.

One can have enlightening experiences and meditate and go into the light, but when you've gone into the light so much that there's really no difference between the light and yourself, we say one is enlightened. The light always flows through you. There's a very near, thin, almost transparent personality structure which allows a sense of independent being and perception, but there's only the light.

So the road out for Arjuna is unexpected. Sri Krishna says you have to face that which you fear the most and that which you're most attached to, and eliminate it. In this case he has to fight a battle, and the battle is his attachments. He says, you can't kill these people you love. This is a game. And in this game, it's like playing Monopoly. You have some good friends who are on the other side. But it's only play money; don't take it so seriously. The way the game has shaped up in life is these guys are going to try and kill you and you're going to try and kill them. That's not your doing. There's nothing you can do about it. You can choose not to play the game. That's a mistake.

He says whatever role we have in life, we have to play it to the hilt. We have to take it all the way. We have to assume responsibility for our role. To run away from it causes misery. To assume responsibility for the role that life has given us and to play the hand perfectly, as well as we can—with all the skill and cunning and knowledge, all the bravado, all the power, all the humor—to do that is what we must do. Those who would lead us away from doing that, we consider the enemy. Those are the illusions. Anything that convinces us to go away from what we know in our hearts is our responsibility, is an illusion. It's blinding you; it's causing you not to see the truth. Those who say, well come on, you don't really need to do that, do this instead. Those are—that's what we mean by illusion. Because only you know what it is that you must do.

So he surprises him [Arjuna]. He says go fight, go kill. Do this because it's only play money. You can't kill your friends any more than they can kill you. But play the game to win. He says it's better to be a winner than a loser, and if you're going to lose, it's OK to lose if you've played as well as you can. It's better to be a loser and have played well than not to have played at all. That's interesting advice. It runs counter to what a lot of people would think because they have a very defined idea of that which is spiritual and have watered-down, quasi-religious ideas about that which creates enlightenment—it's very different than what most people would think.

The world of enlightenment, and that which creates enlightenment, is much different than what most people would think. Most people have Hallmark Card descriptions of what creates enlightenment. And if their descriptions were correct, then everyone who is in religious practice would be enlightened, which is certainly not the case. So it's quite surprising when we find out that in order to become enlightened, to get the big picture, to become free from the transient, what we have to do is face life with a smile and take out our sword and start cutting—and the more we hack down the illusions, the better we feel. And that it's really a game. Life is a game. And there's winning and there's losing in every battle, and there's winning and losing in the battles that comprise a war.

A war is an incarnation. A battle is a day of your life. If we win more than we lose, we say that we've won the battle. If we lose more than we've won, we've lost the battle. So we do one day at a time in self-discovery. Just one. And we win. Because our method is sound. Because our yoga is sound. If we meditate well, then we can't lose because meditation will give us the insight, the power, the integrity, the knowledge and the sense of humor to cut through the most difficult illusions.

When you meditate and you enter the light and you stay in that light as long as you can, using your will and your love of the light and your aversion to that which is of the transient, then that light makes you what you need to be. It's the best trainer there is; it's the best war master. Just sitting absorbed in the light of meditation—if it's deep, bright, perfect light, if there's no thought in your mind—will make you what you need to be, to turn and face the illusions, to face the things that you don't want to do and be able to do them, and not just do them but win.

If we lose a battle, if we lose a day, then we learn from it. We learn from our opponents who defeated us, and we beat them tomorrow. We come at it in a new way. Always respect the opponent. And the more talented the opponent, the luckier you are. Because in order to beat a talented opponent, you have to draw a great deal of strength from your being. And the harder the opponent, the more power you have to pull and the more power you pull, the further you'll accelerate your growth and development. So the difficult opponent is the one that's best. The more difficult the opponent, the better. Not impossible—difficult. No opponent is impossible. Even death can be overcome, simply by seeing that it doesn't matter. It's a hollow opponent; it's a straw dog.

So don't be afraid. Don't grow so attached to the things of the world. Just do yoga. Meditate. Follow the recommendations of the most knowledgeable teacher you can find who will teach you to discriminate and tell you, "Do this and avoid this. This seems important, but it's not important. This doesn't seem important, but it is important." You do those things and you meditate, then you will find you will become more of the light and less of the world. And your pain will lessen and your ecstasy will increase, and this will just continue as long as you are in this incarnation.

Don't be concerned about the next incarnation. The next incarnation will take care of itself, and it will be based upon this incarnation. There's no point in being concerned about it. If you're concerned about it, do well with this incarnation. And if you have more winning days than losing days, then you'll do OK, particularly if your winning days are in the latter half of the incarnation.

Sometimes we get a slow start. But our days and nights can be very powerful. We can meditate very well after we get out of our teenage years. We get more of a sense of purpose. We're not so distracted by the world of parental bonding and societal constructs. We begin to see beyond these transient forms, and we see that there's something eternal, purposeful, worth knowing and worth being, something that really matters, that we love, that empowers us, makes things bright—eliminates the sense of alienation that we experience in life, eliminates the boredom, the dullness, the terrible fatigue. All that comes from just paying too much attention to the transient and from resisting fighting the battles that we should be fighting.

When you pick up that sword and you start to fight, a power comes to you. When you shy back from it, that's when all the little doubts, the insecurities, the terrible deadness of the human condition surrounds you. You can absolutely convince yourself intellectually that you're doing the right thing by avoiding those things that you know you should do, by doing those things that you know you should avoid. The mind is wonderful; you can rationalize anything, but you know.

Sri Krishna's message is eternal—fight. Fight. Everyone is afraid when they face an opponent, so use the fear to make you a better fighter. You'll use that fear to pump that adrenaline. You're so afraid that that opponent may destroy you, that you must destroy them.

It's only illusions that destroy us. It's illusions that convince us that we can't. It's the illusions of the transient that tell us that all of this matters. Mental control is the way out. Strength, balance, a kind heart and a steadfast purpose, a wonderful sense of humor and the correct focus of the will—this is how it's done, this is how you go from the transient to the eternal.

It doesn't happen with good wishes. It doesn't happen because you're a nice person. It doesn't happen because everyone likes you. That means nothing. What occurs occurs because of you. Not someone you know or someone you are married to or someone you are friends with, it's irrelevant. You work it out. No one affects your attention field but you.

If there are forces, powers, people, influences that you focused on that are unimportant, or even that hinder your journey, that tell you that it isn't important, [then] you have to cast them off with all the power you have, and move forward. And if you keep moving forward and you don't open up, they'll leave you alone. They'll go bother somebody else. When they see they can't get to you, they leave you alone. For a while they hang around because they figure if you went for it before you may go for it again, but then, when they see that you won't, then they have to leave. Then focus on those things which matter.

What matters most is to meditate. Then you have to make your physical body very strong to deal with life, the world, and to deal with the energies that we experience as we go into the light. It's very demanding. It's very hard on the body going into the light. You have to be strong. Then we have our work, our careers. Those are our battles.

Then we have our associations to support. We must assume responsibility for the little things that are in each of our lives and do them impeccably. And if you do that, whether anyone notices or not doesn't matter. Infinity is aware, meaning your consciousness will reflect how you've handled your life. Humility simply means that you do a great job at everything and it isn't really a big deal. You do your best. But you meditate and you focus all of your efforts on moving from the transient to the eternal.

In other words, running off to the ashram and meditating doesn't create enlightenment. Talking to gurus and teachers for hours on end doesn't create enlightenment. What creates enlightenment is a person of steadfast purpose who meditates for several hours a day, who has a teacher and who has a sense of respect for their teacher—respect which is shown by the fact that they listen to what they say and follow their recommendations in the practice of yoga. And then they lead a relatively quiet life, just going about the average tasks that are whatever our life gives us. And you do them well, with a sense of serenity, a sense of stillness, a sense of balance, with a kind of a wry sense of humor, knowing that whatever we accomplish is going to be washed away, whatever castles we build down on the sand today at the beach are going to be washed away. But we know that, and that's fine.

What's happening is that we go through those tasks doing them perfectly, even though they're all going to be washed away—it's creating a strength and solidification of our mental processes. So that at the moment of death we can focus on the clear light with the same power that has molded each activity in our life—cleaning the house well, driving the car well, doing our career well, doing our meditation well, controlling our emotions, not getting angry, not getting frustrated, not allowing depression to overcome us. Instead being optimistic and enthusiastic even in the most difficult circumstances because we know that everything leads to the light—remembering that.

By handling everything well, we're developing a hidden power, and as that power increases it stays with us. So every year you file a tax form. You work. And at the end of the year, the work is done. The tax form reflects how we did economically. You could say, "Well, why keep working? I mean all I do is do this, and then it's reflected in the tax form, but at the end of my life I've just worked and I have nothing to show for it. And if I die, even if I have something to show for it, it doesn't go with me." Wrong. If you've worked well and worked hard, then you have disciplined your mind and body. And in the doing of that you've perfected yourself, and that strength stays with you and it leaves the body with you.

People think that—they have funny ideas—they think that, "Well gosh, to be enlightened, to be in these wonderful altered states of consciousness, I have to leave everything and just kind of sit around in rooms with people who are dressed in fancy ochre robes and incense is burning and sitar music is on in the background and we have philosophical conversations." In most cases, that won't do a thing to strengthen your mind. That isn't yoga. That's Hollywood movies.

Yoga means we accept responsibility for the tasks in our life, and we know that being a king, being an enlightened teacher, being someone who sweeps the streets, we know that nothing is a greater yoga than anything else. Whatever we are supposed to have karmically, life gives us.

The question is, how do we handle it? It is in the handling of whatever our tasks are that we achieve greatness inwardly, that we achieve power. You don't need a special task. Every task is special. We always want something glossy. We expect that it has to be different. But what can be different? There only is what there is, in the physical. So it really doesn't matter what the job is, it really doesn't matter which house it is, karma will bring us to whatever one is right, at whatever moment we are in. The issue is, do we handle it?

We may have a tiny little room that we rent, and if we keep it clean and it's impeccable, then we gain a power from that. If we have a giant mansion and we don't keep it as well as that room, then our yoga isn't good and our attention field will be very poor and we won't have power, and we'll be totally hooked into the transient. If President Bush does a lousy job, then he'll lose power. If the guy at McDonald's who's selling burgers does a great job, then he'll be much more powerful than President Bush. It isn't the job that makes us powerful. It's how we handle it.

Naturally, a powerful person should have a job that is on the level of their attention field. Otherwise they won't develop. If you're lifting ten-pound weights but you can easily lift a hundred pounds, your muscles aren't going to get stronger, they're going to get weaker. So we have to take on a task that is equal to our strength and a task that is actually a little more difficult because by lifting weights that are a little heavier than we actually can, we get stronger. And once that's not difficult to do, we have to upgrade the task.

So yes, everything is transient, but no, we gain a strength in each lifetime. And that strength does go with us. So there is no task that's in vain; there is no effort that's lost. And just to not do things well because we think it doesn't matter, because we have some etheric notion of self-discovery and since all this is transient, what difference does it make, let's just meditate—you can do that. You can just meditate. And if you can for 14 or 16 hours a day sit with the mind in a perfect field of attention with total concentration and no thought, then that's the same thing as sweeping a room perfectly, as programming a computer perfectly.

Sure, it's the same thing; you're just using the mind through focus to accomplish the same end. But it's not more powerful than anything else.

Whatever will cause your attention to articulately develop and to learn control is the same. Then you just turn it to the light. The person who's in the Zen monastery, who's doing a kind of poor job at meditating and a half-ass job cleaning the gardens—but he's got the right robes on and he's in aesthetically what we think is the right place to do self-discovery, and he's hanging around with teachers but he may not be absorbing or understanding truly on a deep level what they're saying—is not doing very good yoga. The person in the business suit who works on Wall Street, who does their work perfectly, is probably evolving a lot faster, if they also meditate.

The background is unimportant. It doesn't do a thing. As a matter of fact, it's dangerous. Because when you're in a monastery the problem is you can think simply by the fact that you're there, and by the fact that everyone is talking about the dharma and that's what everyone does, you can think that somehow that automatically gives you a passport to eternity. Wrong. So you don't work as hard. You sit back. You figure, "I'm already on the train, all I have to do is get on the train and I'm there; eventually I'll arrive." Not true.

It is better to be, I think, off in a worldly situation accepting the daily tasks of what we would call human life and doing well with them and then to have a teacher, to have a guru, to have a master, a Zen master, whatever it is, a Buddhist monk—to have someone whom you go to and see regularly and to follow their instructions and then to lead a daily life out in the world—I think that's better. I've taught in monasteries and I've taught outside of them. I think you can make a lot faster progress outside of the monastery. That's my opinion—if you have a teacher and you see the teacher as often as you need to and you practice meditation. While the monastery does, to a certain extent, provide a refuge from the lower human aura, and since there's a tremendous support network, it does certainly, to an extent, allow us to interface with, on a fairly regular basis, higher ideas and ideals—and that's supportive. But the danger is great.

That [the monastery] works well for a person who is a real go-getter, who will not let that environment fool them. But I have observed that more people than not, don't do well in monasteries. The mere fact that they're there, and they have the robe, and because they get up in the morning and meditate from four till eight, and because they work all day and then meditate again in the evening—going through those motions they think is enough. But what's really happening when they're sitting meditating and how well are they working? They may just be sitting there kind of spacing out because they figure they're on the train and that's all they need.

So I think sometimes it's better to be in a difficult situation and you can tell, since the environment is abrasive, it inspires you to do better. If you're in a monastery and everything is great, why try? If you're living out in the world dealing with abrasive things, it reminds you that this is reality and this is why you're meditating and this is why you're going beyond the transient. It inspires you. Because if the person who meditates in the ashram or lives in the monastery is fooled by it, then at the end of the incarnation when they die, yes, they've had a pleasant environment, but no, they haven't worked hard. Then the environment is removed and they're thrown into the *bardo*. The bardo is not sympathetic.

The state between birth and death is not sympathetic. It's strictly—it's a flow system. Whatever your conscious level, automatically, that's how you will reincarnate. So maybe it's better sometimes not to be in a monastery. To have a teacher, to meditate, to follow the instructions—and maybe it's good sometimes to be in painful surroundings because they remind us that that is how life is until we establish ourselves fully in the light. Maybe that's a better motivator. Because most of the monasteries I've visited are slack. Occasionally you'll have someone who's just a go-getter and they use the environment. But more than half don't. They abuse the environment; they're lulled into a false sense of security.

I think it's better—you know when you're in the world where you are. You know how much pain there is. You can tell how established you are in the light. And simply to remove yourself from the things you desire or the things that you find difficult to deal with is no answer. What you need to learn to do is walk among the things that you desire and your aversions, the things that you fear, and be unaffected. That's Buddhism. That means that the reason you're unaffected is because you're so established in the light that you don't give a fuck.

I mean, if you're eating a fantastic food and it's in your mouth, and somebody walks by with a mediocre food, you don't go "Whoa, I want one of those." Because you're so absorbed in the ice cream cone from Ben and Jerry's that you could care less about a cheese waffle.

So the way that you go above the transient, the way you go above pleasure and pain is through ecstasy. When your ecstasy is great, who cares about—you know, who's afraid? When you're established in the light and you see that everything is transient, there's nothing to fear. You see that, so things don't bother you.

You establish yourself in the light through meditation and through work and through listening to the instructions—meaning, following them—of a teacher who is established far more in the light than you are. Obviously, they know how to get as established in the light as they've gotten to. And they can pass that on to you. Then you have to do it, and it will happen to you.

It's good to have companions. It's good to have people who also meditate who are friends. It's good to have contact. It's helpful. When you associate socially with other people who are headed into the light, it's definitely inspiring; it doesn't necessarily make you lax. It's like joining a running club where everybody runs together. You may run more miles because you are spending some time with some good runners. But I think to be in a monastery or an ashram is not always the answer—because we don't fight, we kick back. We don't listen to Sri Krishna.

CHAPTER TWENTY

BUDDHIST ENLIGHTENMENT

Bodhidharma, it is said, brought Buddhism from India to China. He introduced it to China, and it's interesting because Buddhism, which started in India, really kind of died out there. The Buddha lived in India, gave his sermons in India and never left India, and Buddhism first flourished there. But its real growth occurred in China, and then, of course, later in Japan, Thailand, Burma, places like that. Gradually it spread around the world. But it's interesting that it's very much transplanted. A lot of attention is paid to Bodhidharma because he brought Buddhism [to China]. He was not the only one—there are historical records of Buddhism really existing there prior to that time, but he brought the essence. It was considered that he was the first one who perhaps was enlightened, who brought the real essence, not just the teachings, but he was a teacher.

Buddhism has existed forever, just like we have. And occasionally it's codified; it's put together into a system by someone who likes to codify it and put it together in a system. But it's really just a structural understanding of how things work in the universe, inside your mind. The idea really—if I can skip the language that they've translated from and just use my own, which I prefer—instead of getting into Noble Truths and all these ideas, I prefer to play with my own deck of cards and not somebody else's—cards I've designed myself.

The essence of Buddhism is simply that the mind is forever. And that there are endless states of mind. And that we are always experiencing different states of mind in one form or another, in one body or another, in one life or another, forever. And that there are states of mind that are painful and unpleasant, there are states of mind that are wonderful and ecstatic. But there are only endless states of mind—viewpoints, plateaus of seeing life.

Most people exist in very clouded states of mind. That is to say, their minds are very clouded. It's sort of like when you're underwater in a big swimming pool and you open your eyes, and you can't see very far and everything you see is distorted. That's how most people perceive reality. They're under a great deal of water and everything is very distorted. They assume that is what life is, that what they perceive is real. But of course, there are states of mind that are not clouded at all, that are perfect, immaculate, vacuous and clear. Void of illusions. Void of things that make those states of mind cloudy and make them antithetical to reality, to the clear seeing of reality.

The chances are you live in a state of mind that's pretty cloudy. You may not see that or realize that because you're used to it. You assume that the way you see things is the way they are. As a matter of fact, we can't imagine, or it's very difficult to imagine, that anything could be other than the way that we perceive it to be. That's the illusory nature of any state of mind. We assume that what we see is what everybody else sees. But that's not true at all.

I can look through lots of different states of minds. I can look at other people's states of minds and look through them, just like picking up a person's glasses and looking through them. I can pick up five or six different pairs and look through them, and everything looks different. If the prescription is different, life looks different through each pair of glasses—different distortions are apparent. Glasses distort the way things look, unless of course your vision is already incorrect, in which case the prescription corrects it. And then you see clearly. But if you have clear vision, were you to look through someone's glasses, it would distort everything.

It's interesting looking through different people's minds. I do that sometimes. And I see various types of distortion. Distortion is real; distortion is part of the cosmos. But the problem with distortion is that when we see things in a distorted way, we tend to trip and fall and we make mistakes. If our vision isn't very clear, something may take place that we don't see—maybe an opportunity that we don't grasp. Things may not be at all as confusing as they appear to be in a distorted state of mind. Maybe things are very simple. Maybe life is very simple, and all the hubbub and noise that everyone makes is simply because they're in very distorted states of mind.

Maybe life isn't complicated. Suppose it's very simple. But the reason it appears complicated to you is because you're in a very distorted state of mind. That's the basic premise of Buddhism—that you're in a very distorted state of mind. Everything you see looks real to you; you can't imagine it being any other way, but you are so far removed from clear seeing that it's impossible to estimate the distance.

We say enlightenment is clear seeing. When you're enlightened, you have a clear view. A clear view implies the absence of thought or impressions in the mind. When you're not thinking; when you're not seeing things through emotions, through desires, through aversions, through fears; when your vision isn't distorted by egotism and vanity, by just all the petty viewpoints that the mind can embrace; when you just see things as they are, we say that's enlightenment. Not simply seeing physical objects as they are—that's just physical vision—we're talking about inner vision and using physical vision as a symbolic reference to understand inner seeing. Inner seeing has nothing to do with physical vision—it's the perception of life directly. And without thought, without illusions, in perfect states of mind, we exist in a kind of paradise.

Paradise is not the place you go when you die. Paradise is when your mind is in a perfect state. There's no heaven that you go to. There are different worlds that we incarnate in forever, but if you're in a pleasant world in a horrible state of mind, it won't make any difference, everything will appear horrible to you. If you're in, I guess, what one might call a horrible world, if you're in a perfect state of mind, everything will appear perfect to you.

Buddhism is about bringing your mind into a very clear state and from there going to a state that's more clear and so on until you become enlightened. And that's done with a great deal of self-effort. We have to remove all the toxins, all the pollutants from our mind. The mind is originally clear. When you scrape all the barnacles off and get down to the reality of your mind, it's clear. We all have perfect minds. So it's not as if we have to go get something. It's not as if we don't have the right vehicle. But the problem is it's covered over with a lot of barnacles, with silt, with obscurations.

When the mind is perfectly clear, it's like a mirror—it reflects everything. A perfectly clear mirror reflects everything. And since there's no self, when you look in the mirror you just see forever, you don't see a person. The sense of self is one of the obscurations that prevents us from clear seeing—the idea that there is a self, or that we're anyone in particular. To have the illusion of selfhood simply means that when you look in the mirror, you see somebody. When you no longer see anyone, but instead you see life in all of its perfection, then your seeing is clear.

To go within doesn't mean to become enraptured with who you are—or to become enraptured with ideas of who you are. When we talk about going within in meditation, we mean to completely disassociate the consciousness principle of awareness, which is what we are, from any idea of a particularized self. If you stop thinking, if there's no thought in the mind, if the mind is absolutely clear and calm, then there will be no sense of self. The self washes away. The longer we can stay in the thoughtless state, the more the obscurations are washed away, because when we stop thought, a tremendous amount of energy is released and that energy purifies the mind. We also purify the mind through focusing on higher and brighter states of mind when we talk about, think about, engage in activities that have to do with the world of enlightenment. Any action in that direction, any focus in that direction brings us into touch with the aura of enlightenment. The aura of enlightenment is endless light.

We can't say what enlightenment is, we can't say what it isn't, because these are words and words have nothing to do with reality. Words are a human way of trying to describe things. But they're much more of an interference than they are a help in the world of enlightenment. All the *sutras* in the world are useless. All the lectures of all the teachers don't really mean anything, they're only words—they point in a direction, that's their only use. And if they help you in that sense, they're fine. It isn't the words, it's the power behind them that matters. And if the words are spoken by someone who's powerful, if they're spoken by someone who's enlightened, then it isn't the words that matter—they could say anything. It's the aura, the energy field of enlightenment that one feels, comes to know, focuses on and eventually, one day, becomes.

To become enlightened is really quite simple. You have to purify the mind completely; there's no other way. It's impossible otherwise. It's only with complete purification. You have to burn away, with the fire of transmutive energy, anything that's cloudy, any states of mind that are unenlightened. And when they're all gone, there's only enlightenment left. When there's no self, there's enlightenment. Self implies not just a sense of personality, but any state of mind that's unenlightened, that is not enlightenment, that you would view reality through. When you view reality through any state of mind that's not enlightened, you perceive yourself as having a particularized being, which is really a self-reflection of that state of mind. The state of mind reflects itself; it seems to have its own being-ness. When we burn it away, if we burn everything away, at the end of all the burning, there is only enlightenment, and then there are dreams. Dreams. The dreams of eternity.

The dreams of eternity are the states of mind. When we wake up from the dreams there's only enlightenment. There never could be anything else. Humankind has no idea what existence is, at this stage. They're all dreaming, they're all asleep. Occasionally someone awakens from the dream a little bit and tries to awaken the other sleepers—with not much success because it's not their time yet. Once in a great while a fully awakened one is here, observes everybody sleeping and leaves, quietly.

There's only enlightenment. Anything else is a dream. The dreams of the self are manifold and endless and they exist in all the myriad worlds and conditions that appear to have solidity in dreams. When you're dreaming at night, something seems very real. Some terrible thing's happening, some wonderful thing's happening, some nonsensical or boring thing is happening that seems completely real. Completely. You're convinced that it's all taking place, but when you wake up the dream is gone and so is all that apparent solidity, which seemed so real at the time. It's gone.

All the lives we ever lead are only dreams—these waking moments, that look so solid to you when you consider yourself awake, are just dreams. And they'll pass, as they always do. Yesterday has passed; it's gone. You can't find it. It appeared very solid at the moment of its existence. But now it's gone. This day will pass; it'll be gone. Just dreams.

We dream forever unless we awaken. We move from one dream to another—some beautiful, some we're the hero or the heroine, some horrible, some nonsensical, some boring. And then there's enlightenment. To become enlightened we have to purify the mind, we have to gradually move step by step through a series of dreams, and the dreams gradually become less tangible. And we do it by focusing our attention completely, on things that are pure, on states of mind that are pure.

If you want to get someplace, you have to look and see where it is you want to go. And then you keep that viewpoint. And you proceed in that direction and you get there. It's just a question of knowing where you want to go and finding the right direction and then checking once in a while to make sure that you're still on the way. If you keep traveling, you'll get there; it's really not very complicated. And the experiences that we have, we call the journey. And where the journey takes place at any given moment, we call the path.

If you want to become enlightened, you've got to get all the bullshit out of your life. You have to clear up your mind completely. You have to unhook from anything that's impure, and focus only on things that are completely pure and perfect, all the time. And we do it a little at the beginning and then more and then more, and then eventually it consumes us. Literally. Until there's no self, there's only light.

Chapter Twenty-One

THE PATH OF NEGATION

The path of negation is the path of understanding. The path of affirmation, which is the first portion of the self-discovery path, is a path in which we don't seek to understand, we seek to escape. We want to escape the pain of life, the pain of our minds, the pain of our bodies, the pain of the world. We don't really want to ask a lot of questions; we just want to know a way out—and the way out is through avoidance. We don't eat meat, we don't have sex, we don't deal with money, we don't deal with things that we know have caused us pain. The great teachers explain why these things cause us pain—attachment, desire, having a self, you know, all the different things. But—we just escape. We don't really care. You go to the doctor and you hurt. You're not really interested in knowing how the medicine works, you just want it to.

When people seek the spiritual path—which is the path of affirmation, the exoteric path, the first path we walk on, the first part of the path—it's because they're in pain and they want to get away from the pain. So we have a series of prescriptions that we ask them to follow, which causes them to regulate their lives, to separate themselves from the things that cause them pain. The things that cause pain are desire, attachment, egotism, vanity—all the things that religious people tend to avoid.

Now, the avoidance of that which causes you pain does not produce enlightenment. It produces avoidance. The avoidance may lessen or tranquilize the pain, but it will not produce enlightenment. Knowledge and understanding produce enlightenment. Religion is the avoidance of pain and suffering, I mean symbolically, in the hope for a better afterlife, meaning one less painful than the one we're in. So if I don't do this and I don't do that and

I do this and I do that, my next life, be it in heaven or another incarnation, will be better than this. In other words, it's all predicated on the avoidance of pain.

But the path of negation, which is the esoteric or more advanced part of the enlightenment process, is the path of understanding. It's the path of knowledge. Knowledge has nothing to do with avoidance or attraction. In our earlier understandings of life, we're bound by attraction, desire. We go after what we desire, and if we don't get it we're frustrated and unhappy. If we do get it, we're happy, maybe, for a short period of time—till the pleasure ends, till another desire comes and torments us. When it's fulfilled, our expectations were greater and we're frustrated because what we thought we would experience when this desire was fulfilled didn't come up to what we thought, and we're frustrated by that.

Human life is painful because of desire. We desire things and we chase after them. We're afraid of things and we run away from them. And somewhere between the desire and the aversion we exist as a self. The self can be measured by what it avoids and what it seeks and by its sense of history—past remembrances. That makes a self.

Religion offers to people a way to get away from pain. You know you're in pain; that's why you go. You go seeking something, an antidote to pain. You've tried this, you've tried that; it hasn't worked. So you go to religion. What the religions offer you is—it works! Turn your attention away from the sensorial so much, develop the virtues, avoid injuring others, avoid hate, essentially—self-control, compassion, love, understanding—we all know what religion symbolizes. Oh, there are fanatical, crazy religions that tell you to kill people who aren't in your religion. That's not a religion. That's a political philosophy. But a real religion is something that leads us above pain. By following a number of different practices that are always the same—they may be rearranged differently in a particular religion or given different names—but it's always the same, it's structural, it's what reduces pain, the pain that we experience in being, in our being-ness which can't be ended by death since death is just a doorway to another condition that we experience.

When we follow the guidelines of religion, we find that our lives are better; we're happier. Self-control works. Patience works. Kindness works. Love works. All of these things help. And when we lose them, we lose the path and our lives are miserable. When we're selfish, vindictive, angry, when we don't care more for others than we care for ourselves, life is terrible. So we follow the path of affirmation and we find it's better. Life is better. It's beautiful to love. To be loved is irrelevant. But when you love someone, you experience that emotion. It's a beautiful emotion. It has its limitations, but it sure beats hate. To assist someone, to not always have to have everything, to give somebody else the bigger piece of cake—when we do it, we feel better. Practice it, you'll find out.

The religious values are totally important, and as we practice them, to begin with, our lives are better. Then of course, after many incarnations of practicing them, we go into the monastic phase where we just want to really refine the practice. It's worked thus far, and our karmas lead us to a monastery. In the monastery we take a vow of chastity, we take a vow of poverty and we devote our lives completely to the religious condition—more completely. Who knows where our minds are, but outwardly we have accepted certain conditions physically.

Now, just because you don't have sex and because you don't have money doesn't mean that your mind is pure—but you're doing those things in an attempt to purify the mind. Just because someone puts on an ochre robe or a priest's robe means nothing. That's just an outfit, that's cloth. It symbolizes a state they hope to reach. It symbolizes a penitent, basically, someone who's trying to purify themselves through austere religious practices.

But once you've done that or taken that as far as it goes, you will not become enlightened. You will have great self-control. But you will not be enlightened. I mean, go to a monastery and see who's around. There are people who perhaps have self-control, more than most people do, they may be happier, their minds may be a little more still, they meditate; they pray, but they're not enlightened. To become enlightened you have to go much further. You have to deal with the conditions that have arisen in the practice of religion. Sri Ramakrishna used to say, you have a thorn in your foot and you take the second thorn and you get the first one out, and then you throw them both away. You don't keep the second thorn.

Religion is something that eliminates the initial pain that we experience when we're out of control, when we're completely bound by the senses and by our angers and lusts, our petty jealousies and our hates. But then religion, which removes the initial pain, has to be thrown away also. That's the second thorn that gets out the first thorn, when we move into the world of enlightenment and *samadhi,* which is the esoteric, or what we call the path of negation. Samadhi is the path of negation. Not negation in the way that we think of positive and negative. It's just a word that I'm using to try and express a direction. The word itself has no value. No word does, other than expressing a direction.

So then, the path of negation, or what we call *tantra,* leads us beyond self-control, beyond poverty, beyond sexual abstinence, beyond these types of purifications. In the path of negation, principally we're working with what we call power. We avoid power and we learn humility and purity in the beginning.

Someone asked me not long ago, "Gee, in the 1980s and 70s you used to talk a lot about humility and purity and you used to teach those things. Will you teach them again?" And I said it's not likely, because I was working with a group of students who were in the beginning phases of self-discovery. Most of my students now, we've gone through that phase, we've done that. We were doing a lot of basic work, structural work, exoteric work. But now I'm teaching about power because this is more advanced, now that they've gone through those rungs of the ladder.

Anyone who comes and studies with me now, since I really don't teach about those things, has to have learned those things in another life or someplace else. I don't teach the basics anymore. I mean, obviously I teach the basics of meditation and things like that. But the topics are completely esoteric now. I only teach tantra because it's that part of the incarnation where the majority of my students are ready for that. Anyone else who comes in has to pick up the basics someplace else. I don't do that anymore because it's not necessary. My students require a more advanced education now.

The advanced education in tantra obviously has to do with the entrance into samadhi, the negation of the self. That's what the path of negation means—not the negation of life, but the negation of limited states of mind, the negation of anything that is not enlightenment, which is the self. The two principal *samskaras,* perhaps three that have to be overcome—there are more—have to do with sex, money and power because in all those countless incarnations that one goes through in the religious practice, the avoidance factor for money and sex and power is tremendous, and we eventually sort of brand those things as evil. Well, they're not. But we say they are because we're so addicted to them we have to think of them that way for a while.

It's like when you're breaking up with somebody in a relationship, and maybe they're not really so bad but you have to think they are for a while, just because you won't let go of them and you have to do that now, so for a while you just think of them in a worse light than they really are. You really hate them, maybe for a little while. You need to do that to break away because if you don't break away, something very unhealthy is going to happen. Then once you break away, you can let go of it—well, they're really not so bad, you know. But for a while we have to use that. In other words, it's kind of a martial arts move, where we have to use a certain emotion for a while to get away from something. But then we can think of somebody in a nice sense. We have to break our own attachment. It's not their attachment to us, it's our attachment to them.

Self-discovery is realistic. It's not built on ideas and philosophies. It's what works. Philosophies are nice if you like philosophies. But self-discovery is predicated on something that really brings you into enlightened states of mind.

So in *tantra,* in the path of negation, the primary education is exposing the student to the things that they've learned in past lives to avoid, and letting them gain knowledge about these things so that they can accept them as not good or bad. The advanced path is the path of knowledge, not avoidance, but knowledge. In the light of knowledge, all things are equal. All things are good if you will, because in a state of knowledge, that's how life is. Seen through enlightenment, all things are enlightenment. Seen through the eye of purity, all things are pure.

What the student has to do is pursue all their mental obscurations and reach equipoised states of perfect mind, or as perfect as they can get on any given day, and the next day get to one that's a little more perfect. Not a concept of pure or perfect, but perfection—in other words, the reality of the clear *dharma* state, the spotless state of *original mind,* which is inherent within all of us.

Mind itself is pure. The only time it doesn't seem pure is when you're in a state of consciousness that is differentiated, that is not pure. Again, the lack of purity does not imply evil. There is no such thing as corruption. That's just how you see things from a kind of strange state of mind, and if you're in a state of mind that sees things that way, that is how things appear.

I used to have a girlfriend a long time ago, when I was in college. She taught me a few things. She was an artist, and we used to go out walking sometimes. We'd be walking along and she'd be looking at the ground at all the trash people would drop. In my mind I saw all this junk, and I'd say, "Ooh, that's gross. God, people are trashing the environment." You know, it was the 60s, right? How horrible, all this garbage. And she said, "Wait a minute, look at the colors down there. Look at the colors of the M&M box or the—", whatever it was. "Look at the colors," she said, "there's a whole world of colors, there's an art here that's present."

I started to look at it that way, and I just said, "My God! I wasn't seeing it." In other words, I had such a defined way of automatically labeling things that were on the ground—that this was wrong and it was ugly. Then I looked at it from her point of view, and she was absolutely correct in that state of mind. She was seeing art. She was moving through worlds of art and they were moving through her. It was a much more interesting way to look at things because the way I was seeing things was very unpleasant. I was walking around saying, "Oh this is awful, oh, look at this, oh look at that," and it made me unhappy. And the way she was seeing things was, "Look there's no corruption here, there's art." That's tantra. She was tantric, and that's tantra.

In tantra, we see that life is art. But to bring yourself into those states of mind requires power. It's very intricate; there's no way that I can explain to you how this is done. There are no words to explain how you break into the advanced mental states, how you negate—if you will—the self. Not that it's exactly a negation, that's just another word. I can't explain it to you. It's something that I teach; it's something that I live in all the time—that I am. But I can't explain it. Words don't do it.

What we do in tantra is, we go do things. We do things. Words are deceptive. You think you understand something because it's explained to you and now you are under no obligation to do anything because you understand it. That's not what I mean by the path of knowledge. The path of knowledge has nothing to do with words. The path of knowledge means that you have brought your mind into its original pure state, which is the original pure state of the universe.

Original is not time-structured, by the way. When I say "original," that doesn't mean a long time ago. Original occurs at every given moment. Original is a way of trying to explain something; it's a term that we use in Buddhism to suggest that everything is pure. It doesn't mean that things were originally this way and we can't get back to it. It has nothing to do with time. The English translation has a time sense to it.

We are pure. That's all there is, is purity. But you don't see it that way because you're in obscure states of mind. So in the teaching of tantra, what I do is direct people to engage in specific practices, and when they do those things they negate their samskaras and the self goes away because the self that a person has on the esoteric path is propped up by their avoidances, just as the self that a person has before they reach the esoteric path, before they start religion. In other words, in the beginning the self is created by attraction; some aversion, obviously, through fears. That creates a self. That self causes pain, frustration, whatever—the absence of enlightenment. Then, in the practice of the exoteric path we gradually, as we work through it, overcome—we drop the old self. Very often on a spiritual path, they even give you a new name.

Baptism suggests that you're leaving the old life and entering the new. A confirmation name, a Buddhist name, a Hindu name that the teacher gives you means you are on the path and your old life is gone. Forget about it, don't think about it, it's gone. You are new. You are reborn. You are reborn on the exoteric path. But now on the exoteric path you will develop history and you will develop a new self. A happier brighter self, but it still stops enlightenment. After many incarnations of being on the exoteric path, this self becomes as hard, as predicated and as obscure, even though not as painful, as the self you had before the religion. In other words, the good self blocks you.

So then, in the advanced practice, you take a person and you have them go do the things that are their opposites. But they do them in a way that they couldn't do them back at the beginning before they followed any path at all. They used to just go out and get rich but they were bound by it, you see. Now they have to go out and become wealthy or whatever it might be. They have to do that—but with purity, as part of their yoga, not as an attraction. In doing all the things that they've learned to avoid over the incarnations in religion—which has created this new religious, better, prototype self, but which ultimately blocks enlightenment—now they have to go do those things which they think they shouldn't do. It's just intrinsic in the multi-life memory: "I shouldn't be rich. I shouldn't do this. I shouldn't have power," because you know it corrupts, it brings you into very painful states of mind.

So then, the adept, the student, has to go do those things. But they're not doing them like they were all the way back, you see. Because in the doing of them, they erase the current self. In other words, what forges the self is attraction and aversion. Your aversion to the things that used to cause you pain, which has created this happier new self, block you. So you have to now go out and go do the things that you don't want to do. But you have to do them in a way that you obviously couldn't do them in the beginning, because that's why you got away from them.

In the beginning, wealth was causing you pain, your attachment to it, because it created a self that was ugly. Now that you've created a self that's much nicer, through lives of poverty and chastity, great. But that self also blocks you. Now we have to go become wealthy again because you have to overcome your attachment to poverty that was created, and your attachment to the new, happier self. We're not going to go back to the original self that was painful; we're going to move on to no self.

THE PATH OF NEGATION 247

So we give up things for a time, not because they matter but so we can change selves. We develop a kind of a caretaker personality, which is a nicer self for a while, on the road to no self. But then we have to go back when we're strong enough, when our yoga's tight enough, when our power's up, if we really want to break through into higher levels of attention. And we have to go do all the things that we've learned to avoid without being affected by them. So we turn them all to a higher esoteric principle. We go become rich as part of yoga. We use that money only for our own life support and for doing good works, you see? In other words, we put a twist on it, naturally. If we get power, we will only use it in a constructive way, not in a destructive way, per se.

In other words, we learn to handle these things because there's no self. If there's no self, there's no lack of purity, therefore we can't use things in an impure way. Power and money, sex, all of these things are no problem in the hand of innocence, are they? In the absence of self, how can these things be considered obscurations or defilements since they are enlightenment, too. They are void in their nature and in their substance.

All things are void. So how possibly could there be any obscurations, since everything is void, when you're void itself? There's only the void. In the void, there's only the shining, perfect clear light of reality; there's no obscuration. To assume that wealth or sexuality or the usage of power, any of these things, are not void in nature, gives them a reality that they don't actually have. They're void. In the experience of their voidness, of their vacuity, the self, the temporal self, the transient caretaker, somewhat happier self that we've evolved on the exoteric path, vanishes. It dissolves in the clear light of reality, and there's only the clear light of reality.

The final battles are the samskaras of good karma. They prevent samadhi. But you can't just reach a mental understanding where you say, "Oh good, I understood what you've said, I've got it." Nothing will happen; you won't go into samadhi. You have to go do these things but with complete detachment. Naturally, for a religious person, the avoidance is intensive. They just don't want to go do these things; they are so hung up on good karma and on method from so many lifetimes that there's a terrific avoidance. But if they keep the avoidance, they will not become enlightened. They will stay in whatever mental states they're in.

So the path of negation, tantra, has to do with silencing the self that has arisen, in a temporary sense, the wave that has arisen out of the ocean from good karma. The good karma of all those past lives of religious practice has brought you to the path of negation, but you are still attached to it and not necessarily consciously. What you have to do is go and do the things that keep that self empowered, that keep it manifest. You have to go and do the things it doesn't want, which have become reflexive.

In other words, a true martial artist cannot be reflexive because if you're reflexive, then someone else can calculate your reflexes and beat you. Reflexes are fine in the beginning of martial arts when we have no self-control and we can beat an opponent because our reflexes are better than theirs, and faster. We don't think. If you take the time to think in a fight, you lose; a great martial artist can't be reflexive. They've gone through that phase and now they operate purely through voidness/vacuity—no one can predict the move. Because you know, if you've trained in the reflexive schools yourselves, if you feint, if you make a move, you know what the reflex is going to be. Therefore, when they make that [move], you do the feint; they kick, they punch, whatever it is—you know what they're going to do so while they're making that motion, [so] you real quick move the other leg out from underneath them and crunch them. You can lead them into a reflexive move and defeat them, which is what you do in intermediate martial arts.

But in advanced martial arts, you've moved beyond that. You're void. There's no sense of what the combat will be. You don't know what you're going to do, nor are you going to be reflexive. You will perceive the voidness in your opponent and they will lose. You have to go beyond these reflexes that you develop. And anybody who just stays with their reflexes will lose against someone who's gone beyond that. You see? The principle is in all things.

So to go beyond karma you have to end the structure of self. Even a good self will create another good self in the next life and another one, and that good self will never be enlightened. You'll be bound, life after life, by good karma, which is better I suppose than being bound by bad karma, which would imply more pain. That's what we mean by good and bad. So you must—if you find a tantric master, he has you go and do all the things you hate to do. You won't know why you hate them, but it'll just—you don't want to do them. The things that he's having you do are things that just seem totally contrary to you, to anything spiritual. Well, of course they are because all your ideas of what is spiritual are completely based around the path of affirmation, which is where you've been for a long time and that's what caused you to get to where you are to meet the tantric master.

So the tantric master now will say, "OK, good." The things they'll tell you, you don't want to do. You don't even know why you don't want to do them. You don't know why it arouses such hate, anger. It's because the self is so stuck, it's so defined. And it's got to go. Just as the other self went a long time ago before your current memory. Many lives ago you had another type of self that you had for countless lives and you eradicated it. You brought a new tenant in. This tenant is much nicer, which gives you some thought about what the other one must have been like! (Audience laughs.) The other one must have been a reeeal baaad dude, right? You look at this one and you can tell how impure, how uncontrolled, how filled with—you know, whatever it is that this one is. So if this is the new improved model, if this is the one that's much more advanced than most of the people out there on the planet, it tells you what most people are in, which you know already. You know that already. You can see their auras. You can see the grayness and the deadness and you know you're way beyond that.

Then you wonder, well, what am I doing in practice, since I know what I'm like, I'm such a creep. But you aren't, in comparison to everyone else. You used to have one of those dead selves out there. You got rid of it. The reason you see yourself as a creep is because you have an appreciation of what perfection is, whereas no one else conceives of themselves in that way, since they don't even strive. They just are—they exist, like amoebas, globbing along, making little amoebas.

Obviously if you think that you are a vile slime, that means that you aspire to something higher. No, I mean that whole understanding can only come out of a sense of perfection, do you understand? It's because you have a sense of perfection, and you obviously want that, that you find something wrong with anything you consider to be imperfect. But most people don't have that sense at all. Everything's just fine the way it is. They don't realize that they're horrible, in other words, in a sense—that there's limitation. They don't know why they're in pain.

So then, you've created this new self over many lives of practice. But now this one has to go if you want the ecstasy, if you want the enlightenment. You're so attached to your ideas of practice. A tantric master always freaks everybody out, because he says, "Well, you know, let's go do it in the road," whatever it is. Let's do the opposite of whatever you think should be. It's only in the doing of that—you can't fake it, you've got to go do the practice. In the doing of the practice, in a pure state, for the purpose of greater purification and for the purpose of enlightenment, if you're doing it for that reason, then it frees you. If you're not doing it for that reason, it would just bind you further to a self.

There's nothing intrinsically wrong with anything. But if you want to get beyond self to enlightenment, there's a way. Tantra is the advanced way; it's the path of negation. The earlier way is the exoteric method of religion. Tantra is the advanced practice, the esoteric practice, in which we negate the evolved self that we've created through the earlier sections of the path.

Chapter Twenty-Two
TRANSIENCE

Nothing lasts forever, except forever. That's the good news. It's a good thing that nothing lasts forever because things would get terribly boring. Even now they tell us they can recycle plastic. Plastic, while it may last forever in a certain sense, can change forms at least, because otherwise it would be terrible if Tupperware lasted forever. I don't know, it would be tough!

Nothing lasts forever. Everything is transient. Sri Krishna refers, of course, to this world as a joyless, transient world. Obviously he's never been to Disneyland. Disneyland may be transient but it's lots of fun. But we all know what he means. He means that it's a little heavy here sometimes, inside our minds. It gets heavy sometimes, inside our minds. Everything is transient. By that we mean that we are transient. Not the objects of the world—that's apparent. But we're transient. As beings, the self that you now have does not last. Even if it could endure a whole lifetime, it ends at death and you will never be this person or this being again. That's the good news. Because otherwise it would get terribly boring, to just continually be who we've been—because we'd always see life and ourselves in about the same way.

How interesting it is when you're clairvoyant. Because you can look into people's minds and see how they see life, and you see that everybody sees life totally differently. They all think that everybody else sees life basically the way they do, but there's a different film being made in every mind. And of course, the star of the film is the mind, the personality, the self.

Everything is transient and it's a good thing, as I said. I celebrate the transient constantly. I don't find that sorrowful in any way. I don't see anything sorrowful about death. I don't see suffering as sorrowful; it's unpleasant, but it's not sorrowful. The only thing that creates sorrow is attachment to the transient, which is like betting on a horse that you know is going to lose—doesn't make a whole lot of sense. Since you know that everything is transient, it just makes absolutely no sense to be sorry about anything, even ourselves. Mostly ourselves. The good news is that we don't last. Thank heavens! Because to continue the drama of who you are is boring, ultimately. The universe is our friend because it kills us, and that's what friends are for. (Audience laughs.)

Now again, the universe gives us a new self, a new life. We get a new movie to make, we're on to another location, on with the show. Knowing this, we're kind of ahead of the game. You see, most people don't realize that everything is transient and they don't realize that they're going to be making another movie, so they cling to the movie they're in; they never want it to end, even if it's a terribly boring, old stodgy movie. They cling to it.

A famous actress died today. Do you know who died today? (Audience responds.) Who? Greta Garbo. And she is famous for saying? "I want to be alone." Yes, meaning get lost, don't bother me. And true to her statement, for the remaining years of her life she lived a very reclusive life, as many aging film stars do. Sometimes they do it because they're vain. I don't know if that was the case for her or not. But sometimes a film star is very good-looking, very handsome, very beautiful, and that's why they're a film star. And then they get old, and everybody doesn't age real gracefully, I guess. Except for Sean Connery. He's the only man I know who, the older he gets, the better looking he is. There's just no question about it, with or without the toupee.

But some film stars, as they get older, they don't look so beautiful. And since their whole life was built on their beauty and that was their power, then what they do with the money they make is they wall themselves off. They never see anybody except maybe another old, decrepit film star who's done the same thing. Meaning, they don't want anybody to see them. They're ashamed, they're embarrassed because they were once so beautiful, and now they're wrinkled and shrunken—the things that happen to the human body with age. And their identity—they were the femme fatale, he was the most handsome man—and now they're just old and they look like human bodies do when they get old. Old.

But they don't want the film to end. They still want to be that young, bright, vivacious, everybody turns their eye when they walk into the room—"Oh, there's the famous so-and-so." You see? So they hide themselves away because they're so embarrassed by the way they look. They want the film to go on. Even though it's ended, they're still sitting in the screening room, hoping that it might run again. But it's transient. Everything is transient. If their egos weren't quite so big, then they could feel perfectly good being who they are, but I guess it comes with the world of film—sometimes, not all the time. And then there's Sean Connery. He's figured out how to be immortal. Exactly.

So occultists know this and it places us ahead of the game. Therefore we don't get upset by things, or if we do, we don't mind because we know that that's just a part of ourselves, and that part is transient. Everything is transient. It gives you a tremendous freedom to understand this because you can just change your life, you can just go do things. Since you're going to die anyway, and you know that and it could happen at any given moment, why not go do whatever it is you're in the mood to do? Because you are going to die. And to postpone anything is ridiculous, if it's important to you. It's just an absurd way to live. You've just got to go do what you want to do, whatever it may be. Because you are going to die, and if you don't do it now, you may never do it.

Now, there's an argument that well, it really doesn't matter once you're dead. It really doesn't matter what you did or didn't do. Those people don't know about reincarnation. It does matter what you do. If the things you do have power, you can take that power with you; it goes with you into your next life. So if you have a boring, insipid, mouse-like life where you're just afraid to be or do anything, then you don't bring much with you into your next life. You don't bring much power. You get off to kind of a tough start. Whereas if you actualize your life and you live fully at every moment, then you bring the power from that type of life, you accrue an inner power that does go with you.

Money may not travel with you, possessions may not, but power, who you are, does. The personality comes and goes but the power, the energy field that's deeper, that is immortal, that is the part of us that exists forever—that travels. And it has fields around it if you could see them, auras that come from past lives. It's like a report card. It follows you. And while we do get a new slate in each life, the place, the location, and the way it starts off are from the last life.

Meditation is different. It has nothing to do with reincarnation. Meditation is when we go beyond incarnation, beyond all cycles, to immortality, to something that is not transient, to that which is eternal. When we meditate we stop our thought. When your thought stops, the mind is perfect. There is no transience. No thought, no transience. That's what is eternal—when there is no thought, no sense of self and no impressions. That's eternity—what you feel, that reality that you are. That's eternal. That's beyond transience. That's what we really are, of course. Yet, surprise—we get to have two bodies, a transient body and an eternal body. We forget about the eternal body when we're real caught up in the transient body, and things appear very frightening from the transient body's point of view because it knows it's going to die, it knows it's going to dissolve and it's afraid of that. But if we switch to the eternal body, if we bring up and wake up our eternal awareness, then there's nothing very frightening about being transient because we realize it's only a part of us that is transient.

We get rid of the old clothes and we get new clothes. But the body remains. We change from one lifetime to another. The body goes, the personality goes, but that which is us is forever. It's unchanging, meaning that which you experience when there's no thought in meditation. That's the eternal self. I don't know if it's a "self," but it's eternal. That's forever and we are that. That's what we are. We can't really say that we are the transient part. I mean for a short time, sure. For a little while I'm a body, I'm a mind, I'm a personality, I'm a fear, I'm a desire, I'm an anguish, I'm a love, I'm a hate, I'm a dispassion. Whatever it is that we're experiencing at any given moment, whoever is doing the experiencing at any given moment, well, that's who we are for a short time, as short as a moment or as short as a lifetime. But that's not really who we are. I mean we can't really just be who we are for a moment. That's more like a place we pass through; it's a location.

We're travelers, we're mental travelers. We're a mind in time and space. When we drive through an area, we don't say that we're the area. We're the one who drives through. So I don't really think we can say that we are who we experience at any given moment in any given lifetime, because we're just driving through. We're driving through moments. We're driving through bodies, through selves. It helps to know this. The only way you can know it, really, is to meditate. When you meditate you stop thought. When there's no thought, that's eternity. That's the eternal part. To conceptually know this is just another moment that you're driving through. You're driving through the moment when you knew this. Then you'll forget it, and then you'll experience the fear, the obsessions of a transient moment, mistaking it for reality. Whereas when you know that you're driving through, you're just passing through as the song says, then it doesn't matter so much. It matters for a moment, just like driving through any place matters for the moment that you're there. You're there. But the confusion of self is that we are—we mistake ourselves for where we are. We are not the body. We're not the personality. We're eternity, which is passing through all this, all these wonderful forms that we see that we call life. We're the formless. The formless.

If you're meditating, you're not experiencing the formless. If you're not the formless, in meditation, you're not meditating yet. You're practicing concentration and learning to meditate. But only when you experience the formless are you really meditating. And again, you can't experience the formless. That would imply that you, the transient part, is driving and for a moment you're experiencing the eternal part, and you're passing through it. Uh-uh. You're not meditating yet. You're learning how.

No, it's only when you, the eternal part, are eternal and that's all there is, that you're meditating. There's no thought, no sense of self. That's meditation. Up until then you're learning how. You can either meditate or you can't meditate. You know, you can't be a little bit pregnant. Right? So they say. You can't meditate a little bit. You either meditate or you don't. If you meditate, there's only eternity. Then [later] you're not meditating. Well, here we are in the transient again, experiencing a transient body, a transient world, a transient moment. And we forget about the eternal part. But the more we meditate, the less we forget about it. After a while, we have a kind of a dual awareness.

Enlightenment is a dual awareness where we're aware of the eternal as the eternal. We're aware of the transient as the transient, and something else that I couldn't describe to you in words—the void. There are no words. Words don't mean anything in the void—for the experiences that are beyond words, for the reality. Words are terrible traps. They're pretty, but they're terrible traps if we think that in any way they explain anything about reality. They just point us in lots of different directions simultaneously.

So then, when you practice meditation, know that you're not meditating until there's no thought, no sense of self and only eternity. Only eternity. Only eternity. And the more you try and make yourself stand out, the more you try and be noticed by others, that means the less adept you are in meditation. Because it just means that you're clinging to the transient self and trying to glorify it. Well, the only one who does that is someone who doesn't know anything about eternity, who really is mistaking the transient for the eternal.

The more you want to be noticed, that simply means the less you know about meditation. The people who know the most about meditation aren't noticed. There's no need to be noticed because they know they're not the person, so why glorify that? You're glorifying the transient; the transient is God, of course—and Goddess. The transient is perfection. It's not less than the eternal, it's a manifestation of the eternal. But you don't bet on a losing horse—unless you've got tax problems, you know what I mean?

Discrimination, *vivika*, means you know the difference between the transient and the eternal. It doesn't mean you know the difference. It means that you know that you are the eternal, and you are also the transient and you can tell the difference. That's what discrimination means in Shankara's yoga. That's what he's talking about. He's talking about knowing the eternal. To discriminate doesn't mean intellectually you're going to say, "Oh yes, I understand, this is a transient idea, this is something that's eternal." That isn't discrimination; those are ideas. Discrimination is the ability to meditate.

Unless you can meditate, there can't be discrimination because there's only transience and transient ideas of the eternal. Only in meditation is there discrimination.

Meditation is discrimination, the absence of thought, the absence of self. No aggrandizement of the self, not making it big, not franchising it, just the purity and perfect, unbroken continuity of existence which has always been the same—eternal, non-transient. That doesn't mean it doesn't change and have different whatever-it's-in-the-mood-fors. Sure it does. Who can say what it is and what it isn't? No one can describe it. It's just words. It's fun to do, no reason not to. But in meditation alone is there discrimination. It is the discrimination. It is the eternal.

So learn to meditate. Learn to stop your thoughts. It's not just a mental process that you do several times a day. It's a whole way one leads one's life, where we downplay the self, not with a false humility but with power—because we want to know the eternal.

We don't have to hate the transient. We don't have to dislike the fact that we are young or middle-aged or old, it doesn't matter. It just rolls around forever like the seasons. Here it's about to be spring. Winter has passed, finally. Shortly leaves will be everywhere, for six months. And then in six months, they'll all go away and the "bare ruined choirs where late the sweet birds sang," as Shakespeare called them, the branches will dominate again. No leaves. But there are about to be leaves. We're going to go from one condition to another. That's life. In California they have palm trees. Palm trees have seasons too, they're just not as obvious. Unless you're an aficionado of palm trees, which I happen to be.

CHAPTER TWENTY-THREE
PEAK EXPERIENCES

What I'm trying to teach you, what I am in fact teaching you—whether you're learning it or not, I'm definitely teaching it—is how to have peak experiences, how to make your whole life a peak experience. Now, peak implies a plateau. And for me, it's not like that. I was reading a story about a guy who's climbed more of the Himalayan mountains of the highest elevations than anyone else. As a matter of fact, he's only got one or two to go and he's done them all. And in doing this, he's lost several fingers from frostbite; he lost a brother in a climb. He's gone through all kinds of innumerable obstacles. But this guy is probably the most famous mountain climber in the world. He keeps climbing these mountains. He's gone up to the top of Everest without oxygen. He just does these incredible things. And you have to ask yourself, well, why do this? Why does someone become an Olympic athlete? Some people do it for gold and glory, needless to say. And there's nothing wrong with those things. Why push yourself? Why not just be comfortable? Why not play it safe? Why court danger?

It's because there are some individuals who have a peculiar power. I don't know why. Maybe it's from past lives, maybe it's not. Who knows, but some people just have a peculiar power, the power to elevate themselves above the deadness of the human condition. The human condition is not dead intrinsically. We don't start—we're born alive, not dead. But we are deadened by the world. Our world is timid. It's filled with bargaining and deals and everyone plays it safe, or they just follow orders.

You might say, "Well, not everybody plays it safe; how about soldiers who go to war?" Well, they usually don't have much choice. The soldiers who choose it aren't playing it safe, obviously. But after a while, even war can become a routine. Professional soldiers are not necessarily excited by their work anymore. Initially, they may have a moment when they're facing the enemy, when they triumph, when they do something incredible, something that they couldn't imagine doing. It brings them to a new plateau. It can happen in the arts, in dance, music, something where we go beyond who we are. We leave our personality behind, we leave "safe" behind and we encounter a moment. I call it a moment; it's not obviously just a moment, but it's when our perception unfolds and we step beyond who we've been. Our energy just gets so high that it literally lifts us up above personality, and for a timeless time, we merge with life. We merge with something that there are no words for.

Some people experience that moment in sex. Some people experience that moment in athletics. Some people experience it in contemplation and meditation. They're more apt to experience it there, certainly, than any other place. But the life of meditation and religious study is absolutely no guarantee of peak moments. Most people who are involved in religious study and meditation as a lifestyle are downright bored, and they're as stuck in what they do as everyone else is. You can make a routine out of anything. Initially something is exciting, but then immediately we structure it in such a way that we can just repeat the ecstasy and then it's no longer ecstasy.

I am a seeker of what I call perfect moments. I'm not going to define that because, why? There are all kinds. Perfect moments are moments when we, as I said, go beyond ourselves and we touch something immortal. And there are many ways to do it. They involve pretty much the same structural approach, though. These moments don't occur particularly rhapsodically. They occur from a lot of discipline, a lot of pragmatic approach, through building up our power. And if you know how to do it in one place, you can apply that structural knowledge to doing it in any place.

In other words, it really isn't a certain thing that brings us those moments. It isn't mountain climbing. It isn't hang gliding. It isn't bungee jumping. It isn't meditation. It isn't business. It isn't athletics. It's an approach whereby we use something to catapult ourselves into infinity. And once we've done it, the tendency is to want to repeat exactly what we did again and again.

We've baked a great cake, so now we're going to write down the recipe. But it doesn't work that way. It has to be new. It has to be uncertain. If there's no uncertainty, your power doesn't rise.

What I'm teaching you is how to experience the manifold realities of mind, how to surf the Himalayas inwardly, how to go places that very few people ever go, and you come back from those places different. Moses goes to the top of the mountain and he comes back glowing, transformed. He became the vision, you see? That's what you do. There are countless stagings of attention. There are countless levels of reality, call it what you will, that most people, of course, are completely oblivious to because their lives have deadened them, and their societies and so on.

So a person has to have a kind of a weird power. And if they do, they'd look at all the choices that there are and walk away from them. I always remember a story about a poet who I liked when I was in college—Theodore Roethke. He was a little bit crazy, if not a lot crazy, as all good poets are, and one day he was teaching at the University of Washington. He walked into the office and he'd been away for some time, probably in a sanitarium, and he came back into the office and there was a great stack of mail awaiting him. Probably a mixture of the usual forms that you get as a professor—class evaluations, inter-office memos, you know, the boring dead life of the university that keeps it static—and probably some royalty checks. Probably some fan letters, maybe an invitation to speak someplace. And he picked it all up, as the story goes, with a big smile on his face, walked over to the nearest wastebasket and just dropped it in and walked out. Now that's self-transcendence, if you see what I mean.

It's through action, it's through activity, that we go beyond the self. And what makes that a powerful action is not if he [Roethke] does it every day. If he does it every day, his life is going to be a mess. But on one day he felt he was in a certain state of mind. And in that state of mind, on that particular day, had he read all that mail and copiously gone through it, which I'm sure he did day after day, year after year, as a professor and as a poet who won a number of prizes and who had done the hard discipline of writing and pushing his consciousness and all the things that you do to get the

Pulitzer—but one day, his body felt that if he went through the mail that day, it just would have ruined his day. So he just threw it in the basket. I'm sure the next time he came in the office, he went through all his mail.

There may have been an element of showmanship involved. I'm sure someone was watching because we have the story. But it really doesn't matter. Obviously, it had power because I'm talking about it.

What I'm teaching you is how to go beyond yourself. And the world, of course, teaches you the opposite. The world teaches you to conform.

To go beyond yourself doesn't mean to go crazy. To go beyond yourself doesn't mean to be sloppy. It doesn't mean to give up responsibility. It doesn't mean that at all. It doesn't mean anything. It means that you progressively increase your personal power, your energy field, through very complicated means that require a good dose of intelligence, will, and a weird power, as I said. And if you do it just right, if you line everything up just right, you walk through a doorway where the world as you know it collapses. Reality as you know it goes away and you stand in the middle, on the edge of eternity, with a vista that is so incredible, so powerful, so perfect that it's overwhelming, and you are in fact overwhelmed, and you no longer exist. You merge with the reality to a greater or lesser extent and you are renewed by this experience. It purifies you; it changes you. It cleanses your spirit, your mind, your body, and you remember why you're alive—for moments like that.

So I teach people how to do this. A necessary ingredient, of course, is to have a weird power, and all of you have that or you wouldn't be here. And there are lots of ways to do it. I point out the obvious ones—physical development, career development, development of meditation. And through creation, by creating something—something musical, something artistic, something in software. Those are the easiest ways to get to those moments. There are other ways, but it's when you do something that was not in your karmic sequencing and you only do that by leading a completely deliberate life.

If you have a lot of clutter in your life; if your mind is filled with other people, with obscure thoughts, emotions and desires; if you don't know what you're here for—to have moments like that—and if you don't approach it solidly, in a very pragmatic but innovative way, it doesn't happen. The undisciplined person does not have moments like this. They have moments of being undisciplined. The overly disciplined person doesn't have moments like this. They just experience discipline—too much. So we're between two things. We're between the creative, open and spontaneous sense of being and approach to life, and the highly disciplined, pragmatic approach. And between those two there's a doorway, if you can find it, and it leads to immortality. It leads to infinity. It leads to nirvana, to the western paradise, whatever you want to call it.

And it's inside your mind—that's the most curious thing—it's inside your mind. Not inside your physical brain, but inside that which is you, the living presence that occupies the body that you're in, that will leave the body at death. And in order to accomplish this, you can't be drained all the time. In other words, you have to set up your life as a field of power. Most people's lives are set up with so many incessant demands that their power is gradually drained.

I have focused on the things that seem most relevant to me. The thing that increases your power the most is first and foremost meditation—in other words, disciplining the mind so that you can stop thought for protracted periods of time. At the stoppage of thought, a doorway opens to infinite mind and you are empowered. And the longer you can stop thought perfectly, the more power flows through you and the further you extend yourself into other realities, into other "you's."

Career seems to me to be extremely important because I observe that it is in the getting of a living—I would agree with Henry David Thoreau, this was his theorem—that it is in the getting of a living that people drain themselves the most. His response was to simplify your life to such an extent that you don't need to work very much, and you can occupy yourself fully, not with being a bum, but with pursuing things that increase your power. In his case, he was a naturalist, he was a hiker, he was a writer, he was a poet, he was this and that. He didn't just—you know, the American way is to not want to work much so you can kind of hang out. That was not what he was suggesting. He was suggesting [that we] remove ourselves from the deadness of getting a living so that we can live fully. We can pursue things that ennoble our spirits and make us strong and give us these incredible moments of rhapsody.

I perceive that it is the getting of a living that seems to be the principal—the things that drain people the most are making money, romance, their past, their associates, interpersonal relationships, their view of themselves—the "I can't" factor, that view of oneself. And of course, simply not understanding how it's done.

There's a science to the development of personal power that we call occultism, and it's necessary to have a teacher for two reasons, if not three. One, the teacher empowers you and gives you the energy to get yourself going which is hard to get going on your own. [Two, the teacher] shows you what to do and what to avoid because there are as many pitfalls as there are—there are actually many more pitfalls than there are—correct moves. As you go into the different dimensions and different realities, you can become completely lost. You can do just the opposite. You can go down and not up.

And of course, a teacher is there to laugh at you because you have such a high opinion of yourself that you need to be laughed at. You need to sense how small we all are. And [the teacher is there] to teach you to laugh at life and the world because you have to laugh at all these things—yourself, life, the world, occultism—because it's all so vast and so infinite that the only way you can really deal with it sanely is to laugh at it at times.

In order, it seems to me, to have enough personal power to have fantastic moments, you can't be a nine-to-five'er. You can't get up in the morning and enter that huge flood of commutation—people on highways and byways who look so miserable on their way to work, who sort of struggle through the day, get in the big line at the end of the day and come home exhausted. How are you going to have a peak moment? Maybe on the weekend you'll get one or two. Maybe.

It seems to me it's necessary to find a way of making enough money that will give you the freedom and the mobility to do what you want, when you want, the way that you want, and at the same time, the very getting of a living should increase your power. In the very action of getting a living, one should be able to have peak moments. That's what I'm teaching you to do, how to do that—how to use career, since it's the thing that we spend so much time doing, to go beyond yourself and at the same time, how to develop a career that provides you with enough economic resources so that you can go anywhere and do anything.

If, let's say, that next week I wanted to take 25 of my students and go out for two weeks hiking in the desert—you couldn't do it. You've got jobs, you've got responsibilities, you've got payments to make. Your lives aren't fluid. I can do that because my life is set up that way. So that has to change because you have to be able to do that at times. Then there are times when it would be ridiculous to be out hiking around in the desert. You'd just be getting spaced out and it would drain you. You should be pulling off some great business deal, perfecting your art, whatever it may be—and storing and increasing your power and just having moments of exquisite transcendence in the workplace. But it seems to me that if you're working for someone else, punching a clock, it's never going to happen. It's going to be very difficult. You'd have to have an unusual amount of power.

It's necessary to really be employed by oneself. We're always working for somebody, in a sense, but it can be more fluid. And it involves risk, which is precisely why it's worth doing. There's not much risk to coming in every day and operating at about the same skill level and getting a steady paycheck, consequently it deadens you, it's boring, and you get your two or three or maybe four weeks off a year when you're so exhausted—everything is so scheduled, that there's no possibility of an exquisite life.

You come home, you're so tired from work you don't want to go work out. You don't want to go to the martial arts meeting because you're just too tired, you see? People are so tired. The world is set up to exhaust you and drain you. That's how humankind has devised their world. Life is not necessarily that way.

There are moments of exquisite power everywhere we look. But we have to know how to get to them and use them. That's what I teach. I call it "Tantric Buddhism" just because it's the system that's been devised to do that. It's a methodology for increasing your personal power and directing it—directing the will and the conscious mind. And over a number of years, you learn to direct your will to such a fine and perfect point that you can literally do anything. You can do things that are not within the realm of human reason, thank God.

At every moment, you have the opportunity to crap out and not do it and run away from it, or to move to the next moment. The world will always tell you to play it safe and just be dead. You know, roll over and play dead. On the other hand, I suggest that you're capable of doing things you can't conceive of, that most of life is really that way, but this world we exist in is populated by these people who have really shut themselves off from life. They've destroyed their environment, by and large. They've eliminated most other species on the planet, which is just an indication of their sloppiness and their deadness and their oblivion—but even more so, they've cut themselves off from happiness.

Human beings are not happy. They're miserable creatures. And that's not necessary. My role in life is not to illumine mankind and womankind. It's not my job. I don't really have a job, I just find that there are moments in teaching that are exquisite and there are certain moments I reach in the teaching of self-transcendence that, for me, takes me through that doorway. That's why I do it. If I don't have moments like that, if it becomes more of a drain than a game, why teach? I don't feel a noblesse oblige. I don't feel a requisite duty as a being to transmit what I've learned to anyone. I'd rather hang out with squirrels than people. They're much more enterprising and much more interesting. Their social lives are better too, yeah.

I teach because I get a kick out of it. And also, it's fun to watch someone who's been shying away and shying away from that barrier, just go through it—to go through that doorway and spin and become somebody else.

I'm teaching you the art of self-transcendence through a method that I call Tantric Buddhism, which is a continually evolving series of methods that each of us adds to. There's a body of knowledge that we learn, that others who have experimented along the way have passed on to us. But essentially it's not something that you learn by reading and then tell others about. It's something that you have to do yourself. Because the transmission and the teaching, of course, is mainly nonphysical. There are directives, there are directions to the student, to the adept—do this, don't do this, try this, try this, see what this does, play with the chemistry of your life. But most of what is taught, is taught—well, you know how it's taught. It's not taught through words. It's taught in other realities, in other levels of mind.

I don't feel it's my responsibility to successfully bring one person into enlightenment. I don't feel I have any responsibilities. I think that's a rather weighty role to feel that you are the Buddha of all times and all places and that in some way the salvation of anyone, including yourself, depends upon you—I think there's a lot of ego involved in such a view. Not much self-transcendence. Not much fun. I think that the only thing that I have to do in life is keep myself perpetually spinning through infinite realities, each more amazing and incredible. And it's a constant challenge in a world that's running in the other direction with so much deadness, so much boredom, such a lackluster place. It's not easy. But it's exciting.

You're learning that art from someone who does it and it's not an easy thing to learn. You don't learn it in a day, a week, a month or a year. You've had many, many years of living another life. You've just been living another way. Every day you're around people, and you're reading their books and reading their magazines and their newspapers and watching their television shows and their films, and picking up their vibration which says the same thing over and over—conform, give in, don't try, be mediocre.

We applaud the people who are film stars, who get elected to an office, who are very athletic—the small group who play with power in a very limited way. But we're completely oblivious to what can be done, to the infinite realities that exist in front of us. We deny them.

The mind is infinite. It's made up of light. It exists forever. There's no end to its thresholds. You've found very few so far. They're endlessly present everywhere, always. But you have to approach them in a certain way, with a very, very strong degree of respect. Without respect, not much happens. You have to respect power, the bearer of power, the experience of power, and at the same time you need to keep your sense of humor.

So what are you learning here? I have no idea. I don't really keep tabs. I have no idea why you come here at all. I know what I do—I teach people how to transcend themselves. You can sit and come up with your version of all this, which won't do a damn thing, or you can actually pay attention to what I'm saying and if you do it exactly, with your own good shot of creative flair, you will have incredible moments that will spin you into universes that are beyond imagination, beyond wonder. You're unlocking the power of eternity and allowing it to flow through your mind and your body. You're allowing your spirit to rise with the wind into infinity, above this dead, drab human condition. But you have to listen exactly and do it precisely. Step by step, not all in a day, but yet each day you can revolutionize your being in some way. And if you just keep doing that, your power increases and increases and then—snap! You transmute. The world becomes light.

The mind is light, and there's only infinity. There are no words, there's only the possibility of a moment even more incredible a little bit further down the road.

Chapter Twenty-Four

SOLSTICES AND EQUINOXES

We're coming into a very interesting time. The summer solstice is approaching, and I'd like to talk to you a little bit about the summer solstice. There are four times of tremendous power that occur every year. There are others that occur at different times, but there are four that you can count on, and those are the solstices and the equinoxes. Without going into the structures of why that is so—it just is—I'd rather look at what it means.

The summer solstice is the time in the physical world of greatest light. The winter solstice is the time of the greatest darkness, if you will. The equinoxes are equal day and equal night in the fall and spring. But while this is occurring in a physical sense, in the physical universe, in the inner universe, meaning in other dimensional planes, something else is happening at that time also. The manifestation may be more sunlight or less sunlight or half and half in the physical world, but in the subtle planes there are doorways and powers that open and come into view. And if we can hook ourselves onto those powers, they can carry us a long way.

Occultists are intrinsically lazy like everyone else. We would much rather hitch a ride than walk—unless we just are in the mood to walk. The way we accomplish things is by hooking ourselves and unhooking ourselves to powers, to forces, to energies. And we focus on those energies, we blend our aura, we extend our luminous selves psychically into those forces and powers and we hitch a ride. When we've ridden to the destination we want to get to and the destination, if we stayed with it, would take us someplace we don't want to be, we let go. We hook ourselves onto things and we let go of things. It's a very unemotional process. We just do it.

The summer solstice is a time in the physical plane of great light. In India, in every yoga center, every master, every ashram has a big celebration. Some celebrate the winter solstice also. The summer solstice tends to get more play. I feel equal about them, to be honest. They're very different.

We have a summer solstice coming now; it's the solstice of 1990. It's a very strong solstice. Just as there are times when there are sunspots, the geysers of fire that spew forth from the sun that are more powerful and they affect the electro-magnetic field of our planet and of our universe, they affect radio waves and all kinds of things—there are times when the sun is very active and there are times when there aren't many [sunspots]. All solstices are not the same. This particular summer solstice is a very, very powerful time. There's a tremendous power that's present. There is in every summer solstice and every winter solstice and every equinox. But this is a very active one; there are a lot of sunspots. There are a lot of pillars of fire.

It's a time when it's easier to change, to erase personal history, to do what I call "transit." It's an astrological term, to go through a transit—that is to say, to shift yourself, to adjust the foreground and the background of your mind, to take aspects of yourself that you don't find interesting, that drain your power, that are just a pain or that are boring and put them in the background, and to bring other things into the foreground. It's a very, very strong solstice. It's like all of them, yet more so.

The last really strong solstice was around '85 in the summer. It's been about five years since we've had one like this. And it's a time, I suppose in a sense—we have the longest day, June 21st or June 22nd, there's more sunlight around—in a way that reflects inwardly because during the summer solstice, it's very easy to see things that might be difficult to see at another time. It's like everything comes out in the wash, if you know what I mean. It's a time when you will find it very easy to see your imperfections and your perfections. It is a time to see what has to be done, and what's done.

What a good occultist does, is they hook themselves to the summer solstice. It's a very powerful time. It's a feeling. You know it's coming internally because your mind is quiet, because you meditate and your life is not filled with a lot of things that distract you, because you're centered and you have your goals set forward and that's what you put your time and energy into. Because you've eliminated anything unnecessary from your life and your mind isn't cluttered, you can feel things that other people don't feel. You can feel the power of the solstice.

Most people's lives are so disjointed and they've got so many loose ends in their lives that they can't feel these things, even though they're very powerful. But a good occultist, who has their life in order, is sensitized. They're more sensitive to the energies of the universe and the energies of life. Consequently, if you're aware of these energies, you can hook onto them and utilize them to pull you or push you to different places, either physically or in terms of outer world accomplishments or just in terms of shifting mental states—flipping from one plane of consciousness to another, flipping from one self to another, things like that.

This solstice is really strong. And the way you do it is—as we do everything in occultism and Buddhism, advanced Buddhism—the way we do it is with a feeling. You have to feel the solstice. Now we're about a month away, five weeks, and it's going to get stronger every day. But if you're sensitized, you can already feel it. You can already feel it coming. It's sort of like when you see something in your peripheral vision, see it out of the corner of your eye, you just sort of notice something. That's how an occultist feels energies, as a rule.

Now, we don't really want to look directly into the sun. If you look at the sun long enough you go blind. If you look at anything powerful directly for too long, you tend not to see it. Power masks itself. When you look into power for too long, it almost overcomes you; it kind of enchants you and you don't really see it carefully. Sometimes when you look directly at a thing you can't see it very well. When you look at it out of the corner of your eye, you see it better because you're not distracted by its appearance. In other words, what we want to look at is not the way the thing looks, but the way it is. Appearances are oft times deceptive. Very often the appearance of something has nothing to do with its reality.

So when you look into the solstice, when you look into that energy field, you might not see it. You may become so caught up with the feelings, the intensity, that you won't see where it's going and how you can hook yourself to it. What a good occultist does is feel; you feel the solstice. You know it's very powerful, and so you just—it's like having a program operating in the background—you just put a part of your second attention, part of your inner self there. There's no way to explain these things, as I'm sure you know. You do this every solstice and every equinox.

In other words, what you should always be doing is focusing, feeling—without becoming obsessive—the next solstice or the next equinox. You should set up your life mentally so that you always are apprehending the next solstice or the next equinox. Those are the measurements by which an occultist gauges their life. Those are our time increments. Not so much the calendar, the names of the months and the days, but more the lunar cycles and the solstices, things like that. We're more concerned with internal energies that are in this universe that affect us very strongly.

The sun has a very strong gravitational field and without it, none of us would exist right now, we'd all not be here. But inwardly it also has an energy field, it has an aura, you see? So does the earth, so does the moon, so do all the planets. We're affected by those auras. It's not something that you really want to reason out. It's not necessary. What you want to do is always hook yourself to the next solstice or equinox and set up your own personal calendar in that way. In other words, it's good to set goals and achieve those goals for every equinox and every solstice. It's a nice way to set your life up, so you know that, "Well, I just passed the equinox, I have three months to the solstice, so in the next three months, I'm going to focus on—, I'm going to accomplish—." You know, you have ideas like that. Then, of course, you do it. And you're more apt to do it if you do it that way, because you're hooking yourself onto that power, and the power of the coming solstice or equinox, if you're aware of it, will enable you to accomplish more of those goals.

Let's say that you wanted to make a career jump. The average person would just go out and try and get a job, get their resume together, submit it, try and get any information they can. An occultist doesn't go about things that way. We use internal energies to accomplish what we do. That's what occultism means—it means hidden, the other side of things. Hidden not in the sense that somebody's trying to hide it from you, but what is not apparent to the senses. You can't see it with the physical eyes, feel it with the hands, taste it, touch it or smell it. But it's there. It's more real, perhaps, than anything else.

An occultist who is trying to make a big change in their life would build that change around the energies of the next solstice or the next equinox. They'd hook themselves to it. We have a very powerful solstice coming up, which is why I particularly draw your attention to it. At this time it's very easy for an occultist to make a major shift of any kind they choose because so much power is going to be available from the solstice. Not the day of the solstice.

The day of the solstice is just totality. It's a very interesting and powerful time of course, but as you get closer to it, if you just think of it as a four-point ratio—we've gone through an equinox and you've hit the totality of the equinox on the 21st of March or September, but then you will stay in the field of the equinox for about another month as you leave it; you're still really in it. We define it as a singular day but it isn't just a day, it's a time period.

But then about a month out, you start to pick up the radiance of the coming solstice, which is two months down the road. And then, of course, about halfway through that next month you're right in between, which is a midpoint. There's a secondary power spot, there are four more, that are directly between the solstices and the equinoxes, and there's where you get involved with retrograde energies. There's an in-between power when you're directly between a solstice and an equinox; there's a power there that's even harder to talk about. You have to be more advanced to use that power.

So around the middle, you shift. In other words, it's as if we launch a spacecraft and we're trying to get from one planet to another—we aim it at the gravitational pull of a planet. Even though we're not going to stop at that planet, we pick up its gravitational pull and it will accelerate the spacecraft. Then when we get close to that planet, instead of smashing into it, we fire our rockets, bounce around it, escape its gravitational field and push past it. Then a little bit further along, we'll pick up another planet, we'll let it pull us along. See what I mean?

Except that in the case of a solstice or during the equinox, it doesn't trap you. It pulls you to it and then it pushes you away. So let's say the summer solstice is coming, which it is, you can let the summer solstice pull you to it. But then once we hit the 21st of June, it will start to push you. Then you can use its energy to push off. There's an energy that you can then use from that solstice, now that we're into July. You can continue to gain a power from it, but now, instead of pulling you it'll push you, if you use it properly. And it'll push you till about halfway. Halfway to the equinox. Then around that time, you'll pick up the line of the equinox and the equinox will pull you until you reach it, and then it'll push you, if you know how to use it, until about halfway, in which case you'll pick up the line, then you'll let go of the line to the equinox and you'll pick up the line of the solstice. See?

Occultism is really a science whereby we are able to accomplish incredible things, things that other people can't imagine, because we're dealing with forces and powers that they're not aware of—we train our bodies and our minds and our spirits to be aware of these powers. We do this by continually cleansing ourselves. We purify ourselves endlessly so that we become empty, so that we're not filled with ego, we're not filled with vanity, we're not filled with a lot of stupid desires. And we do this by meditating, leading very deliberate lives. By doing that, we become pure enough to be conscious of these forces and powers. And it's much more difficult now to do this than it used to be because the population is so great. There's so much human aura on this particular planet with 5.3 billion people that it's very hard to feel these things. Human aura is just like a kind of gray smog that covers over things.

In the time of ancient Egypt, or whatever, it was a lot easier to feel these things. You could feel the solstice coming much more strongly. Now, you have to be very, very sensitized. The power is there, it's just as strong, but there's so much interference, there's so much gray sludge from the overcrowded earth that it interferes with your ability. An occultist today has to train themselves to a much higher degree than an occultist did even a hundred years ago.

That's why we call this a dark age. It's a dark age in the sense that there are so many people on earth who are so unattuned that they create such a level of white noise, in a sense, that it drowns out things that we'd like to see.

They [astronomers] try and use telescopes, and in a lot of cases they've had to move them, when they built the telescope, because a city appeared nearby and there's so much light from the city that if it's a reflective telescope, they simply can't see the sky anymore. There's too much light, even at night. You have to put your telescope in an area, unless it's a radio telescope, that's very dark. They just can't see the stars.

So occultists depend upon—for their very existence as occultists—the internal powers and energies of the universe. We train ourselves; we go through a long training process and purification process, whereby we become highly sensitized. Then we have to guard that sensitivity because once you're sensitized, you can also pick up a lot of junk. In other words, we have to become so much more sensitive now because the earth is so polluted, but that pollution poses a tremendous danger to someone who's sensitive. It's always been that way. An occultist, in other words—once as an occultist you sensitize yourself, you now have to guard the sensitivity. Sensitivity is a two-way street like everything, and the sensitivity will enable you to do amazing things but it can also be incredibly painful if you don't guard it properly.

Today it's necessary to become much more sensitive than a hundred years ago, let alone several thousand. But also because the toxic residue of humanity is so much stronger, you have to guard yourself, guard that sensitivity even more heavily because otherwise you become so psychic. In other words, if you don't guard that psychic sensitivity, you can pick up so many pollutants that you'll become more toxic than before, if you see what I'm saying.

We spend a tremendous amount of time doing two things, three things, really. One, we spend a lot of time as occultists purifying ourselves, eliminating all the crap from our lives so our purpose is straightforward, we know what it is, our intent is straightforward. We're honest people; we work hard and we have our own specialized interests. There's nothing vague in an occultist's life. There's no down time. There's no, "Gee, I'm not quite sure what to do today." We have our projects, our development, and we just do it. That's what being an occultist means. It means there's no vagueness in your life.

You don't start that way. You start as an average human being who is filled with vagueness and not much purpose or definition, who is controlled by their desires, their mind spins all over the place, their senses spin all over the place, out of control.

If you have an apprenticeship with an occult teacher, the teacher will then teach you how to become sensitive. But the teacher will also have to teach you how to guard that sensitivity. And so we spend a lot of time developing things that are extremely beneficial to focus our minds on, because once we've developed the sensitivity, if we don't have those things that are very positive to always put our mind into, our mind naturally is going to pick up the toxic residues that are around from humanity and it'll make us very ill, or it'll drive us absolutely nuts.

In other words, when I go into New York City—hey, I'm completely clairvoyant. I've eliminated all traces of self through countless lifetimes of purification. When I go into New York City, if I was not careful—if there are seven million people there, I am so psychic that I could be thinking and feeling all seven million minds. Simultaneously. So when I'm in New York City, I stay completely focused on certain things that shield me from picking all of that up. The same is true at home. You know someone who is unhappy, someone who's depressed. Now if I think of that person for a few seconds, my mind will enter their mind and I will pick up everything that's in them and it'll make me very depressed. Suddenly I'll be filled with their thoughts, even if I was happy and radiant and feeling great. And if you pick up enough of that, it begins to affect your physical body. It makes you very ill because these are plasma energies that are very, very strong. You may not be able to see them, but it's like radiation. You can't see radiation but if you were exposed to too many rads, you'll die.

We're dealing with inner radiances. And just as there are radiances that are harmful, there are radiances that are extremely helpful. When I meditate, I generate a tremendous field of energy. I've spent lifetimes in monasteries refining my ability to push a lot of *kundalini,* a lot of high gradient, radiant light through me, and anyone who is around me when I do that, picks it up. It's like a transfer. They pick up a lot of energy and power, and the more sensitized they are, the more they have developed their ability to focus, the more they pick up.

But at the same time, you have to be very, very careful not to pick up too much of the lower energies, the toxic energies, because they'll make you very ill. They can kill you. They can cause cancer, debilitative diseases of all types. Or, if you don't have a very strong mind—if you've developed the sensitivity side of your being but not the mental strength—then when you just walk down the street, all the thoughts of all those people will flood your mind, their desires and their ideas, and there may be some people with some very strange thoughts and ideas and desires. If you can't separate those out and sift those out and recognize them as being other than your own and push them aside, then they will overpower you.

Somebody's thinking about eating; you've just eaten. You pick up those desires and suddenly you have to go eat because it seems like it's coming from you. Somebody has very strong sexual desires. And if you're around somebody and you're highly sensitized, suddenly their desires become your desires and suddenly you may find yourself having sex with someone who you really didn't want to have sex with. They weren't even your own desires. Naturally, it'll be a deleterious experience because it's something that your own being did not want. But you find yourself doing things because you have not developed your mind to an extent to filter out and recognize and eliminate the psychic pickup, the desires and thoughts and feelings of others—you follow?

As a teacher it's even more complicated because what a teacher is, is someone who meditates with you, who transfers a tremendous amount of radiant high energy, which enables you to complete your occult tasks much more rapidly than you would on your own. It [the energy] enables you to enter layers of mind that at this time you don't have the ability to enter, to make structural changes, to overcome bad habits, to tighten yourself up and to bring yourself into high radiant states of mind—it speeds it up. But as a teacher, it's really quite impossible to just send out radiant energy without picking up a certain amount of the energy of the people you work with.

Now, when I do a meditation, if I just go do a public meditation and I'm sitting down in a room with a bunch of people who I'll just see once, I don't pick up that much. A certain amount. But what I do is, I go in, sit down, meditate and I just project energy. And if you're just projecting you really don't pick up much.

But when you have apprentices, when you have people you work with on a regular basis, part of what you have to do is escalate their development very rapidly, and the way that is done is not only by transferring something to them, but you also absorb a certain amount of the negative elements in their psyche and it goes into your body, and then it's necessary to burn that off. And if you have a lot of students, of course, and if your students are not doing their homework and if they're just hanging out in low states of mind continuously, it's extremely toxic. It can make a teacher very sick—a lot of teachers die quite young, for that reason. But the same is true of every individual.

In other words, the teacher is just doing it in a larger capacity, in a larger way, but the same thing really affects every apprentice. So what a teacher does, is they set their lives up in such a way that that doesn't have to happen. In other words, I come in, I do five nights of meditation with my students. I come in feeling good and looking good. By the end of the five nights I've gone very, very high, as high as I could, to transmit as much energy as I could to the people who are there. But at the same time, after the five nights, I've also picked up—I've cleansed their psyches, I've pulled everything out of them which, in most cases they're unconscious of; it's in your subconscious. I pull out all this stuff, and at that point my whole body is toxic. It's like—I'm very high on the one sense because I've really had to push it to transmit the energy of enlightenment to several hundred people simultaneously, which is no easy thing. It's fun, you know, it's great, because I have to go even higher than I would for myself and I get to enjoy the ride. I love it.

But if they're apprentices, if it's not just a public meditation, I'm also—because I want them to advance—pulling all their energies through my body. So then it's necessary for me to go—normally I spend a great deal of time alone after that. I go off into the mountains or to a power place and I cleanse myself. I do a lot of physical exercise, which helps purify the body. I do a lot of meditation. It's a lot of work! No, I mean seriously, it's a tremendous amount of work, which obviously one would not have to do if one were just meditating for oneself.

But it's understood—there's an unwritten contract between student and teacher as there is between parent and child—that yes, with a child, I'm willing to change your diapers and clean up your shit for a couple of years, but it's not going to be a lifetime thing. Then after a while you're going to be toilet trained and you're going to dress yourself and you're going to clean your room and eventually, there's a level of payback. You'll clean the house, you'll go out and mow the lawn; no, it's a symbiotic relationship. That's how it should be. That's proper. So with a teacher's students, what should be occurring is initially, when they first come in, you're just going to pick up for the first year or two a tremendous amount of their toxicity. But as they advance and enter their third, fourth, fifth, sixth, seventh and so on, as they go further and further, every year they should be less toxic, because if they're following the prescriptions of occultism, they're purifying their lives and purifying their minds. They're cutting themselves off from everything that's impure and only focusing on things that are highly radiant. And then after a while, they can assist the teacher in a lot of different activities and projects that are fun for everybody. That's the basic theorem.

So we're approaching a solstice, and a solstice is a time when you can hook yourself to something. That's what an apprentice does with a teacher. The teacher is a continual solstice. You hook yourself to the teacher—not as something that is always going to be there. It's not—I drive my car and every time I need gas I go to the gas station and it'll always be that way, since my car is never going to produce gas. But in occultism, what you're learning to do is develop energy for yourself. And you have to go through a period of time where you have a teacher who transfers power to you in a massive way. But the purpose of that is to enable you to develop your own power and then, if you do what the teacher suggests, you will learn, over a period of years, to develop your own power. As time goes on the teacher will still continue to transfer power, but the power will take you higher and higher because you have more of your own, if you're developing power yourself. Then anything that I add is on top of that.

If you come in and you don't have much power, which is how people come in, the transfer takes you to a certain place. But then, as you apply the dictums of occultism to your life, gradually you'll be—it's as if I'm giving you a thousand bucks a month and you have no money. You spend the thousand every month; you just need it to survive. But now you're making money, and now you're making a thousand a month because I've shown you how. Now when I give you a thousand a month, guess what, you have two, see? You can do more things. Soon you're making ten thousand a month. So now, if I give you a thousand a month, or maybe five thousand a month, then you have fifteen thousand, and so on and so forth.

A teacher continually, as long as they work with an apprentice, augments their power, but the way that we get you there sooner is obviously because you are developing power. If you're not developing power, you're going to stay at about the same level. You'll always get your thousand; you'll always spend it. You won't get anyplace new. And if the teacher goes away, you've got nothing. You haven't learned to develop power.

So in occultism, we hook ourselves to things, but not just to do it again and again and have the same ride. But we hook ourselves to something to take us to a place we've never been because we enjoy that. We want to reach levels of mind we've never been in. We want to transmute ourselves. We want to become perfect, enlightened, whatever these words are.

We do that every day by gradually eliminating the negative energies in our being and augmenting the positive energies. It's just a balance sheet, really. And if you continue to do that, even without a teacher, you'll go higher and higher. But, of course, a teacher can show you ways to develop power that you would probably not find yourself and they can augment that process with massive transfusions of energy.

In some cases we have students who do what we call "ride the energy." What they do is, they come in, pick up some energy, ride that energy till they see the teacher next time, and they don't develop power themselves. This is a very dangerous practice—because power is a weird thing. I didn't invent it, just as I didn't invent the atomic structure; it's just there.

Power works in certain ways. And a person who's given power of this type, occult power, who does not use the power properly—if you just ride the energy and you don't use that energy to do the practices that would evolve you as an occultist, clear you out and enable you to gain more power, if you don't use the energy—in other words, I give a person power not just to have a fun life. But I give them power to do things that would be very hard—it [power] makes it easier. These things are to practice occultism. I give a person power to practice occultism, for no other reason. It's like giving a kid a scholarship in college. If you give a kid a scholarship, instead of having to work at the local grocery store and wait on tables, the kid can be home studying. The scholarship is not intended to subsidize the kid to go to the local bar and party every night. It's not. It's to enable that individual to spend more time studying.

So a teacher transfers power to enable an apprentice to go through their apprenticeship more rapidly. But in the West, we seem to see, I've observed, that people take a lot of things for granted; they don't understand this. In the East, occultism has been practiced for a long time and it's more popularly understood. More people understand it.

It's considered very, very bad karma, if I can cut to the chase, to take power from a teacher and not use it for something very positive. Now, bad karma is not a moral, ethical idea. In other words, in the world of power, we're not philosophical. You may believe in God, you may not; you may believe that a good person does such and such, a bad person does such and such. I don't know about all that, that's human philosophy. Maybe it's true; maybe it's just somebody's idea that they like or they're laying on other people. Occultists are scientists. We deal with cause and effect.

The reason someone in the Far East—if they went and visited a teacher and they were empowered—would then use that energy in a beneficial way, is because they know something. They know that to use that energy in any other way, or to not use it, will cause the energy to reverse. This is how occult energy works.

What occult energy does is intensify everything. So if I were to transfer power to a person who was just your average person—their average desires, average loves, average hates, average mess—and if that person did not say,

"Oh great, this guy gave me all this power so I can get out of this average mess and become an exceptional being and open my horizons in ways that I didn't know they could be opened and become something far more interesting than the normal human usually becomes"—if a person just sat with the energy and just stayed as they are but just had more energy, what happens is that power will intensify their humanness. A person's desires will become stronger, their hates will become stronger, their angers—in other words, if we're assuming that the person, when they start out, has more negative energies than positive energies in them, then if you just amp 'em up, what's going to happen is those negative energies are going to increase and if there are more of them, the person's gradually going to become more negative than positive. After a while the negative energies and propensities will totally overwhelm them.

Let's say a person is your average angry, hateful, spiteful, feel-sorry-for-themselves type individual. That's what most human beings are like. You know, "the world owes me a living," and all that kind of stuff. If you empower a person like that and you just keep doing it and they don't do yoga, they don't do Buddhist practice, they don't do occult practice, meaning they don't spend a number of hours a day meditating and all of the time monitoring their thoughts, eliminating negative thoughts, only having positive thoughts, reading books, focusing on things that are extremely positive—if they don't do that, then what will happen is their hate will become overwhelming. After a while, they will be nothing but hate, they'll be nothing but desire, they'll be nothing but frustration. In other words, you'll create a monster.

Power by itself without direction makes everything worse. On the other hand, power with direction makes everything fantastically better. So a teacher really spends most of his time admonishing his students to employ the methods of occultism. Not because they have some philosophical idea about, "Gee, let's be nice," but because they're smart. They know what happens if you don't use the power. If you don't use the power properly, it reverses; it goes retrograde. It pulls you down. A person may say, "Well gosh, I don't use this power negatively. I just don't do much at all. I just sort of continue to be my usual human self." Uh-uh. If there's a rape taking place and you just stand and watch and you don't try and stop the person, you're culpable also. You get locked up, or you should be.

In other words, just the excuse that, "Well, I don't do anything wrong"—power doesn't care about what your rationalizations are. It's intensifying everything in you and if there's more negative than positive, then gradually you'll become more and more negative. So it's incumbent upon a person who practices occultism to realize that power is exactly that, and it has to be treated with intensive respect. You can't idly be empowered and then just go your own way. It's necessary to make an extreme effort to utilize that power to practice the occult exercises and to lead the life an occultist leads, which is bright, efficient, beautiful, humorous, filled with radiant light, energy and positive beyond belief. You have to do that. The energy is given to you to do that. If you use this energy in any other way, if you allow it to enter into your angers, if you don't control your anger, your anger will become hate, your hate will become obsession.

An occultist has to have complete emotional control. You get the emotional control that would otherwise be very hard to get because someone is showing you what emotional control is, explaining it to you, and they're giving you the power to do it. The average person—how can they get emotional control? Emotion is like a wind, it comes and it blows them wherever it is.

But the empowerment gives you an edge. The empowerment enables you to control your emotions. So if Sally's a new student and Sally's your typical angry, frustrated, confused, "I want this"—she doesn't know what she wants—you know, average human being. Her mind is guacamole. Every two minutes a new idea, a new desire. That's how people start.

So I say, "Now, Sally, I'm going to give you power. OK. Let's meditate together." We meditate, she sits in the room with me, I amp her up. "Now Sally, go be a better person." In other words, no more hate, no more anger, no more jealousy—when those thoughts come in your mind, push them out.

Now, normally your average person couldn't do that. It's a nice idea but it takes a lot of willpower. Ah, that's what I just gave her. I just gave her willpower. Some of mine. I've got enough to keep myself going to do what I need to do, and because I work extra hard and earn extra money, I make extra power, I can also give some to someone else.

So now Sally has power and with that power she can do what would be unthinkable for an average human being. She cannot hate anymore. Oh, the thoughts will come in. She's also learning to be psychic; she's meditating every day and she's becoming sensitive, and she could pick up the thoughts, angers and frustrations of the world more readily than before. But if she's been paying attention to the lessons that she gets on a regular basis from me, then she will be able to distinguish her feelings from the psychic things she picks up either in dreaming or in waking, eliminate them by meditating twice a day and by monitoring her mind all the time. With this boost I give her, she will be able to purify her emotions. And in doing that, of course, she will eliminate the negative aura from her body and her mind and her spirit and become a being of light, become a being of radiant happiness.

As an occultist progresses, they're given tasks. In the beginning you're just told, "Do this, avoid this." You know, the kind of do's and don'ts. You're offered suggestions on how to develop power. You learn about places of power, places to live, lifestyle, all kinds of ideas that are just very energy efficient. That's what a person learns, usually in the first year.

But then after you've been an apprentice for a year or so, you are given tasks. These tasks augment your power incredibly because they come from the world of *seeing*. An occult teacher can *see*. He can stop his thoughts, or she can stop her thoughts, completely. And when thoughts stop completely for protracted periods, it's possible to *see* beyond one's own desires and ideas and to *see* the designs of the universe. The universe has designs. In other dimensions, things just are. An occultist can *see* that and know what should be done.

In other words, occultists don't do things because of desire. I might have a desire to do something, but I won't do it because desire means nothing to me. Everything an occultist does, if they're more advanced, comes from the world of *seeing*. We can stop our thoughts and stop our desires and *see* past them and *see* what is appropriate, what will lead to more power, more enlightenment. We only view things that empower us and enlighten us and we avoid things that drain our power and bring us into lower sentient mind states of confusion, delusion, hate, anger, psychosis, neurosis, whatever it might be.

We become completely psychically whole and we hook ourselves to higher and higher bands of auric light until eventually we hook ourselves to enlightenment itself. And whatever we focus on we become, particularly if we're empowered, particularly if we're very sensitive—if we refine our sensitivity.

An occult teacher sees things that the student should do. Not some paltry desires that they may have, that they want fulfilled by their students, but in seeing in other planes they can see what will be the best for that student to develop. They then will provide that opportunity and in doing that, the student will become more empowered because the task comes from not the human world but the world of *seeing*. It has a very heavy charge, aurically. So now you're not only picking up the empowerment that the teacher gives you on a regular basis, but your own meditation is improving, which is causing you to gain more power, plus you're learning to avoid things—those are lifestyle recommendations—how to be more energy efficient, you know, avoiding negative people, negative emotions, negative experiences that drain you.

Gradually what you're doing is—it's like taking an unhealthy corporation that has more money going out than coming in. We gradually cut out the expenditures except those that are necessary and we increase our balance of payments, we have more money coming in. The United States is unhealthy. We have more money going out than coming in. We should reverse that. It has to be the other way. So an organism, in order to stay healthy, let alone become more healthy and more empowered, has to have more energy coming in than going out. Meaning we have more good aura coming in than bad aura, you see?

In the beginning, the teacher gives you some power and teaches you basic concentration, gazing, meditation, ways to create power. As you practice you'll be creating more power, plus the teacher is handing you power, so you're getting more power, plus you're losing less power because you're becoming more energy efficient. And there are other ways to gain power that I'm not going to discuss right now.

So you're getting more power, and then at a certain point when you should have some level of self-control and understanding, and if you've survived the first year of your apprenticeship, you're given a task. The task gives you a lot more power. A lot—because it comes from not the human world, but the world of *seeing*. As you perform the task it interfaces you with other dimensional realities. The task obviously is always something that's either beneficial to the apprentice or to the world at large or to other apprentices, or whatever it is. We only do things that assist others because that's the only way we see life. We're not mean, angry, petty people. We get all of that out of ourselves. We live in higher auric states where we only see beauty, light and perfection and we have no negative intent towards any organism. We remove that from ourselves. We also remove the self, the ego.

We refine ourselves completely by going into the light again and again and again, and focusing on it totally until there's only the light. But an apprentice who not only doesn't follow the direction of the teacher to go through the purifications, meaning monitor their mind, use this energy to control their thoughts—if they just use this energy—you can use it in a lot of ways. You can use it to look better and have people admire you. You can use it to make a lot of money. You can use it to be successful. You can use it to hurt others. You can use it to injure others. This is a powerful energy. You think very badly about something, someone, some pretty terrible things can happen to them. It's power.

A person who doesn't monitor themselves properly as they continue to meditate and gain more power and particularly once they've started doing the tasks of occultism, which gives them even more power, such a person is headed to disaster. Because as more and more power flows into you, if you're not using that power as you should be to continually refine yourself to even higher levels, sooner or later something's going to happen.

Now the teacher, for a while—because teachers understand how difficult it is, how confusing the world is, and how weird the whole path to enlightenment is—they have a sense of humor about it and when they see the apprentices getting in too deep, they pull all that—everything that was supposed to happen that would be awful to the apprentices—they pull into their bodies so the apprentice doesn't have a major disaster. And that goes on for some time, because it's hard. It's confusing sometimes. It's hard to sort out the thoughts, the emotions, the desires. It's hard to stay on the path. It's the "razor's edge," as we used to say in Tibet.

But still, there comes a time when you must be culpable as an apprentice. There comes a point where you have to bear the responsibility for your actions and your thoughts, and the teacher will not step between you and your karma. Meaning, whatever you're drawing to yourself, finally, you have to experience. Because if you still are screwing around, if you're still not doing your homework, in spite of everything the teacher has said, and they've absorbed all kinds of disasters for you time after time; if you still continue to not do the right thing, obviously this could go on perpetually and you're not getting your hand burned, so why should you be motivated to straighten anything out? So what the teacher finally does is step out of the way. And they say, "OK, sucker, I've pulled the karma for you. I've taken this bad energy in my body, you know, it hasn't been much fun, but I've done it because that's what we do for each other." The same way a parent changes the diapers and does a lot of things for kids that may not be fun, but that's what we do as a race—we help each other out, if we're at all intelligent, as a species, in order to survive, we do that. It's just a life process.

But there comes a point where you've got to figure something out and for the teacher to continue to absorb your problems, if you're not going to do anything to straighten them out, is not going to help. You've got to experience your karma. And in that experience you will learn something. You will learn how unpleasant it is, when someone is not always cleaning up your messes. You know, the mother gets tired of picking up after the kid and finally says, "OK, you want to live in a slum, live in a slum. That's your business. OK, see what it feels like." You see?

So we're getting near the solstice—this is one of these multi-level Rama conversations—and it's a very powerful time. It's a very good time for you to examine your life and ask yourself what you're doing as an occultist. What are you doing? And you should ask yourself this question every time you get near a solstice or an equinox—every day. But particularly four times a year you really need to go through yourself and really look—with a cold eye, with no condemnation, no guilt, just you want to know what's what.

It is most important that you understand that there are tremendous repercussions for using power improperly. And you could say, "Well, I don't use it improperly." Well, to not use it properly is to use it improperly. It's not like money that you can just leave in the bank. Maybe you're not buying guns to shoot people. Good for you. But in this case, if you don't use it, if you don't use the power to improve your occult practices, it will intensify what's already there, which is obviously going to be more negative than positive. This is not the intention of the occult teacher, and it should never happen. It only happens when you have an apprentice who doesn't understand the repercussions. Now, the Far East people understand the repercussions.

In the West, my experience has been that people are basically oblivious to power, solstices, enlightenment and everything that matters. They don't understand the multi-life sequences; they don't understand anything. And anything that they can't see in a laboratory, they think is nonsense. But I'll be interested to see how they do when they die, these great empiricists. We'll see what all this great empirical stuff is worth at the moment of death, you see?

The powers of life could care less what you think. They are what they are and they work the way they do. Life is wonderful; it's amazing, but it has to be taken very seriously. And we draw repercussions from our actions, not just in this life and at this moment, but in our future lives, and there are definitely future lives just as there have been past lives. The karma that you bring upon yourself, if you don't use occult energy properly from a teacher, is stronger than most karmas. If you use it really improperly, if you use the power that was given to you to become enlightened, and you use it for the destruction of others, if you let it flow into hate, anger, violence and things like that, deception, whatever it may be, what will come back to you will be horrible beyond imagination. I'm not trying to scare you, I'm just telling you—that's how karma is.

If the President of the United States or someone to whom we've given power commits a crime, or the head of the police department, his punishment should be much worse than the average person's because they're in a position of responsibility. So a person who works with an occult teacher is in a position of responsibility. You're given a power that human beings can't imagine, that you wouldn't be able to develop for countless lifetimes. Someone's giving it to you to augment your self-discovery. The purpose is pure. Now if you think, "Well, ha, ha, that person's just sort of an asshole and they're a goodie-goodie and I can now go do what I want," you're in for a big surprise, buster. You're going to have a lot of problems for a long time.

You don't understand the repercussions because in the West they don't believe in reincarnation. They don't believe in energy. This is the consumer mentality. "I'm just going to grab what I want and screw everybody else." You may be able to do that with things that don't have a lot of power to them, but in the world of occultism, you can't bring that mentality in. You have to bring a very severe respect for the power of the occult. If you don't, if you don't have the respect, obviously, then you will not pay attention to it. If you don't know what it can do either way, it will still affect you. The effect of the occult energy doesn't depend on your awareness. You may not know that there's an area where they had a nuclear test that's radioactive, but if you walk through it, you're going to die. Your awareness is not necessary. Your lack of awareness is what kills you.

An occult teacher will, for some time with apprentices, come between them and their own foolishness because that's part of learning. But there comes a point where, if you want to keep putting your hand in the fire, sooner or later somebody is going to stop grabbing your hand out because they see that that's not teaching you anything, and I guess you've got to get burned.

The solstice is coming. And what a good occultist does is they hook themselves to the next solstice or equinox and they let it pull them. By that I mean they allow it to work—that power to work through them—to accomplish their occult tasks. And the occult tasks—there's only one—and that's to get as high as you possibly can. That's the only task worth doing.

Everything we do is designed to bring ourselves into continued states of newness and brightness and beauty and perfection. That's the only task there is. Everything we do is supplemental to that, aids that; anything that gets in the way of that we eliminate.

We want to see the universe in its absolute, pure, naked perfection. We want to know its wonder. We want to know the totality of ourselves. That's done in steps and degrees and not in one day—gradually, with a great deal of common sense, a lot of hard work, a happy sense. A wonderful sense of humor is necessary. It's a very complicated study, the study of enlightenment, the study of power, the study of perfection.

So as we approach the solstice, and this particular solstice being as powerful as it is, perhaps the power of this solstice will enable you to understand this. Because I've talked about this before and it's obviously gone over people's heads, by and large. But we haven't had a solstice this powerful for about five years, since 1985. There's a power that you can use now to understand things that maybe—it's hard to read in the dark, but if it's really bright, it's easy to read. It's about to be really bright, and that brightness, if you don't cover your eyes, will enable you to see what's what.

Occultists just like to know what's what. We're—inquiring minds want to know. We're your basic consumer. We just want to know what are the good choices, what will make us happy, how can we avoid unhappiness, what will make us healthy, how can we avoid disease, how can we make money and not lose money, how can we be successful. But in addition to all that, we also want to know what will bring us to fulfillment, what will bring us to the totality of ourselves, what will bring us beyond all the limited states of awareness into those perfect states that are even beyond ecstasy itself. And so we study that, we learn that, and it's a very specific art, and it involves complete control of the mind and the body and the spirit.

At the same time, we learn to hook ourselves to powers and forces that make it easier. It would be very hard to do otherwise. We use the *ki,* we use the flow of the universe. The energy of the opponent is used to throw him. You can only beat a bigger opponent if you use that person's energy. So we use the gravitational forces and powers of the universe to escalate our evolution, and the downward energies are avoided. We use the uplifting energies.

Chapter Twenty-Five
TENACITY

An individual has to be tenacious enough to become enlightened. Everyone lives down at the bottom of the hill, in the city—in India everybody lives in these huge cities or off in the country, but whatever it is, it's all a fairly low auric level, with certain exceptions, Benares, things like that. But even that's kind of the costume jewelry of enlightenment.

But way up on top of the hills—this is how it was a while back if we can use geography as kind of a symbolic representation of the mind—there are the Himalayas, up top, snowy ranges, way up top. And people are living down in the city. And the cities are hot and crowded and they're filled with the thoughts, feelings and desires of humanity. We could even go so far, perhaps, as to say that the cities are representative of the human condition. In other words, you might say, "Well God, these cities that we have, they're so crowded, there are slums, there are nice neighborhoods, there are—." They're all just reflections of the human psyche. They didn't just occur at random. These are the by-products, these are the auras, the creations of human beings. The earth in its current state reflects the consciousness of humanity. It's an imprint of their evolution. What else could it be?

There are some individuals who are born, like we all are, in a city—be it the city, the farm, but down at the low altitudes of mind. They lead their lives like everyone else does until one day, they just sort of look around. You look around yourself and you know that this isn't it, and thus the spiritual quest begins. Oh, I'm sure in past lives the person did the same thing, all that sort of stuff. But—the spiritual quest begins.

A person then has to be very tenacious if they're going to overcome it, because the entire world they know—it's like everybody subscribes to the same magazines and everybody gains their view of the world from the same magazines. But suddenly one day, you've been reading these same magazines and they've always been very entertaining. You've been watching the television shows, you have all the props of humanity—the families, the friends, the things to look forward to, the things to dread, the good times, the bad times, the menu-driven world of humanity. Then something in you one day just looks around and goes, "Oop! This is not it!" It's been "it" up until now but suddenly it doesn't feel right anymore; it just doesn't feel good. In the old days in the Far East, such a person would then want to get away from the crowds because they felt something, an awareness, a feeling, that was very difficult to pin down in words, but it certainly would be very hard to experience in those cities or on the farms around people. It's real hard to experience it around people.

So the individual would then leave the cities. They'd leave the family, and probably they'd be shocked by what they were saying, "Mom, Dad, I'm out of here."

"Well, what's going to happen? We need you to take care of the farm, or run the business, or you're supposed to get married to Susie," or whatever.

"Sorry, I just gotta go. I just gotta go. I just can't handle this. It's not me, you didn't do anything wrong, or maybe you did. But in any case, I'm out of here. It's been OK, adios!"

So, suddenly an individual finds themselves doing that. It doesn't necessarily happen in a day. It's a long process, but a day finally comes when it hits you. You just can't do this anymore. You just can't do it because it doesn't mean anything to you anymore. It doesn't have a pull. You watch all these other people who are obviously very, very much engaged in living the human life. They seem to be having a good time with it all, or a bad time. But whatever it is, it drives them. And you're just looking at it. And one day you look at it and it just doesn't make any sense to you. We're not discussing whether it's qualitatively good or bad, it's just, you're looking at it and saying, "Wait a minute, what a—what is this? I watch TV and I don't enjoy it. I go to the places I'm supposed to go, I dress the way I'm supposed to dress, I do all the things, but I don't—these other people seem to get off on it, but it's just not doing it for me this week."

Such an individual then will obviously look for something that does do it for them. And usually that involves a great deal of solitude. This is how it used to be. You see, it's very difficult to get solitude on the earth, but we're taking you back a thousand years or so here. Such an individual, in India, the subcontinent, would then leave and would usually go up in the mountains. You climb up the mountains. You don't know why. It's just because—it's not going to be very comfortable up there, and you don't climb the mountains because you're avoiding comfort. You're looking for purity, a purity of a kind, a clarity. Something that just isn't all garbled. Someplace where you can feel the earth again, maybe. Where you can feel what the wind feels like. You can see the stars at night and actually not just look at little dots in the sky, but you can feel an energy from them. When you're around the aura of humanity in those cities, you can't feel anything. You feel the thoughts and desires and auric formations of human beings.

So you climb on up the hill, you take the trip, you go up to Nepal or Bhutan or Tibet or someplace up there, and you get up there because you've heard the rumors that there are other people like yourself who are up there; they're up on top and they are doing something different up there. They wanted to get away from it all.

Now, needless to say, there are going to be two kinds of people up there, really three. One is the structural, organizational people. These are people who went up to the top, they had the vision and after a while they couldn't maintain it. They kind of missed the cities. They like being up there, and they like self-discovery and they like meditating. They like the experience of consciousness. So what they do is they get together and they form a community and they put together a little city, a monastery. And pretty soon the monastery develops history, customs, scriptures. Oh, all this is doubtlessly based around the religious teachings of one Buddha or another, but after a while the monastery takes on a kind of a functional autonomy, and the people in the monastery don't necessarily have very strong or powerful experiences. It becomes another way of living, and perhaps it suits that person. If it does, they'll stay there.

Now there's another group of people who have kind of a wilder look in their eye. These guys and gals are a little further out, right? These are the people who are seeking the peak experience. And once the monasteries were built up there, initially when they probably got up there, they tried out a monastery for a while, met a couple teachers. They were handed the beads, the bowl, they put on the ochre robe, shaved the head and started doing all the exercises and the practices. But then after a while, they probably noticed that initially it gave them a new clarity, a new purity, the self-discipline was fun, the meditation was fun. They developed a new orientation and it felt better than it did before.

But after a while they noticed—they look at all the people doing the beads, they look at everybody singing the songs. Everybody's looking good, you know, they've got the good monastery, the right outfits, the good looking ochre robes. No, I mean there are lousy monasteries where they're real scummy. They're not well run at all and the people are really flaky and the vibration is terrible. But let's say you got a good one, everything is kind of pristine and looking good. And it's all looking good, and you do it for a while, and it's feeling good, but then a day comes when suddenly you're looking at everybody doing the beads and singing the songs, and you know that prayers are in two hours, and then it's time to go work in the kitchen, and you know it's all scheduled out, and suddenly you're looking at everybody, and they're all really involved in it. I mean they're getting into it heavily.

But you look at it, and it's like you're down in the city again, and you say, "Wait a minute, this is not it, for me." And of course you doubt yourself, "Well, what's wrong with me because all these other people obviously seem to be having some kind of great experience here and they're all totally getting off on it," right? I mean, they're sitting in those lectures on the dharma and they're just eating it up, and you're sitting there kind of looking around. Because you don't feel the pulse, you see, enlightenment isn't there. Practice is there, and practice is good and it's a necessary step, but I guess you're through that step.

So then you hear about some weird radical group that is way up on the left, and they don't have a real fancy monastery. It's kind of basic. And you go there, and there's some teacher there. Now the teacher there is real different. Doesn't necessarily have all the robes and artifices and conch shells and all the good stuff, OK? And you walk into the room, and he kind of looks at you and says, "What do you want?" You know, they give you a harder time. I mean it's not predictable. Oh, they might be very nice, or they could be into anything, but the teacher there is not exactly what the other people were like down on the real classy, Mercedes Benzy kind of monastery. The teacher is just a little off, a little weird, see? And the people there all look a little bit strange—they're all a little bit off, too.

But you'll notice when you sit there, even though it doesn't look like you figure it should in the storybook version you have of the enlightenment experience, as you're sitting there, you're looking at the teacher, you notice that the room starts to change colors. You see the guy's auras are flipping through and the room is spinning and suddenly you're moving into different mindstates. You won't have necessarily the prayers at five in the morning, and you won't hear the beautiful dharma singing and all this jazz, but the people are flipping through different levels of consciousness. In other words, they're avidly pursuing the enlightenment experience.

So what I've done is given you a few levels. I've given you the level of common humanity—having children, having families, growing old, dying, the endless samsara. Then we have, of course, the local religions down there, which I really say are part of the same thing. They're just custom houses, social situations, something to hold onto, funeral rights, marriages, christenings, nice ways to live, moralities. That's one level. I don't really separate the local churches from the local people.

Your second level is your fancy monastery, OK? In the sense that it's very well run, very antiseptic and it's a place for people to do serious practice. They work real hard there. It's not flaky. There are the flaky monasteries, but they're not worth considering. They're just like bad restrooms in the service stations. The less said about them the better. No, you know what I'm talking about—as opposed to the nice, clean sparkly restroom in the Exxon station. We don't have to talk about the bad ones, we don't even talk much about the good ones. But the bad ones, we all know about that. So the real flaky monasteries, we don't have to talk about those. Those are just, they're not even monasteries. And there are bad teachers who run them sometimes who are just mean, nasty people who try and get power over people for their own egotistical little reasons, or do black magic and sorcery, all kinds of weird stuff. But it's all egotism and vanity, and it's gross.

But there are some nicely run Buddhist monasteries, the kind you always see in the *Kung Fu* movies. They just do practice there. Nobody's really enlightened. Maybe they had a guy who was enlightened a thousand years ago who started the monastery and since then they've been doing their best to keep up with it, but they don't have somebody to really show them how to become enlightened. I mean, you don't just go find out on your own.

It's a very complicated matter to become enlightened. If it happens to a person without a teacher in this lifetime, you can bet their boots they've had about a thousand teachers in their last thousand lives because it's a very complicated thing to do, to become enlightened. Very complicated. I mean, you don't just sit down and design a supercomputer. You take a lot of classes before you get to the point where you design a supercomputer. See what I mean? Now, a lot of people will take the classes—that doesn't mean they can design a supercomputer. That's obviously going to be a certain kind of mind.

So we have the basic humanity, we have the posh ashram and then we have the wild-eyed types who actually have a teacher who's enlightened or very close, who are all sitting around really not stuck in any particular way of doing things. Now there's no suggestion that one thing is better than another. But the person who felt uncomfortable in the other situations will probably feel more comfortable there. There, people really practice and their teacher gives everybody a hard or a happy time constantly, depending upon what he or she is into. But you're dealing with real enlightenment. Real enlightenment doesn't fit into your storybook ideas.

Then there's one other group that's worth mentioning. It's not a group, it's an individual, and it's a solitary individual who goes off on their own in the mountains and doesn't get involved with the posh ashram where it's well run, obviously avoids the flaky ashrams and knows where they are, nor do they go down to the local enlightened teacher with all the bright-eyed types who are on their way to enlightenment, working through various solutions. That individual wanders alone and just meditates by themselves. They might stop by a monastery once in a while, visit, listen to a talk, but they feel that their path is strictly solitary. And they roam by themselves. There are some enlightened teachers like that, too. Once in a while there's an enlightened teacher who doesn't take students, and they just roam. Whomever they meet they do their best to confuse, you know, that sort of thing, to teach something to. No, I mean it goes without saying, but they don't really have a fixed abode and they don't accept students at all.

You're dealing, here, with a guy who's involved with the wild-eyed group. It's the actual practice of enlightenment, which has nothing to do with religion at all. It has nothing to do with the well-run monastery at all where everybody is doing practice. Everybody is practicing in the other one, but the real—the real enlightenment experience draws very few individuals. You have to be terribly tenacious. There's a certain drive you have, that you will never be placated by illusory forms of self-discovery. You won't settle for the town with the local churches. You won't settle for the really well-run monastery. You want the peak experiences.

Naturally, people who are involved in peak experiences are not what you might think. In other words, the way of humanity is to turn everything into a marketable product, and religion and enlightenment are no exceptions. But when we turn something into a marketable product, it loses something. Christianity is a marketable product. It has very little to do with Jesus Christ. I'm sure it has nothing to do with Jesus Christ at all, what that experience was like to be around the guy when he was walking around, for the three years he was teaching. This has nothing to do with it—these churches, edifices, robes, cardinals, Vaticans, popes. It is whatever it is, but it has nothing to do with any of that. I mean that was a bunch of wild-eyed guys who were just walking around with the guy. He was doing miracles, talking to them, telling them about other ways to live and be. That was very different than the well-ordered, "Let's go to church on Sunday." He didn't say anything about going to church on Sunday. They all gave up everything and just roamed around with the guy while he did what he did. See? That's what the study of enlightenment is like.

Enlightened teachers are not logical. They don't function from levels that are understandable to the human mind. They're not religious. Religions form around them, usually after they've died, because they've said interesting things and obviously they had a power and it left an impression on the minds of some of their students who wrote books and set up scriptures and ways of being and the structures.

But real enlightenment is something that, you have to be there. In other words, the only way it really happens is, you have to be there. You've got to find an enlightened teacher. And you're with them and you go through whatever they happen to be into at the moment. It's very vicarious. Whatever they're into, everybody does—just because they're into it. It's not a clone situation, it's just because that's where the teacher is at the moment.

In other words, in this culture it seems that the student wants the teacher to be in some way available for them and feels that it's the teacher's bound duty to turn into what they want them to be. Somehow, in other words, you walk in and you want the teacher to be a certain way because this is how teachers are. You've got it all figured out. So now the teacher's going to be one of "these" because you've decided that's what the teacher's supposed to be this week. You've got it all figured out before you arrive. Your Hollywood images are all in your mind. "Well, the teacher's going to look this way, talk this way, act this way, this is what I'm supposed to feel," you see? You've got this very defined idea before you ever arrive.

Now, there are people, of course, who are imposters, phonies, who know all that and they will act that out. They will portray that part completely, knowing that that's what someone wants. And of course, they'll fulfill that expectation; everybody will love them, they'll be very popular. But a real teacher is not there to be of service to you. In other words, there's a weird idea—teachers in the Western culture, by and large, are viewed as impotent. In the Western culture, the profession of a teacher—who becomes a teacher? Let's say an academic teacher in high school, college—they're usually kind of laid-back, scholarly, somewhere between a yuppie and a nerd. Right? Unless they're a P.E. teacher. Right? No, I mean, think of what a teacher is in your mind. Whereas you think of a billionaire, someone who makes a lot of money, a corporate executive or a corporate raider, even better, an Olympic athlete—that's a virile, strong person. But this is not the case necessarily in the East.

This is a very Western notion that teachers are impotent. They're these kind of—they're like Mom, after she's kind of burned out. You can always go to her, she's not going to create any trouble, she's there to just take her energy, clean up after you, say everything is all right, then you can split. That's Mom. Mom is impotent, basically. She might have been hot to trot before she had the kids, she was a real hot little number, wore the miniskirts, looked good. But now she's—if I can step into the world of cartoons— *Calvin and Hobbes?* And the mother and the father there are great. They're the mother and the father of the 90s. The father's an attorney; he's kind of a yuppie type. He's kind of burned out. Just wants to sit in his easy chair after working all week and being completely drained. And the mother is the same thing, and they have this wild kid who they really don't want, who is Calvin. Calvin has a lot of energy and he's kind of wild-eyed and crazy. And mom and dad just are listless, tired, mellow types. They just wanted listless, tired, mellow kids. But instead they got Calvin. He's totally frenetic; he eats the sugar bombs by the carton just to mellow out! They've got this crazy kid, see?

So in the West you expect a teacher to be a very impotent person. You expect, usually, they'll be from the Far East, very old, lots of wrinkles; you'll come in and you'll get what you want out of them and leave. That's your idea. They're here to be of service to you. What bullshit. What vanity. What egotism—to think such a thing—in the world of enlightenment.

I don't know about scholastics. In scholastics that's largely true because we hire the wrong people. We should hire virile men and women who are tough, who are fighters. That's what a teacher is—it's someone who has worked their way to the top and can transmit that spirit and that information to someone else. That's a teacher.

But in the world of self-discovery, if it's real enlightenment, not religion, you're dealing with someone who has done what almost no one on earth has ever done. You're dealing with someone who's broken through every rule, every barrier, every "do" and "do not," and they've reached an apex of consciousness. They've broken through all the conditioning, all the timidity. They don't buy any program. Someone who's fought their way through to that is virile, is tough, is one tough hombre. Now, that's not going to be your little image of the kind of quiet teacher who just kind of walks up (Rama playfully imitates an East Indian teacher), "Oh, is very good to see you today, students. How nice, please sit, we will have darshan, close your eyes and repeat the sacred mantra!" (Back to normal voice.) And then you'll walk out with kind of a passive, dead feeling, with no energy involved and you've done your religious enlightened bit, and they'll say some nice words about truth or maybe even about emptiness, something for you to think about that will confound your little simplistic mind for a while. Which isn't hard! (Audience laughs.)

But if you have someone who's intense, who's virile, who's just like—when I say "virile," I don't mean that necessarily sexually; I don't mean it not sexually, but I don't want to limit it to that definition—but someone who's strong, which is what you have to be to become enlightened. You have to have fought through every limitation inside yourself. Such a person is not going to sit there and just be passive. And they're not going to be around for you to get what you want out of them in your way, when you don't even know what it is to get or what is there to get. You don't know anything about it. You're coming in looking for something. You have no idea what's involved. This person does.

Such a person is going to tell you what to do and how to do it if you're interested, and if you impress them that you even have the potential. But you in the West expect someone is just going to be here; it's going to be like your high school teacher was. They're going to sit here, you can ask them all the questions you want, get whatever you want and walk out. That has nothing to do with the enlightenment experience. Nothing.

In the enlightenment experience you're dealing with someone who's done what no one does. They've overcome the self. That doesn't make you passive, that doesn't make you anything that can be verbalized. It makes you everything. Yet there's still a body there for some reason, with an infinite consciousness floating through it. You can't comprehend what it means. Don't try. If you want to become that way, you're going to deal with someone who's very intense. Not off, not out of balance, not someone who will take advantage of you, just someone who's operating from levels you can't even imagine.

Now that shocks most people. That shakes them up; that scares them. Padmasambhava is the classic teacher. Oh, you can read accounts of his illustrious miracles, which have been embellished about a thousand times over, to the point where it's ridiculous. But if you can get past that, you've got a guy who came to—you know he brought Buddhism to Tibet, and this was one tough motherfucker. This guy is tough, this Padmasambhava; he's a hot dude. He goes off, he meditates in a cemetery for five years, then spreads the dharma, then he kills a couple of people, throws a rock off a tower and somebody dies, and then in court he wins because he informed everybody that this guy had it coming from a past life, right? (Audience laughs.) You know.

Padma's hanging around with the princess and he's all over the place, but he's pure as can be. He's coming from a place human beings can't imagine. Human beings want you to be orthodox, to fit into their ideas of purity and spirituality. Fuck that. Just fuck it. It's bullshit. In other words, human beings want to deaden you. They want to turn you into something that's porridge, that's palpable, that works into the 50-minute timeslot on TV at night.

Enlightenment is X-rated, honey, if you haven't checked it out. It's hot, it's vivacious. You're going to take your mind and merge it with the entire cosmos—your idea of the word "cosmos" is what you can perceive with your senses.

You're going to merge your mind with the mind of eternity that goes on forever? You're going to do that? That's not easy. It's very intense. I mean sitting on Mount St. Helens when it went off would have been small talk. You're going to refract your mind through the endless refractions of infinity, constantly, forever? That's not exactly your timid type who does that, or your mellow type.

A real enlightened teacher is intense. And they could care less what you think about anything at any time since you are lost in illusions. They understand that because they were once in the same place. Of course there's understanding. But if you want somebody timid and dead like yourself so you can feel comfortable, well there are lots of them out there. But real teachers are very intense, if they're enlightened. They're very strong. They don't take shit from anybody. Yet they'll take shit from anybody if that's what they're supposed to do. It's complicated, it's complicated.

The world of enlightenment is for very few people. It's for people who have what we call an edge. They're not people who want the religious imagery—oh, you may have gone through that phase. They're not people who want the human deadness. They don't really want somebody to pat them on the shoulder and tell them everything that they want is acceptable. A lot of religion and a lot of the pseudo enlightenment is just people who are kind of practicing psychology. Originally, before there was psychology and psychiatry, there was religion. And there still is. It's just saying that it's OK, or whatever you believe is OK. It's peer group acceptance.

Real enlightenment has nothing to do with this world. It has nothing to do with this world. It's the entrance into infinite consciousness. Beyond the body. Outside of time and space. That doesn't fit into any pragmatic program, and almost no one has the guts to try it. Which is OK—that's why there are very few who reach that point, and those who reach that point are indifferent completely to all others. But because there's a tradition, because someone once helped them when they were a complete asshole lost in illusion, you do that for someone else. It's sort of a payback, I guess, to the universe. A karmic chain of some kind that isn't really karmic. It's just how it works. I don't have words for it.

The enlightenment experience is not what you think. It can't be, or it couldn't be enlightenment. How could it be anything that you can configure, anything you can imagine, any way that you think it should be, any way that you want it to be? Nor is it necessarily what you don't want. It just is what it is.

Your entrance into enlightenment begins where you are at any given moment. And the outer forms, symbols, are completely irrelevant. They might be there, they might not be there. What matters is—is there enlightenment? Yes, everything is enlightenment. Yes, there's enlightenment inside of you. Yes, there are numerous pathways, forms of yoga, Buddhism, Taoism, blah, blah, blah, that lead to enlightenment. But they all are dead ends, of course. They just lead you to a certain point where you have to make a leap yourself.

But the experience of enlightenment is something that rubs off. It's transferred. Now, it isn't really transferred, that is to say, you don't really transfer it from teacher to student. The student has to find it on their own, just as the teacher did. But it's transferred in the sense that the steps, the alignments, the melding of the mind with infinity is a complicated maneuver, or series of maneuvers, that you learn from a teacher. You don't learn it physically, I mean, it's nothing that can be explained in words. It's something that you learn occultly or inwardly or mystically. It can't be discussed. And a person who seeks it will find it.

Very few people seek it, and that's just fine. It's not something that's supposed to be sought, necessarily. It's not something that, "Oh gee, isn't it too bad, there aren't a lot of people seeking enlightenment now." There never were. There probably never will be. That doesn't matter. If someone has the impetus and the drive, they seek it. And if they seek it, they'll find it—if they don't stop.

Chapter Twenty-Six
Buddhist Yoga

The essence of all practice is to be cool. Life is not worth getting excited about because whatever you perceive is an illusion. If you like getting excited, then you can get excited. But if your excitement is anything more than enjoyable, then you're making a mistake. The essence of all practice is to be relaxed, to be at peace with yourself. Now, you can't really be at peace with yourself if you're trying to hold onto things that are illusions. Think about it for a second.

Nothing lasts. Consider everything that you've gone through and experienced thus far. How many things did you really get upset about in your life thus far? How many things have you freaked out about? A lot of things—that are completely gone now. The amount of emotional trauma that you've gone through over things that today have no importance—and they didn't have any importance then, except that you gave them importance by magnifying situations and giving them a power over you. It's understood that nothing lasts.

This universe is just like the sky. Clouds come and go, but the sky remains. The universe is unchanging. It takes countless forms. To be perturbed about whether there are a lot of clouds in the sky today is silly because whatever is in the sky is going to change. That's the nature of the sky. One day it's clear, the next day it's cloudy. One day it rains, the next day it snows, the next day it's sunshine.

Human beings affix themselves to things that are of little or no importance. They affix themselves to the transitory, to things that are impermanent. And in doing so, they get all upset. Nothing lasts; everything changes. Life changes into death, death changes into life. So the essence of all practice is to be cool, to be relaxed, to be poised, to be at one with the changeless and to go through the experiences of transience, the experiences of daily life and nightly life—to go through them with a very balanced, open viewpoint.

You're much too hung up, you human beings, on all of your ideas and your desires. You still have not penetrated the essence of yoga. You think that yoga is in some way going to make everything you want to happen work out, and you're going to be able to avoid what you don't want. That's not yoga. That's desire and aversion. The purpose of yoga is not to care about things, to detach ourselves from the ephemeral world, which causes us pain. The world doesn't cause us pain by the fact that it exists, but we cause ourselves pain because we attach ourselves to circumstances. And when those circumstances are in conflict with what we want or don't want, we experience pain. The answer is to pull our attention, our awareness, our focus, back from the physical world and to place it on something that's changeless and ecstatic, which is the pure and perfect light of reality, which exists inside all things.

There's another world other than this world. Oh, there are countless worlds, dimensions, planes, but there's another world that's formless. It doesn't have a form. It doesn't really change. That doesn't imply that it's static; it's beyond change and changelessness. The purpose of all yoga or Buddhism, Taoism, practice, enlightenment, occultism, whatever it is, is to reach into that plane, world, call it what you will, with our minds—to enter into that reality through the conscious focus of the mind. Just to experience that reality is to be free.

In order to experience that reality, we have to remove ourselves from this reality. That is to say, what creates the world is our focus. If you focus on getting a job and you're all hung up about it, and if you don't get that one particular job, your world is ruined. Then you'll go through a lot of misery and torment. You'll go to an interview; you're waiting to hear, biting your nails, you're all upset. If you get the job you're happy and smiling; if not, you're depressed and suicidal. But the person next to you could care less about that job. That's not even in their mind. You could be the person next to you. You could forget about the whole thing.

In other words, we assume that the things that are important in our lives are intrinsically in some way important, and the things that are unimportant are unimportant. That's not true at all. We produce importance and unimportance by bringing to bear the power of our life, of our attention field, of our mind on something. What we focus on becomes reality. We give reality to things through the venue of our perception. When we withdraw our perception from the world, then our perception will go someplace else.

In other words, you can't meditate on the clear light of reality, you can't put your mind into *samadhi*, you can't experience ecstasy if you're all caught up in the things of the world. Obviously, if your feet are on one side of the street, they're not on the other side of the street. So if you're all caught up in this world, there's no way you can experience ecstasy; you're in this world. But this world really doesn't exist, per se. Obviously, the world exists. If it exists, it exists. If you see something, you're perceiving it. But that's a way of saying that the only reason you're perceiving it is because you're there and if you change your perception, it's not there. You know—if a tree falls in the forest and there's no one there to watch it, did it really fall? Well, it really doesn't matter. If you weren't there, it's not of consequence.

The world of here and there is completely dependent upon you. You see, a lot of you are trying to use the power of yoga to improve your lives. This is a terrible mistake. Because all you're doing is binding yourself more. You're putting more of your attention into the transient world. In other words, if you increase the volatility of your mind through the practice of meditation and you focus that volatility into the physical, into the realm of desires and aversions, then you're going to make everything more important. When you increase the volatility of the mind, whatever you focus it upon, the mind is going to interact with more.

The purpose of increasing the power of the mind through the practice of meditation and occultism is not to then be able to force and push our way, to get the things we want more and to avoid the things we want to avoid more. That's going to be a major pain in the ass. What we're trying to do is not care. We increase the power of our mind because our mind is hung up in a nasty little routine, and that routine is to try and get everything it wants and to avoid everything it doesn't want. Yoga means we go a step further back. In yoga we go to the cause. The cause of pain is not the world. The cause of pain is us.

All pain comes because of frustrated desire. I mean, obviously there's physical pain—you put your hand in a flame, you get burned—that's not what I'm talking about. That's sensorial pain that's caused through contact with things that are obviously not pleasant to the senses. But we're discussing mental and emotional pain. Mental and emotional pain come because we focus on things, we desire them. And either their possible loss—just the thought of it—or the actual loss causes us pain.

In other words, suppose—right now you're caught up in the trauma of your life, totally. Each one of you has a scenario going; you're making a movie. Listen to me, I'm talking to you. You're making a movie right now in which you're the star. And you've got your whole life figured out. You've already figured out what you want to have happen and what you don't want to have happen, therefore you're completely screwed. Because the likelihood of what you want occurring the way you want it to is highly unlikely. And even if you get it to happen, it won't last, see? Or the mind will shift and then it'll want something else. In other words, what you want to do is just be indifferent. You don't want to be bound by the movie. The movie is always a bad movie; it's always a B movie.

The answer is to withdraw from the stage of life and to place your attention somewhere else. In other words, if you really don't care what happens here, it won't affect you, it won't bother you. Now, that doesn't mean that one just doesn't care. That's absurd. You can't not care. Of course you're going to care. But what you do is, you move your caring to a safe place. There's nothing safe here. Everyone and everything dies. Anyone you care for is going to die and that will cause you pain. If you care for yourself, you're going to die and that's going to cause you pain. This world only brings things apart that come together, and it brings things together that weren't together.

The solution is not, as Charlie Brown once said to Lucy in a comic strip, "Don't you wish sometimes we could take all the people we love and bring them all together and put our arms around them and just hug them forever?"

That's not the solution, because that's not going to happen. Or even if it does, it's not going to last. The solution is not to care.

I irritate my students whenever I make a suggestion that's contrary to their current view of themselves and the world, which is the only kind of suggestions I ever make. They immediately get upset because they feel that what I'm suggesting runs contrary to their desires and their aversions. They're so fixed in their view of themselves and the world that they don't want to let go of it. So they experience mental suffering and emotional suffering at the mere mention of anything that they had not already scripted in their internal movie. This is ridiculous. What you're trying to do is free yourself completely from the trap of selfhood, from the trap of being.

There's no such thing as a better life. All of life is either wonderful or horrible. I mean, call it what you will. But no one life is better than another. All lives are equally painful, it's just some people don't let on how much pain they're in. Oh yes, you can be in the cancer ward and it's very painful physically. And we all go through the pain of having a body and of living and dying. But the real answer is to move our perception someplace else. You've come to study with a teacher because you've realized that no matter what you do, it's a bad deal. You can be happy, but it won't last, it just sort of opens you up for the sucker punch. Now this isn't a negative way of looking at life, it's just accurate. It's just realistic. It's just a clear perception of how things really are.

Pleasure and pain are transient. Look around you. Happiness here is limited. But there are realms of light, there are realms of perfection, from which all of this comes, this world, you. We all come from a place, which we remember intuitively, that's perfect. That place always exists. It's inside us. It's the nexus of our minds. It's the central core of our being. But we don't see it because our focus is external. Just changing the focus to an ideal life won't help; it'll make things more painful later when the ideal life falls apart. Then the pain of the loss of the ideal life will totally floor you. Nor should you avoid the ideal life and seek a painful life. That's equally stupid. The answer is to live as best you can, following your intuition and your feelings, but not to get caught up in it.

In other words, there are some people who practice in the Far East. And they feel that, "Well, since everything here is painful or it's just transient pleasure, and what I have to do is remove myself and my attention from the sphere of this world, what I'm going to do is just not care about anything. I'm not going to take showers anymore; it's useless. I'm just going to focus all my attention on the other world. What happens here is of no importance. Why bother? Why get involved? Why try?"

That doesn't work. That doesn't cause one to be happy either because you really can't run away from the world and the body. They think they can, but they can't. They're experiencing the external world constantly. They're experiencing their thought forms, their desires. Just because you deny yourself something doesn't mean you really don't want it. Who are we kidding?

The answer lies deeper. It's really a change in psychology, our own psychology. What yoga teaches us, what Buddhism teaches us, is not to want things, not to avoid things, not to be upset by the loss. In the "I Ching," there's a hexagram that says, "Be like the sun at midday." View all things as being equal. It's the hexagram of abundance. "The king attains abundance" is the judgment. You get everything you want. Everything works out real well.

Normally, the sage, who is a little deeper than the average person—you win the lottery, you're totally ecstatic, you're going to get everything you want—the sage would immediately get depressed because he knows that if you get everything you want, it's not going to last. The stock has gone as high as it can. Now it's going to start to go down.

But that's really not a correct view either. The guys who wrote the old "I Ching," they say, no, that's a mistake. It's as much of a mistake to rejoice at getting everything as to be depressed at the thought of, "Now that I have everything, sooner or later it's inevitable that it's all going to go away." Both are erroneous. The right view is just to enjoy everything, but not to be stuck on it. The right view is just to say, "Look, everything is transient. And great, I've got everything! Good! I'll have fun with it. Great, it's not going to last. That's OK, then I'll enjoy that experience." Life is a circle. Today you have it, tomorrow you don't; the next day you have it, the next day you don't.

It's easy to say, "Well, just feel equal about all things and don't mind gain and loss and pleasure and pain." You can have that idea, but that doesn't mean you can do it. Because the winds of desire, the winds of aversion are very strong.

In order to do that so it's not just a neat idea that you'll forget about as soon as something really goes wrong, or really goes right, in order to be able to attain the equanimity of perfect dispassion you have to have something to distract yourself, essentially, from this world. You've got to have something that makes everything here seem unimportant. That's the secret. In other words, you're not going to move to another neighborhood until you find one better than the one you're in. It's all well and good to say, "Well, have an equal mind and view all things equally, pleasure, pain, loss and gain." You know, that's the classic yogic aphorism. But the answer is that you have to have something much more wonderful to absorb yourself in, and then you won't notice. If you're having a wonderful dream, the house can be on fire and you won't notice.

So what we do is shift our attention to a realm that's so wonderful that it really doesn't matter what happens here. And that's what the practice of meditation is. The practice of meditation is when we shift our mind through the use of the will to a realm of pure and perfect light. We learn to sustain ourselves in that realm, which actually exists. We go to another place, just like you physically walk from one room to another. We walk with our minds from the habituation of the senses, which takes us into the sensorial world or the thought world, habituations of the mind or desires or aversions or the egoistic cravings. We learn to take our mind to another place that most people don't know about. It's a place of perfect purity, peace, light and ecstasy, happiness beyond your comprehension that never ends. We call it the "clear light," *nirvana*. There are different names for it. And the more we touch that world, that endless abode of happiness, the less we care about what happens here.

That's what yoga is. Yoga is a removal of the conscious awareness from the world as you know it—meaning the world that you've constructed through your focus within your mind—to something else. Then you wonder, "What do I do here, does that mean that nothing matters? Should I act, should I not act?"

Well, you have to act. This is what Krishna says in the *Bhagavad-Gita*—karma yoga. He says that you can't avoid acting. Even if you don't move, you're going to think, you're going to sense things. You really can't avoid action. If you can't avoid action, you might as well act. Meaning, the avoidance of action is just another hang-up. So is being stuck on acting.

The answer then is to do things without being attached to the result. That's an easy line. I've read it, as probably some of you have, hundreds of times. Do things without being attached to the results. But what does that really mean? Well, what they're saying is that you should put yourself into such ecstasy that you don't really care what happens. You can happily do whatever has to be done. Your happiness is not dependent upon what happens here, on outcomes.

Imagine that you're working and you're making $100,000 a year. You really need that $100,000—that pays your bills. Now, if you don't get the $100,000, you're going to be very upset. If you get it, that's OK. But suppose you found another source of revenue. Suppose you were now making $1 million a year. It was just arriving. It was being put into your bank account. It wouldn't really matter a whole heck of a lot anymore whether you got the $100,000 or not. But yet, in life, now that someone's giving you a million, you still have to do something. You could just sit at home all the time, but maybe you like to do things. Maybe that would get to you after a while. Maybe you would still work. But it wouldn't really matter whether you got paid or not.

That's the essence of all yoga, in other words, of all *karma yoga*. If you're working for rewards, you're screwed because that's why you're working. If you get the reward, great. You live in anticipation of something. If you don't get the reward, you're unhappy. It puts you in this whole transient phase. The answer is to have so much money that it doesn't matter and you can go do anything that you want to. Money is no longer an issue.

I see a lot of people worried about money. They spend their whole lives worrying about money. My answer to worrying about money—if you're worried about money, why don't you go make so much money that you can just get anything you want? I mean, if it's such a big issue, how hard could it be to be rich? If you have any mental control, if you really put your will and your mind and your body and your spirit for a while into making a vast quantity of capital, then you'll never have to think about it again. If money's such a hangup for you, why not get too much of it? That's a yogic attitude. If it doesn't matter to you at all, then you don't need to think about it. It's not an issue.

Obviously, if the ups and downs of the transitory are driving you nuts, the answer is to get beyond the transitory. Go make so much happiness that nothing here will matter. You won't take it seriously. Loss and gain just won't matter. As I said, millions and millions of people read those lines in practice—loss and gain are the same, don't focus on the transient, be unattached to your work. But no one does it. You read the lines, you say, "That's a great idea." But then, you know you really care. You're all hung up.

I could right now say, "I want you to do the opposite of everything you're doing," and you'd freak. Whether it was better or not wouldn't matter, if it went against your desires or your aversions, you'd immediately become upset. Which tells you that you are completely into loss and gain. You're stuck completely on results of your actions. You're completely into avoidance. That means you don't really practice much yoga. If you'd practice a lot of yoga, you'd be really happy all the time and you'd have equanimity, and then if someone who knew a little more than you do pointed out a course of action which might lead you to an interesting experience, you'd be happy to take it, since it doesn't really matter.

In other words, a real yogi or yogini can at any point drop everything in their life because they know it doesn't matter—because they've realized that nothing makes you happy. And nothing makes you unhappy. What makes you happy or unhappy is to depend on happiness from activities, from experiences. Once you get to the point where you've established your awareness, you've moved it from the transient into the eternal, into the formless, and you just are happy all the time because of your experience in the formless, then you can just have fun with what's going on here. You can get highly involved, if that's what you want to do, with the world and activities. And if everything falls apart, it doesn't matter. And if everything comes out well, it really doesn't matter. If you just get a kick out of doing things, you might as well do them.

In other words, I don't really think a person should work at a job if they wouldn't do it without pay. What a bad idea, to go do something you obviously don't want to do because somebody's paying you. It's time to rethink it. I do what I do because I enjoy it. If I'm getting paid for it, fine, but I would be doing it if I wasn't getting paid. It's what I have chosen to do. Otherwise I'm working for a result. Everything I do in my life, I like. I wouldn't do it otherwise. I don't do it for a result because I know that's ridiculous.

Nothing works here, in the transient. Everything changes, everything shifts. If you bother to study the nature of reality, if you wake up for a moment and look around at life, you will observe that nothing here lasts, nothing works out. There are no happy endings. There are happy moments. But everything culminates in death; all accomplishments are washed away by death or by the next moment.

All beings are egotistic and vain, driven by their desires and aversions, and they have very little knowledge of how the whole system works, or what it could possibly lead to. If you happen to be just a little bit wakeful, then you back up and say, "Wait a minute, no matter what path I walk down, there's going to be happiness and unhappiness—unless I walk down a path that isn't in this world. That isn't in any world. If I place my mind in the midst of eternity, in the midst of eternal ecstasy, then it really doesn't matter where I am or what I'm going through. Well, then, what should I do?" How will one choose?

Well, your nature will guide you. There's a part of you that will always know, intuitively, what you should do and what you should avoid. We don't have to be concerned about that. If you're still thinking about that, that means you still think it matters. You'll just know. You'll wake up in the morning, you'll know what to do. You'll find yourself doing it.

So what yoga and the practice of Buddhism is, is the removal of the mind, of the focus of the conscious attention, from the world to infinity, to a realm of pure light. To simply increase the power of your mind through the practices that are engaged in yoga—gazing exercises, meditation, empowerments from teachers, from power places, from karma yoga, whatever it is—to simply increase the volatility and power of your mind without then using that power to move your mind to a formless realm, is going to cause you much more pain than you had prior to practicing.

We've got somebody who's running—every chance you give them—against a wall. They just keep running into the wall. Great, let's take the guy down to the gym, make him a lot stronger. Now he can run against the wall with twice as much speed and hurt himself even more and cause himself more pain. Great accomplishment!

Well, that's what I observe most people are doing with yoga. That's all they're doing—they're increasing the power of their minds, but then they are going back to or they never left the world of desire and aversion. Consequently, now that they've refined and developed the power of the mind, the pain will be all the greater, the attachment will be all the greater. Desire will completely overcome them.

It's [yoga is] through the conscious removal of the focus of the mind and the body, to the realm of spirit, to the realm of happiness. Now, when I talk about the realm of spirit, happiness, nirvana, enlightenment, I'm not talking about something ideal or imaginary. There are realms of light that exist that have always existed and will always exist. They're much more solid than the transient, sensorially perceived or mentally perceived reality that you're currently experiencing. They're just behind the world that you see. Oh, there are countless dimensional worlds, but they're no different than this one, really.

All form worlds are the same. Meaning, they're painful, ultimately frustrating. There are some good moments, some bad moments. Just to shift dimensions isn't going to make a difference, really. You'll be in the appropriate one—you'll find your way to it, for your level of evolution—where you're supposed to be in the cosmos. What really is important is to remove yourself from this world. Death doesn't help because it just places you into another world. One reincarnates. Reincarnating to a better world does not necessarily—there really isn't a better world. There are worlds that one should be in according to one's evolution. To not be in one would be somewhat painful; it's appropriate of course. Or if a world becomes inappropriate, then it would be time to shift to another plane.

But the real way out is within. It's through the practice of meditation and through leading a pragmatic life doing the different practices of yoga, Buddhism, occultism, that one frees oneself from the world, from the self. In other words, you have a habituated focus on a certain level of reality, and that certain level of reality is always painful—occasionally pleasurable, but always painful. So you have to change the way—like you get an old horse and he is used to going around the track in a certain way because he's done it so long. He can't even understand that there could be another possible way. That's what the mind is like.

The human mind is very habituated. It creates reality in very specific ways. But that doesn't mean that that's all there is. Yoga is the exploration of other states of mind, other realities, other ways of perceiving things. Those who have practiced yoga have come to know and see that there are countless ways to perceive. And you can get stuck and have fun in all of them. But if you keep searching—you can wander endlessly in the *bardo* of the *samsara*, you can wander endlessly through countless perceptual levels and have varying experiences. But it won't really make you happy. Good moments and bad moments, depending upon what's going on. Horror or ecstasy. But it's all temporary.

If you really want to be truly happy, then you have to remove your mind from all *samskaric* worlds; all worlds with formations, with aggregate formations; all worlds that have dimensionality, in which you have a self. You have to place your consciousness in the realm of the *dharmakaya,* the pure light of the void. Void means formless. You have to separate yourself from yourself, because the very self that you perceive as you, is created by the world that you're in. The world adjusts to itself.

Yoga means we train our bodies, minds and spirits to enjoy everything, to not get hung up about what happens and what doesn't happen. The way we can do that is by bringing our attention into the world of enlightenment, into enlightened mind. We do it a little bit more every day, so every day what happens to us here affects us a little less, and we're independently happy regardless of circumstances. That's the only way to happiness that I'm aware of. Everything else is just temporary. When you realize that, you stop taking shortcuts, you stop doing things poorly. You relax a little bit, you look at yourself, you look at your imperfections, you look at your life and you realize that everything has to be done right to get out of here, and so there's no point in trying to do anything poorly because it simply means that they'll send it back to you and you'll have to do it over again.

You have to completely perfect your nature. When your nature is perfect, meaning it's void, when you've completely managed to move your mind—another way of saying the same thing—away from the world and you've placed it completely in the worlds of ecstasy, in the formless plane of nirvana, whatever you want to call it, then you'll be free.

To perfect your nature doesn't mean to have some idea of what a perfect person is and simply be that. That doesn't work. To perfect your nature means to let go of this world and place your attention fully in the plane of ecstasy, in the plane of enlightenment. That's what "perfect your nature" means. Any way you can do it is valid. There's no way that it has to be done. Whatever works, works. There are methods that some of us have found that we pass around to each other who have been exploring this for a while, and that's called "the teachings." It's a very loose collection of methods that have worked for some of us. And we pass them around since no one has a copyright on them.

Chapter Twenty-Seven

LIGHT

There is only black light, between the stars. It may seem that it's darkness, but it's really black light. There's no such thing as darkness. Darkness is a human concept. There's only black light between the stars.

There is no evil, there's no bad, there's no good. These are human ideas. There's no creator, there's no creation, there's no God, there's no nirvana, there's no perfection. These are ideas. Everything is transient. That's an idea. Everything is perfect. That's an idea. Everything is imperfect. That's an idea.

Beyond ideas there's reality. That's not an idea—that's real. There's no way to talk about it, there's no way to describe it. But there's a way to get to it, a series of ways. The pathways to enlightenment are numerous and they're all in front of you. If we stand back with wide eyes and look, we'll see some of them.

Our life is a pathway to enlightenment, every moment, every experience. Everything is a pathway to enlightenment. But if we think that there is good and evil, if we think that there is blackness and we don't see that it's black light, then we see ourselves that way. We see life that way.

To go to that place that's beyond all this—all these ideas, all these abstractions—that's what I chose to do. You can do that. Beyond perfection—you could be there—beyond both truth and illusion.

The mind is a complicated thing. Very complicated. To you it seems simple. There are thoughts, there are feelings, there are emotions, there's memory, desire, self-importance, ideas, your life, your moods. The mind lives beyond death though. Anything that ends with death isn't really the mind, just the things that pass through a mind. The mind is like a diamond. It's very hard, very cold. It just is. It's like the black light. It is the black light.

There's nothing to learn in life that's important because all of the things that we learn are forgotten at death. They're important for a lifetime, perhaps, but not in the sense of eternity. But it is possible—it is!—to experience the refulgent, ecstatic perfection of all, that which never ends and never begins. It's not a fairy tale, or if it is, it's one that I live in that's rather wonderful. When I die all this will be forgotten or it will become a past life memory. And something new will happen. Something wonderful, as it always does, because creation is perfection, beyond ideas.

Beyond the shoestrings of human consciousness, there's the black light and the white light, and they only seem different to you. They're not really different at all. There's only light. Light in the mind and light outside the mind. All these shapes, these appearances that you call existence, the things that trouble you, the things that look promising, the things that you're indifferent towards, are refractions of the one light. You're a refraction of the one light. You're a waveform of light. You're a fractal, a pattern, that life has created, and that continuously changes.

The only reason you feel pain is because you're so busy looking at yourself instead of looking at the wonderful patterns of light. If you become absorbed in the wonderful patterns of light, then there's no pain.

The creative imagery of existence, life to itself, is what we are. We're made up of light. To know that, is self-knowledge, the conquest of the ego. Call it what you will.

You see, I'm a believer in the rhapsodic. I like things that are happy. For no particular reason, I just like them. Most people don't seem to be like that in this particular place, in this world. You can tell by what they focus on. Read a newspaper, watch a TV show, go to a movie, look at a life. People seem to thrive on misery and unhappiness. I seem to be a minority of one.

It's a question of discrimination, what we do with our mind, what we do with our life. You have a choice. You do. You don't believe me, I can tell, but you do [have a choice]. You can choose to look at beauty, to look at hope, to look at ecstasy, and if you look at it long enough there's nothing else. There's nothing else. In the eye of Vishnu, there's only Lakshmi. In the eye of Lakshmi, there's only Vishnu. You see?

The effort to lift one's self into perfect enlightenment is a profound thing. It has nothing to do with individual will. It's a refraction of the cosmos. The cosmos delights in itself. It's a complicated thing; no one understands it. It delights in its pain, it delights in its frustration, it delights in its boredom, it delights in its ecstasy.

But I know that if you look at a thing long enough, you become it. If you wish for a thing long enough, it happens. If you ache for something, if you long for it, it comes to pass. No matter what it is, of course, then, there you are—you're stuck with it. It pays to be mindful in what you long for and wish for because it will come to pass but you'll be, of course, the thing you wished for. You'll become that. If you wish for revenge, then you'll become that. You'll become revenge. You'll live in that all the time. You'll be that.

So it's really not worth bothering with, is it? Anything limited, that is. It's really not worth getting stuck in anything. Everything is so transient here, in this world, in this life, on this earth, in this *samsara*. Why bother? Infinity has a lot of faces; you'll see them, it's inevitable. But what you focus on, what you are enamored of, will determine what your ecstasy is. Where you focus is your ecstasy and also there is your unhappiness. It's just the way it works.

If you focus only on light, both black and white, then there's only ecstasy. There's nothing else. The dreams of human beings are dark, heavy and morbid and simplistic and boring. The dreams of immortality are endless and shining. They shimmer. They shimmer. They glow. They unfold themselves in themselves forever. There's only forever. You think there's time, you think there's space—there's no such thing. It's an illusion; it's not true. There's only the perfect glimmering of the moment.

To celebrate the moment in happiness or unhappiness and pain or ecstasy, in enlightenment or in transience is the only possible solution to anything. It's to celebrate—to continually celebrate existence. It leads you to the fountainhead of yourself. That is the riddle. The riddle is the riddle of self. What is self? What lies beyond self? Self is the perception of perception. Beyond self there's no perception of perception. That's the riddle. The only way to answer the riddle is to go beyond perception and, of course, then there's no answer because there's no perception, there's only silence.

So soon we'll all go into that silence. It won't be long. We'll all be in it. Again. Back in the flux.

Also By the Author

BOOKS

Surfing the Himalayas

Snowboarding to Nirvana

Lifetimes: True Accounts of Reincarnation

Total Relaxation: The Complete Program for Overcoming Stress, Tension, Worry, and Fatigue

The Bridge Is Flowing But The River Is Not

The Lakshmi Series

The Wheel of Dharma

Insights: Talks On The Nature of Existence

Rama Live In LA

Talks and Workshops

The Last Incarnation

A Workshop With Rama

On The Road With Rama

Psychic Development

Zen Tapes

Tantric Buddhism

The Enlightenment Cycle

Insights: Tantric Buddhist Reflections on Life

MUSIC

Atlantis Rising

Breathless

Canyons of Light

Cayman Blue

Ecstasy

Enlightenment

Light Saber

Mandala of Light

Mystery School

Occult Dancer

Retrograde Planet

Samadhi

Samurai

Surfing the Himalayas

Tantra (2 vols)

Techno Zen Master

Urban Destruction

Zen Master

Tantric Buddhism

2020 © The Frederick P. Lenz Foundation for American Buddhism (the Foundation). All rights reserved. This product is published under exclusive license from the Foundation.

ALL RIGHTS RESERVED

No part of this publication may be reproduced, distributed, stored in a retrieval system, or transmitted in any form or by any means, including photocopying, recording, scanning, or by any information storage and retrieval system, or other electronic or mechanical methods, or otherwise, except as permitted under Section 107 or 108 of the 1976 International Copyright Act, without the prior written permission of the publisher, except in brief quotations embodied in critical articles and reviews, and certain other noncommercial uses permitted by copyright law.

Published 2003 by The Frederick P. Lenz Foundation for American Buddhism

Published 2020 by Living Flow
www.livingflow.com
Boulder, CO 80302 USA

Paperback ISBN 978-1-947811-21-8
Ebook . . . ISBN 978-1-947811-22-5

Publisher's Code r73-v08

Cover art & design by Meg Popovic
Interior dragon art by Janis Wilkins
Back cover photo by Greg Gorman

www.ingramcontent.com/pod-product-compliance
Lightning Source LLC
LaVergne TN
LVHW020925090426
835512LV00020B/3209